Data Analytics for Cybersecurity

As the world becomes increasingly connected, it is also more exposed to a myriad of cyber threats. We need to use multiple types of tools and techniques to learn and understand the evolving threat landscape. Data are a common thread linking various types of devices and end users. Analyzing data across different segments of cybersecurity domains, particularly data generated during cyber–attacks, can help us understand threats better, prevent future cyber–attacks, and provide insights into the evolving cyber threat landscape. This book takes a data oriented approach to studying cyber threats, showing in depth how traditional methods such as anomaly detection can be extended using data analytics, and also applies data analytics to non–traditional views of cybersecurity, such as multi domain analysis, time series and spatial data analysis, and human-centered cybersecurity.

VANDANA P. JANEJA is Professor and Chair of the Information Systems department at the University of Maryland, Baltimore County. Most recently, she also served as an expert at the National Science Foundation supporting data science activities in the Directorate for Computer and Information Science and Engineering (CISE) (2018–2021). Her research interests include discovering knowledge in presence of data heterogeneity. Her research projects include anomaly detection in network communication data, human behavior analytics in heterogeneous device environments, geospatial context for IP reputation scoring, spatiotemporal analysis across heterogeneous data, and ethical thinking in data science. She has been funded through state, federal, and private organizations.

Data Analytics for Cybersecurity

VANDANA P. JANEJA

University of Maryland, Baltimore County (UMBC)

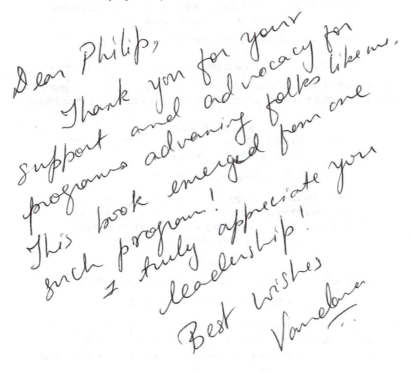

Dear Philip,

Thank you for your support and advocacy for programs advancing folks like me. This book emerged from one such program! I truly appreciate your leadership!

Best wishes
Vandana

CAMBRIDGE
UNIVERSITY PRESS

CAMBRIDGE
UNIVERSITY PRESS

University Printing House, Cambridge CB2 8BS, United Kingdom

One Liberty Plaza, 20th Floor, New York, NY 10006, USA

477 Williamstown Road, Port Melbourne, VIC 3207, Australia

314–321, 3rd Floor, Plot 3, Splendor Forum, Jasola District Centre, New Delhi – 110025, India

103 Penang Road, #05-06/07, Visioncrest Commercial, Singapore 238467

Cambridge University Press is part of the University of Cambridge.

It furthers the University's mission by disseminating knowledge in the pursuit of education, learning, and research at the highest international levels of excellence.

www.cambridge.org
Information on this title: www.cambridge.org/9781108415279
DOI: 10.1017/9781108231954

© Vandana P. Janeja 2022

First published 2022

A catalogue record for this publication is available from the British Library.

ISBN 978-1-108-41527-9 Hardback

Contents

Preface

Cybersecurity is a pervasive need in our connected world to counter threats affecting individuals, organizations, and governments. The acceptance and adoption of technology on multiple types of nontraditional devices force cybersecurity solutions to address challenges emerging in the areas of not only computer networks but also sensor networks, industrial control systems, and user devices. Data are the common thread across all these types of devices and end users, especially data generated during cyberattacks. Increasingly, the focus of cybersecurity is shifting to analyzing data in not only a retrospective manner but also a prospective manner across different cybersecurity domains. This data-driven understanding of attacks can potentially prevent future cyberattacks and provide insights into the evolving cyber threats.

Data analytics pushes beyond the traditional themes of security to seamlessly weave the analysis of threats across several applications. This book applies data analytics concepts and techniques to the domain of cybersecurity, discusses methods to evaluate data sources in cyberattacks, and provides insights into data mining methods that can be utilized for cybersecurity. Finally, this book also looks at nontraditional views of data analytics for cybersecurity in time series and spatial data, discussing the need and application of big data analytics and offering a human-centered analytics perspective to cybersecurity.

Although there are several books on network security, information assurance, and forensics and other books on data mining, there is a need to address both cybersecurity and data analytics in a synergistic manner. In addition, I have developed a graduate and undergraduate course on data analytics for cybersecurity. I taught this course for several semesters without a textbook. While developing this course, I reviewed several very good books. However, there was a gap in the material available for the data analytics perspective of cybersecurity in depth. This motivated me to write a book that looks at the different domains affected by cyberattacks, spanning computer networks, industrial control systems, sensor networks, drones, and other connected devices. Data analytics provides a window of learning into such systems by looking at the massive amounts of data being generated that may go untapped. For instance, this book addresses the human-centered perspective to cyberattacks, and it addresses the multiple facets of data analytics for cybersecurity, such as anomaly detection across spatial and temporal data.

I expect the book will be primarily useful for teaching graduate and undergraduate cybersecurity courses that take a data analytics perspective. It should also be relevant for the industry and government as it discusses the potential avenues of understanding and discovering cyberattacks and additional knowledge about them to better inform future decision-making.

The need for data analytics is also evident from Information Assurance requirements such as those stated in federal frameworks[1,2] and security directives for Information Assurance Training, Certification, and Workforce Management,[3] where various technical cybersecurity positions and their functions are outlined in detail. For instance, the Computer Network Defense (CND) Service Provider Incident Responder (IR) position has functions such as (CND-IR.2) – collect, analyze, intrusion artifacts – and (CND-IR.7) – correlate incident data and perform CND trend analysis. Similarly, the CND-Analyst (A) position has functions such as (CND-A.4) – perform analysis of log files – (CND-A.5) – characterize and analyze network traffic to identify anomalous activity and potential threats to network resources – and (CND-A.8.) – perform event correlation. These and many other security functions, such as forensics, threat hunting, and such clearly indicate the need to incorporate an analytics perspective to cybersecurity.

What Does the Book Cover?

The book spans from introductory concepts of cybersecurity, foundations of data analytics, and applications of data analytics concepts to cybersecurity applications.

---

[1] Workforce Framework for Cybersecurity(NICE Framework), NIST Special Publication 800-181 Revision 1, https://nvlpubs.nist.gov/nistpubs/SpecialPublications/NIST.SP.800-181r1.pdf, Last Accessed May 2021

[2] Workforce Framework for Cybersecurity (NICE Framework), https://niccs.cisa.gov/workforce-development/cyber-security-workforce-framework , Last Accessed May 2021

[3] Information Assurance Workforce Improvement Program, DoD 8570.01-M www.esd.whs.mil/Portals/54/Documents/DD/issuances/dodm/857001m.pdf; 8140.01 reissues and renumbers DoDD 8570.01, Last Accessed May 2021

Chapter 1 introduces the basic concepts of cybersecurity and the data analytics perspective to cybersecurity. It lays out the areas of study and how data analytics should be a key part of the spectrum of cybersecurity solutions.

Chapter 2 focuses on understanding sources of cybersecurity data and the end-to-end opportunities for data collection. It goes onto discuss the sources of cybersecurity data and how multiple datasets can be leveraged in understanding cyber threats.

Chapter 3 gets into the techniques of data analytics focusing on the three pillars of data mining, namely clustering, classification, and association rule mining, and how each can be used for cybersecurity. This chapter can be seen as a crash course in data mining. It begins with an understanding of the overall knowledge discovery and data mining process models and follows the elements of the data life cycle. This chapter outlines foundational elements such as measures of similarity and of evaluation. It outlines the landscape of various algorithms in clustering and classification and frequent and rare patterns.

Chapter 4 focuses on the big data elements of cybersecurity, looking at the landscape of the big data technologies and the complexities of the different types of data, including spatial and graph data. It outlines examples in these complex data types and how they can be evaluated using data analytics. Chapter 5 highlights the various types of cyberattacks and how data analytics methods can potentially be used to analyze these attacks.

Chapter 6 and 7 holistically focus on anomaly detection. Chapter 6 focuses on what anomalies are and more specifically what anomalies are in the cybersecurity domain, and what some of the features of anomalies are. Chapter 7, on the other hand, focuses on techniques of detecting anomalies starting with some of the basic statistical techniques, going into data analytics techniques.

While Chapter 4 introduces the complex types of data, Chapter 8 delves into the specifics of spatial and temporal analytics with topics such as spatial neighborhood and temporal evolution of large amounts of network traffic data. Chapter 9 extends the ideas of complex data by looking into cybersecurity through network and graph data. Chapter 10 brings in the human-centered data analytics perspective to cybersecurity. Finally, Chapter 11 discusses several key directions, such as data analytics in cyberphysical systems, multidomain mining, machine Learning concepts such as deep Learning, generative adversarial networks, and challenges of model reuse. Last but not the least, the chapter closes with thoughts on ethical thinking in the data analytics process.

Acknowledgments

The views expressed in this book are my own and do not reflect those of the organizations I am affiliated with.

I want to thank Carole Sargent, who planted the seed for this book and helped me learn the ropes of the process. Many thanks to my editor at Cambridge University Press, Lauren Cowles, and the Cambridge University Press team, Amy He, Adam Kratoska, Johnathan Fuentes, Rebecca Grainger, Andy Saff, and Neena S. Maheen, who were patient with the many deadlines and generous in their time reviewing the book and its many facets. Many thanks to the reviewers of this book who helped improve it with their detailed feedback.

The work in this book is built on the foundation of my work with many of my students, and the many conversations with them have inspired the writing of this book. I would like to thank my PhD advisees, Josephine Namayanja, Chhaya Kulkarni, Sara Khanjani, Ira Winkler, Faisal Quader, Mohammad Alodadi, Ali Azari , Yanan Sun, Lei Shi, and Mike McGuire; my master's advisees, Henanksha Sainani, Prathamesh Walkikar, Suraksha Shukla, Vasundhara Misal, Anuja Kench, Akshay Grover, Jay Gholap, Javad Zabihi, Kundala Das, Prerna Mohod, Abdulrahman Alothaim, and Revathi Palanisamy; my graduate students who worked on research projects with me, Yuanyuan Feng, Ruman Tambe, Song Chen, Sandipan Dey, Tania Lobo, Monish Advani, Ahmed Aleroud, Abu Zaher Md Faridee, Sai Pallaprolu, and Justin Stauffer; and my undergraduate research students, Gabrielle Watson, Olisaemeka Okolo, Aminat Alabi, Mackenzie Harwood, Adrian Reyes, Jarrett Early, Alfonso Delayney, David Lewis, and Brian Lewis.

My thought process and contributions are also framed by work with advisors, collaborators, colleagues, and industry affiliates who have contributed to my research and thinking in the area of security and data analytics, including Lucy Erickson, Carolyn Seaman, Aryya Gangopadhyay, Anupam

Joshi, Susan Sterrett, Krishnan Chellakarai, Yatish Joshi, and Raghu Chintalapati. I also want to thank my advisors and mentors: Vijay Atluri, Nabil Adam, Jaideep Vaidya, Erwin Gianchandani, Keith Bowman, Philip Rous, Patrice McDermott, Erin Lavik, and Chaitan Baru. This work is also built through the support of Dr. Freeman A. Hrabowski III, who has always been generous with his time as my mentor.

Last but not the least, my heartfelt thanks go to my biggest allies and pillars of support: Neelu, Suhasini, Harish, Deiptii, Nisha, Viraj, and Mukul, and my single most avid cheerleader, Vihan, who kept encouraging me with timeline prompts to complete this book.

1

Introduction

Data Analytics for Cybersecurity

1.1 What Is Cybersecurity?

Cybersecurity refers to securing valuable electronic assets and physical assets, which have electronic access, against unauthorized access. These assets may include personal devices, networked devices, information assets, and infrastructural assets, among others.

Cybersecurity deals with security against threats also referred to as cyber threats or cyberattacks. Cyberattacks are the mechanism by which security is breached to gain access to assets of value.

The first aim of cybersecurity is prevention of cyberattacks against critical assets. The second aim of cybersecurity is detection of threats. The third aim is to respond to threats in the event that they penetrate access to critical assets, and, finally, the fourth aim is to recover and restore the normal state of the system in the event that an attack is successful. Cybersecurity is achieved by addressing each of these three aspects to prevent, detect, and respond to threats against critical assets. Essentially, it deals with securing everything that is in cyberspace so these assets of value are not tampered with.

What really are these assets? Are they the data on a hard drive, a contact list on a cell phone, an Excel sheet with sales numbers, or a program to switch on a device?

It is all of these and more. With the ever-increasing use of electronics for every possible function of life, cybersecurity is becoming a pervasive problem permeating every individual's life. If you look around yourself, there are several electronic devices that you may see or use, and each electronic device may in turn be connected to another device physically or virtually. This connectivity enables us to access additional functionalities on the device.

1

However, this also makes the device vulnerable since it has external connectivity and access is fragmented through multiple external applications.

Now the obvious question is, does cybersecurity apply to connected devices only? Although a big part of cybersecurity is a result of the high level of connectivity, it also includes threats resulting from compromised physical security. For instance, a highly secure desktop in a secure room, which is not accessible via the traditional internet but only through a biometric authentication or a card swipe, is also at risk. An unauthorized access to the secure room poses a cybersecurity threat due to the electronic assets at risk and potential risk to the systems providing access to the room. This is primarily because some form of connectivity is always possible in this highly connected world. Another example is that of an insider threat where an authorized user accesses materials with a malicious intent.

1.1.1 Assets Affected

Cybersecurity is a major challenge due to the potential of damage. An empty hard drive that is stolen is a theft, but a hard drive with data accessed in an unauthorized manner poses a much bigger threat due to the value of the information stored on it. A sensor controlling a chemical flow into a vat that breaks down accidentally may lead to a hazmat accident, but an authorized access leading to tampering of the program controlling the sensor is a cybersecurity risk. This is because the intent and extent of the tampering are uncontrolled and may be much more catastrophic than a sensor breakdown. Thus, cybersecurity aims to prevent unauthorized access to electronic assets and physical assets with electronic access.

Let us look at some types of assets – personal, public, and corporate – that can be impacted by cybersecurity risks, summarized in Figure 1.1. We are now referring to the electronic access to physical assets or electronic assets. This list is a small sample of such assets in the highly connected world that we live in. These include the following.

- **Personal assets (mostly used for personal needs):** Phones (home and mobile), tablets, personal computers (desktop and laptops), external physical hard drive, cloud drive, email accounts, fitness trackers, smart watches, smart glasses, media devices (TiVo, Apple TV, cable box), bank accounts, credit cards, personal gaming systems, blogs, vlogs, photos, and videos.
- **Public assets (for managing public utilities and services):** Smart meters, power grid, sewage controls, nuclear power plant, rail lines, air traffic, traffic lights, citizen databases, websites (county, state and federal), space travel programs.

Personal	Public	Corporate
• Phones (home and mobile),	• Smart meters,	• Customer database,
• Tablets ,	• Power grid,	• Websites,
• Personal computers (desktop and laptops),	• Sewage controls,	• Business applications,
• External physical hard drive,	• Nuclear power plant,	• Business network,
• Cloud drive,	• Rail lines,	• Emails,
• Email accounts,	• Airplanes and air traffic,	• Off-the-shelf software,
• Fitness trackers,	• Traffic lights,	• Intellectual property
• Smart watches,	• Citizen databases,	
• Smart glasses,	• Websites (county, state, and federal),	
• Media devices (TIVO, Apple TV, cable box),	• Space-travel programs	
• Bank accounts,	• Satellites	
• Credit cards,		
• Personal gaming systems,		

Figure 1.1 Sample assets at risk due to cyberattacks.

- **Corporate assets (for managing business needs):** Customer database, websites, business applications, business network, emails, software, intellectual property.

Some overlap may occur as corporate assets may link to public assets or personal assets may be connected to corporate assets or public assets. As such, these assets should be clearly separated through well-defined security policies. However, with the level of connectivity through multiple devices, it is becoming more and more difficult to keep assets completely discrete and disconnected.

Thus, cybersecurity is securing everything of value that exists in cyberspace, which includes computer networks, mobile devices, cloud data storage, sensor networks, industrial control systems, emergency devices, railway lines, and air traffic controls, to name a few. It is not simply limited to our own private data or banking information but goes beyond to critical infrastructure and corporate assets.

Certain geological regions are more prone to attacks than others due to the availability and richness of such assets. Many tools are available to depict attack maps of popular cyberattacks. Examples include ThreatCloud showing real-time attacks based on monitoring sensors across the world (Check Point

2020), Digital Attack Map depicting top distributed denial of service (DDoS) attacks worldwide (Netscout 2020), and Kaspersky Lab's 3D interactive map of cyberattacks (Kaspersky 2020). These are helpful in visualizing the spread of types of attacks and level of activity in a region.

1.1.2 Motivation, Risks, and Attaining Security

What is the motivation behind such attacks? An unauthorized access to secured resources may be due to various factors. Some such factors are summarized in Figure 1.2 and listed as follows:

- Stealing intellectual property: The majority of corporate product development strategies are stored on highly secure infrastructure. Small companies and large corporations alike devise novel products, and their intellectual property holds the key to revenue in the future. Loss of such information could be devastating for the sales and profits for an organization.
- Gaining access to customer data: Banks and retailers are constantly at the receiving end of cyberattacks due to valuable customer data, which can then be sold. Recent notable examples include Target (Washington Post 2013).

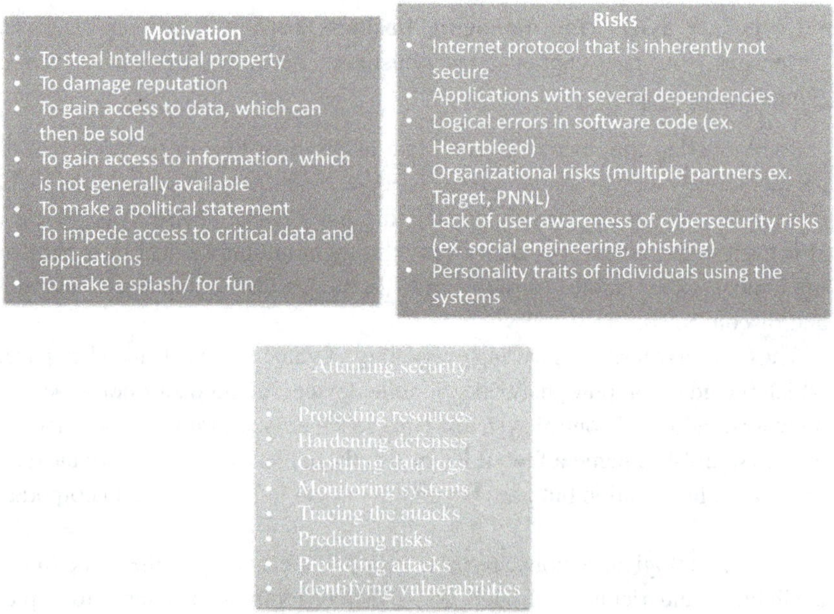

Figure 1.2 Unauthorized access motivations, risks and attaining security.

- Making a political statement: Hacktivism, or hacking for activism (Samuel 2004), is an act carried out primarily to send a political message. An example included the cyber war in Estonia in 2007 (CSMonitor–Estonia 2007), where a series of DDoS attacks were directed toward official websites and even mobile phone networks. Estonia has several e-government initiatives, which had to be shut down for access from foreign locations due to the massive scale of the attacks. The Estonian foreign minister has also been quoted blaming the Russian government for facilitating these attacks.
- Performing cyber espionage: These attacks originate from government-supported cells, which target state secrets. Unlike theft of intellectual property, cyber espionage is geared toward gaining access to sensitive information. An example is the Titan Rain attack (Lewis 2005, Chi 2014), a type of advanced persistent threat (APT), believed to have been initiated by government-coordinated cells in China targeting US defense networks and contractors such as Lockheed Martin, Sandia National Laboratories, and NASA, among others. The SolarWinds hack led to a massive impact for federal systems believed to be directed by the Russian government (Stubbs et al. 2020). In some cases, this becomes a global supply chain attack, where the hack from a trusted vendor leads to a major attack, such as in the case of FireEye, which was impacted by the SolarWinds attack (Geenans 2020)
- In addition to the aforementioned motivations, cyberattacks may be aimed at damaging reputation (Townsend et al. 2014), which can lead to substantial losses; making a splash for fun (Gesenhues 2014), such as a traditional search example using Google dorking; and impeding access to data and applications (Risk Based Security 2014). Most of these scenarios are carried out to gain unauthorized access to information.

1.1.2.1 Why Do We Have Security Risks?

Security risks arise due to various factors, which include the following: applications with several dependencies, logical errors in software code (such as Heartbleed), organizational risks (multiple partners, such as in cyber-attacks at Target and the Pacific Northwest National Laboratories [PNNL]), lack of user awareness of cybersecurity risks (such as in social engineering and phishing), personality traits of individuals using the systems (phishing), and inherent issues in the Internet protocol being used.

1.1.2.2 What Is the Level of Damage That Can Occur?

According to a McAfee report, the monetary loss resulting from cybercrime costs about $600 billion, which is about 0.8% of the world Gross Domestic Product (GDP) (McAfee–Cybercrime Impact 2018), with malicious actors becoming more and more sophisticated. Such large numbers are difficult to estimate, and the report outlines a sound strategy for reaching the estimated loss.

The loss due to cyberattacks is not simply based on direct financial loss but also based on several indirect factors that may lead to a major financial impact. As an example, let us consider the Target cyberattack. According to a Reuters news article (Skariachan and Finkle 2014), Target reported $61 million in expenses related to the cyberattack out of which $44 million was covered by insurance. Thus, the direct financial impact to Target was $17 million. Now let us consider some other factors that led to the indirect loss for Target: there was a 46% drop in net profit in the holiday quarter and a 5.5% drop in transactions during the quarter, share price fluctuations led to further losses, cards had to be reissued to several customers, and Target had to offer identity protection to affected customers. All these losses amount to much more than the total $61 million loss. In addition, the trust of the customers was lost, which is not a quantifiable loss and has long-term impacts.

1.2 Handling Cyberattacks

Now the key question is how one secures the resources against unauthorized accesses. Understanding and preventing such risks can be done in several ways, including protecting resources, hardening defenses, capturing data logs, monitoring systems, tracing the attacks, predicting risks, predicting attacks, and identifying vulnerabilities.

Several subdisciplines of cybersecurity deal with these aspects.

1.2.1 Subareas of Cybersecurity

Various areas of cybersecurity have developed techniques to prevent and respond to cyberattacks. There are several overlaps in these areas of cybersecurity. These include the following (shown in Figure 1.3):

Application security: This area deals with incorporating security in the software development process. This includes following best practices for code development, designing strong and comprehensive test cases, and following rigorous maintenance practices.

Data and information security: Increasingly with the advent of cloud data storage and remote access to data warehouses, data and information are at a risk of unauthorized access and misuse. Data and information security deals with securing data from such threats.

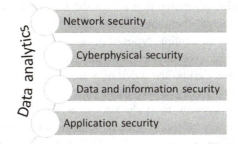

Figure 1.3 Areas of cybersecurity.

Network security: This deals with the challenges faced in securing the traditional computer networks and security measures adopted to secure, prevent unauthorized access and misuse of either the public or the private network.

Cyberphysical security: This focuses on the emerging challenges due to the coupling of the cyber systems with the physical systems. For example, the power plants being controlled by a cyber system present new security challenges that can arise due to the risk of disruption of the cyber component or risk of unauthorized control of the cyber system, thus gaining control of the physical systems.

Data analytics: This crosscutting theme can apply to each of these areas to learn from existing threats and develop solutions for novel and unknown threats toward networks, infrastructure, data, and information. Threat hunting (Sadhwani 2020), which proactively looks for malicious players across the myriad data sources in an organization, is a direct application of using data analytics on the various types of security data produced from the various types of security streams. However, this does not necessarily have to be a completely machine-driven process and should account for user behaviors as well (Shashanka et al. 2016), looking at the operational context. Data analytics can provide security analysts a much focused field of vision to zero in on solutions for potential threats.

Cybersecurity affects many different types of devices, networks, and organizations. Each poses different types of challenges to secure. It is important to understand and differentiate between these challenges due to the changing hardware and software landscape across each type of cybersecurity domain. While hardware configurations and types of connectivity are out of scope for this book, it is important to understand some of the fundamental challenges to study their impact and how they can be addressed using techniques such as data analytics, which is crosscutting across the many different types of connectivity since data are ubiquitous across all these domains. In the current connected environment, multiple types of networks and devices are used, such as computer networks, cyberphysical systems (CPS), Internet of Things (IoT), sensor networks, smart grids, and wired or wireless networks. To some extent, IoT and sensor networks can be seen as specialized cases of CPS systems. We can consider these systems to study how data analytics can contribute to cybersecurity since any of these types of systems will generate data, which can be evaluated to understand their functioning and any potential benign or nonbenign malfunctions.

Computer networks are the most traditional type of networks where groups of computers are connected in prespecified configurations. These configurations can be designed using security policy deciding who has access to what areas of networks. Another way networks form is by determining patterns of use over a period of time. In both cases, zones can be created for access and connectivity where each computer in the network and subnetworks can be monitored.

Cyberphysical systems are an amalgamation of two interacting subsystems, cyber and physical, that are used to monitor a function. cyberphysical systems are used to monitor and perform the day-to-day functions of the many automated systems that we rely on, including power stations, chemical factories, and nuclear power plants, to name a few.

With the ubiquitous advent of connected technology, many "smart" things are being introduced into our connected environment. A connected network of such smart things has led to the evolution of Internet of Things. IoT has become excessively pervasive and prevalent from our smart homes to hospitals. These new types of connected systems bring about new challenges in securing them from attacks with malicious intent to disrupt their day-to-day functioning.

Throughout this book, we will use examples from various types of such connected systems to illustrate how data analytics can facilitate cybersecurity.

1.3 Data Analytics

Data analytics deals with analyzing large amounts of data from disparate sources to discover actionable information leading to gains for an organization. Data analytics includes techniques from data mining, statistics, and business management, among other fields.

The large amount of data collected has led to the "big data" revolution. This is also the case in the domain of cybersecurity. Big data (Manyika et al. 2011, Chen et al. 2014) refers to not only massive datasets (volume) but also data that are generated at a rapid rate (velocity) and have a heterogeneous nature (variety), and that can provide valid findings or patterns in this complex environment (veracity). These data can also change by location (venue). Thus, big data encompasses the truly complex nature of data particularly in the domain of cybersecurity.

Every device, action, transaction, and event generates data. Cyber threats leave a series of such data pieces in different environments and domains. Sifting through these data can lead to novel insight into why a certain event occurred and potentially allow the identification of the responsible parties and lead to knowledge for preventing such attacks in the future.

Let us next understand how data analytics plays a key role in understanding cyberattacks.

1.3.1 Why Is Data Analytics Important for Cybersecurity? A Case Study of Understanding the Anatomy of an Attack

Cyberattacks evolve very fast. Let us consider a vulnerability in software code. A software patch can be developed to address the vulnerability; however, a slight modification may lead to a new vulnerability. There is a constant back and forth between the conspirators and the legitimate users. In several cases, the more serious attacks are not just a one-stop exploit that breaches a system through a single vulnerability, but a multipronged attack that uses several different channels to gain access to the secured systems.

To understand the intricacies of such a complex attack, let us consider the anatomy of an attack based on a scenario motivated from a recent attack on a federal lab (Dark Reading 2011). This example demonstrates the challenges posed by multiple aspects of cyberattacks coming from multiple sources and spread over time. Similar patterns of threat propagation have been seen in other attacks (such as Skariachan and Finkle 2014, FireEye 2020).

Figure 1.4 shows the flow of a multipronged attack. Despite the lab's well-protected information technology (IT) security perimeter, the attacks made it through in a very coordinated and prolonged process. Similar to a global supply chain attack (FireEye 2020), in the PNNL case, first there is an attack on the organization, and second, there is an attack on a partner that shares key resources. In the first part of the attack, intruders take advantage of vulnerabilities in public-facing web servers. In addition, hackers secretively scout the

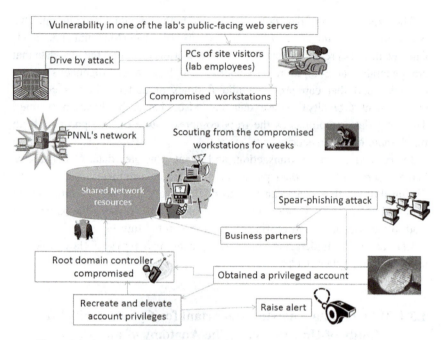

Figure 1.4 Anatomy of a multilevel attack.

network from compromised workstations that have already been targeted beforehand as part of a coordinated prolonged attack. The second part of the attack starts with spear phishing. Instead of casting out thousands of emails randomly, spear phishers target select groups of people with something in common, such as a common employer, a similar banking or financial institution, the same college, etc. So potentially a second group of hackers institutes a spear-phishing attack on the organization's major business partners with which it shares network resources. The hackers are able to obtain a privileged account and compromise a root domain controller that is shared by the organization and its partner. When the intruders try to recreate and assign privileges, it triggers an alarm, alerting the organization's cybersecurity team.

This scenario clearly demonstrates that simply looking at one dimension of the attack is not enough in such prolonged attacks. For such multipronged attacks, a multifaceted approach is required. Events of interest can be identified using a combination of factors such as proximity of events in time, in terms of series of communications, and even in terms of the geographic origin or destination of the communication, as shown in Figure 1.4.

For this specific example, we can evaluate three important aspects of analysis of the cyber traffic data, which can potentially generate new insights in detecting unusual events of interest. The three aspects are temporal, spatial, and data-driven understanding of human behavioral aspects (particularly of attackers):

- Firstly, computer networks evolve over time, and communication patterns change over time. Can we identify these key changes, which deviate from the normal changes in a communication pattern, and associate them with anomalies in the network traffic?
- Secondly, attacks may have a spatial pattern. Sources and destinations in certain key geolocations are more important for monitoring and preventing an attack. Can key geolocations, which are sources or destinations of attacks, be identified?
- Thirdly, any type of an attack has common underpinnings of how it is carried out; this has not changed from physical security breaches to computer security breaches. Can this knowledge be leveraged to identify anomalies in the data where we can see certain patterns of misuse?

Utilizing the temporal, spatial, and human behavioral aspects of learning new knowledge from the vast amount of cyber data can lead to new insights of understanding the challenges faced in this important domain of cybersecurity.

Thus, simply looking at one dimension of the data is not enough in such prolonged attack scenarios. For such a multipronged attacks, we need a multilevel framework that brings together data from several different databases. Events of interest can be identified using a combination of factors such as proximity of events in time, in terms of series of communications and even in terms of the geographic origin or destination of the communication, as shown in Figure 1.5. Some example tasks that can be performed to glean actionable information are the following:

(a) **Clustering based on feature combinations**: One important piece of data collected in most organizations is Intruder Detection System (IDS) logs such as SNORT. These can be leveraged, and a keyword matrix and a word frequency matrix can be extracted to use for various analytical tasks. For example, the keyword matrix can be used to perform alarm clustering and alarm data fusion to identify critical alerts that may have been missed. Instead of clustering the entire set of features seen in a snort alarm, we can perform clustering based on a combination of features.

(b) **Collusions and associations**: Using the keyword matrix, we also extract associations to identify potentially repeated or targeted communications. This information in conjunction with network mapping can also be used to determine which attacks are consistently targeted to specific types of machines.

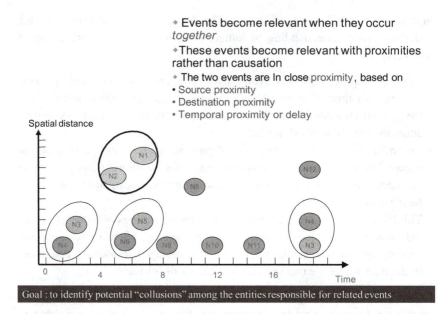

Figure 1.5 Multidimensional view of threats.

(c) **Time proximity and network evolution**: Clustering can be performed after creating time intervals that accounts for time proximity. This not only allows mining the data in proximity of time but also evaluating how the networks evolve over time and which time interval may be critical. For instance, we might want to identify if there are repeated events of interest in certain time periods. Lastly, looking at the clustering in different segments of time, we can look at mining for possible attack paths based on variations in cluster content and cluster cohesion.

1.3.2 How Can Data Analytics Help?

The attack case study shows the potential of data analytics and how data from multiple sources can be used to glean novel information. Data analytics can help in several ways to support the defense of cyber systems: mining system logs, monitoring systems, tracing the attacks, predicting risks by identifying critical systems in a network flow, predicting attacks based on prior or similar attacks, identifying vulnerabilities by mining software code, understanding user behavior by mining network logs, and creating robust access control rules by evaluating prior usage and security policies.

What this book is not about: This book does not address the traditional views of security configurations and shoring up defenses, including setting up computer networks, setting up firewalls, web server management, and patching of vulnerabilities.

What this book is about: This book addresses the challenges in cybersecurity that data analytics can help address, including analytics for threat hunting or threat detection, discovering knowledge for attack prevention or mitigation, discovering knowledge about vulnerabilities, and performing retrospective and prospective analysis for understanding the mechanics of attacks to help prevent them in the future.

This book will provide multiple examples across different types of networks and connected systems where data can be captured and analyzed to derive actionable knowledge fulfilling one of the several aims of cybersecurity, namely prevention, detection, response, and recovery.

2

Understanding Sources of Cybersecurity Data

Cyber threats often lead to loss of assets. This chapter discusses the multitude of datasets that can be harvested and used to track these losses and origins of the attack. This chapter is not about the data lost during cyberattacks but the data that organizations can scour from their networks to understand threats better so that they can potentially prevent or even predict future attacks.

2.1 End-to-End Opportunities for Data Collection

The information systems used to perform business functions have a well-defined process spanning over connected systems. In a typical client server scenario, as shown in Figure 2.1, a user connects to a system via an internet pipeline. The system has built-in application functionality important to run the business function. A return pipeline sends a response back to the user. The functionality of the system allows the delivery of the information commodity requested by the user.

As the example layout in Figure 2.1a shows, the logical view of the user requesting access to a business application can appear to be fairly straightforward. However, within this pipeline there could be several points through which the request and response pass, as shown in Figure 2.1b, leading to several opportunities in the end-to-end process for data collection to help understand when a cyber threat may occur in this process.

As we can see in Figure 2.1b, when the user requests a resource, it has to go through a complex networking pipeline. The user may have a firewall on their own system and the router through which they send out the request. This request can be filtered through the internet service provider, lookups can be performed in the domain name system (DNS) and the data can be routed through multiple paths of routers, which are linked through the routing table.

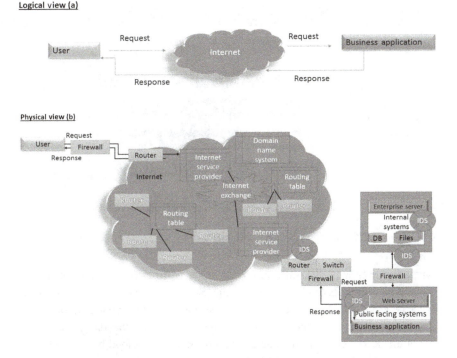

Figure 2.1 Logical and physical view of user request and response in a network-based environment.

The request on the other side may again have to pass through the routers and firewalls at multiple points in the system being accessed by the user. There may be multiple intrusion detection systems (IDS) posted throughout the systems to monitor the network flow for malicious activity. This is just one example scenario; different network layouts will result in different types of intermediate steps in this process of request and response, particularly based on the type of response, the type of network being used, the type of organization of business applications, the cloud infrastructure being used, to name a few factors. However, certain key components are always present that allow for multiple opportunities to glean and scour for data related to potential cyber threats.

There can be several opportunities to collect data to understand potential threats. Data collection can begin at a user access point, system functionality level, and commodity level (particularly if the data is being delivered). For example, at the user level, we can utilize data such as the following: (a) Who is the user? The psychology of the user, personality types, etc., can influence

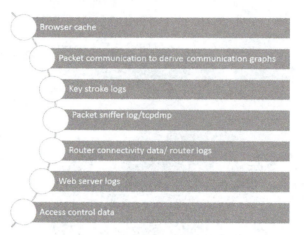

Browser cache

Packet communication to derive communication graphs

Key stroke logs

Packet sniffer log/tcpdmp

Router connectivity data/ router logs

Web server logs

Access control data

Figure 2.2 Common types of cybersecurity data.

whether a user will click on a link or give access to information to others. (b)
What type of interface is being used by the user? Is there clear information about
what is acceptable or not acceptable in the interface? (c) What type of access
system is being used? Is there access control for users? (d) What data are available
about the access pipeline, such as the type of network or cloud being used.

Several common types of datasets can be collected and evaluated, as shown
in Figure 2.2, including various types of log data such as key stroke logs, web
server logs, and intrusion detection logs, to name a few. We next discuss
several types of such datasets.

2.2 Sources of Cybersecurity Data

Cybersecurity-related data collection will vary across the type of networks,
including computer networks, sensor networks, or cyberphysical systems. The
method and level of data collection will also vary based on the application
domains for which the networks are being used and the important assets being
protected. For example: (a) social media businesses, such Facebook, are
primarily user data driven, where the revenue is based on providing access
to user data and monitoring usage data; (b) e-commerce businesses, such as
Amazon, are usage and product delivery based; (c) portals, such as Yahoo, are
again user data driven but more heavily reliant on advertisements, which can
target users based on what they see and use most often; (d) cyberphysical
systems, such as systems for monitoring and managing power grids, are based
on accurate functioning of physical systems and delivery of services to users
over these physical infrastructural elements.

In each of these types of systems, the underlying infrastructure has to be monitored to ensure accurate functioning and prevention, detection, and recovery from cyber threats. The level of monitoring and management of such data will vary with the level of prevention, detection, or recovery expected in the domain. Some domains have a high emphasis on prevention; others may have a high level of emphasis on detection or recovery. In all such cases, multiple types of datasets can be collected to provide intelligence on the cyber threats, and user behaviors can be evaluated to prevent future threats or even identify an insider propagating the threats.

In the following discussion for each dataset, we examine the following: (a) What is the data? (b) What is an example of its use in literature? (c) What type of detection can it be used for? In the chapters throughout this book, we will discuss how some of these datasets can be leveraged to discover anomalies identifying potential threats using data analytics methods.

2.2.1 Log Data

The nature of electronic communication and activities allows for several types of datasets to be logged. Some examples include the following: (1) intrusion detection system (IDS) logs including alarms raised by IDS; (2) key stroke logs; (3) router connectivity data/ router logs; (4) web server logs; and (5) firewall logs. This is not an exhaustive list but includes some of the major types of logs that can be collected.

2.2.1.1 Keystroke Logs

Keystroke logging or *key logging* is a mechanism to capture every key being pressed on a keyboard, but can also go beyond key presses to actions such as copying materials to the clipboard or other interactions with the user system. Key logging has been extensively studied for many applications, from writing to cognitive analysis to security threats. A survey on key logging (Heron 2007) outlines mechanisms, including hardware installation, kernel-level, system hook, and function-based methods, for key logging.

Key logging has also been studied for smart phones (Gupta et al. 2016, Cai and Chen 2011). A recent survey (Hussain et al. 2016) extensively outlines motion-based key logging and inference attacks that can result from smart phone key logging. This survey classifies key logging as in-band logging through the main channels of the keystrokes and out-of-band logging using side channels such as acoustics, power consumption, etc. Thus, key logging is not necessarily limited to keyboard-based data collection but can get quite sophisticated.

This type of data collection allows studying user behaviors but may also be used to maliciously detect user credentials, user preferences, or other sensitive information. Thus, it is also essential to understand the capabilities of key loggers to create any type of defense against threats utilizing key loggers.

2.2.1.2 Intrusion Detection System Logs

Intrusion detection system (IDS) log data (e.g., from Snort) provide data about alerts that are raised by matching any known signatures of malicious activities in the header and payload data. Generally, IDS will also provide an alert level of low, medium, or high. IDS logs analyze the packets based on malicious signatures and provide information on time stamp, service used, protocol, source, and destination. IDS can be placed at various points in a network, and multiple such datasets can be collected and correlated (Deokar and Hazarnis 2012). IDS logs are also commonly used for anomaly detection methods, which are utilized to detect threats beyond signature matching. Here anomalous packets indicate an unusual behavior with respect to the normal, where the normal can be discovered and predefined through various analytics methods.

IDS log data lends itself well to secondary analysis such as through data mining methods including association rule mining (such as Vaarandi and Podiņš 2010 and Quader et al. 2015), human behavior modeling (such as Quader and Janeja 2014 and Chen et al. 2014), and prediction of attacks, to name a few examples. Multiple IDS and other types of logs are also correlated to detect significant anomalies, which are not otherwise detectable (such as illustrated in Janeja et al. 2014 and Abad et al. 2003). Visualization of logs (such as in Koike and Ohno 2004) has been explored to facilitate the analysis of the logs by looking at the information selectively, slicing and dicing the data by certain features, such as by time or by event.

2.2.1.3 Router Connectivity and Log Data

The internet is a network of networks or subnetworks. The networks at each level are connected by routers. A router connects computer networks and forwarding data across computer networks. Each of these routers is connected for data transmission. This can range from a simple home router to corporate routers that connect to the internet backbone. A routing table stores information about the paths to take for forwarding and transmitting the data. The routing table stores the routes of all reachable destinations, including routers, from it. Various algorithms devise an efficient path through these connected routers (such as Sklower 1991 and Tsuchiya 1988).

A router provides not only route information but also all the raw IP addresses that pass through the router. These IP addresses can be mapped to identify possible malware activity when data are sent to suspicious geolocations in an unauthorized manner (Geocoding-Infosec 2013). However, care must be taken in using the IP addresses in isolation as they can be subject to IP spoofing, which hides the identity of the sender. Router data can also be utilized to study and possibly identify traffic hijacking (Kim Zetter Security 2013) and bogus routes by looking at historic route data stored in a knowledge base (Qiu et al. 2007).

2.2.1.4 Firewall Log Data

Firewalls act as a first line of defense that can stop certain types of traffic based on firewall security policies. In addition, these policies also have to be maintained to stay up to date with the changing landscape of the network usage. Essentially every access entry can be logged as it has to pass through the firewall. Some threats can be directly identified and blocked based on a clearly defined firewall policy or rule. For instance, if there is a clearly unauthorized access to an internal server, a well-configured firewall can block it to prevent access to the system. Major threat-related activities such as port scans, malware, and unauthorized access can easily be filtered through robust firewall rules. It essentially filters traffic based on the configuration of access to the systems protected by the firewall. Firewalls are typically designed to look at the header information in the data packets to match against prespecified rule sets. Firewalls can be host based or network based depending on whether they are deployed at an individual user's system or at a network interface.

Firewalls differ from IDS since they are generally limited to header information screening, whereas IDS can look at the payload data as well and block connections with malicious signatures. However, there has been a convergence in these functionalities in more recent times.

Firewall policy rules are one area where data mining may benefit by allowing the creation of a dynamic set of rules based on the traffic passing through the firewall. Analysis of policy rules and network traffic is used (Golnabi et al. 2006) to generate efficient rule sets based on the network traffic trends and potentially identify misconfigurations in the policy rules. This particular work uses association rule mining (ARM) and simple frequency counting of rules to generate firewall policy rules. In addition, it also identifies different types of policy anomalies, including blocking of legitimate traffic, allowing traffic to nonexisting services or redundant policy anomalies.

Similarly, Abedin et al. (2010) regenerates firewall policy rules and compares them with existing policies to discover anomalies.

2.2.2 Raw Payload Data

Any data sent over the network are divided into multiple parts. Two key parts include (a) the header information, which stores data about source and destination among other things; and (b) the actual content being transmitted, referred to as the payload. There are several privacy concerns in accessing these payload data since these data are the actual content that is being sent, which may be under strict access control. Such payload data can be accessed only where legally allowed and users have provided permissions to access the data. Additionally, the data may be encrypted, so its usefulness as raw data to be mined is limited.

Payload data are accessible through packet sniffers such as Wireshark,[1] where the data dump of the traffic can be retrieved. Payload data can be massive even for a few minutes of data capture. Thus, it provides a strong motivation for using big data technologies to collect and mine such data where permissible. In addition, for web-based traffic the browser cache is another way to access the payload data from the client or end user's side.

Payload data have been shown (Wang and Stolfo 2004, Kim et al. 2014, Limmer and Dressler 2010) to be effective in identifying anomalous threats in network intrusion detection systems. For example, one recent study (Limmer and Dressler 2010) selectively analyzed parts of the payload, thus reducing the challenges in high-speed network intrusion detection systems. Parekh et al. (2006) utilize suspicious payload sharing in a privacy-preserving manner to identify threats across multiple sites.

Payload data can be used in multiple ways, such as to discover an individual user's behavior, the presence of malwares in the payloads, and other security threats that can be detected based on the actual content of the payload. One common use of payload data is to identify threats based on signatures of malware that may be present in the payloads. For example, if a virus is embedded in a packet and this virus has a known signature, then this can be captured by traditional intrusion detection system rules. One such open-source network intrusion detection system is Snort, which provides Snort rules (Snort 2020). Snort can also be used as a packet sniffer, like Wireshark, but can also be used as an IDS. Packets with malware embedded in them can be detected using multiple mechanisms such as simple keyword searches or complex regular expression matches and flagged. The traffic can be blocked or marked for further analysis, such as using Snort alarms or Wireshark coloring rules (Cheok 2014).

---

[1] www.wireshark.org.

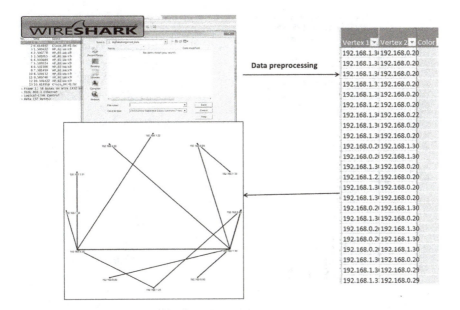

Figure 2.3 Example extraction of a communication graph from network traffic.

2.2.3 Network Topology Data

A computer network can be represented as a graph in terms of the structure of the network and in terms of the communication taking place over the network. Network traffic data dump can be used to generate the communication graph of all exchanges taking place over the network. As shown in Figure 2.3, for example, header data collected from a traffic dump file through Wireshark can be utilized to plot the communication between the source and destination IP addresses, which become the vertices, and the exchange between the two vertices forms the edge in the graph. In this example, NodeXL[2] is used to plot the graph data.

Once the communication data are in the graph form, graph metrics (for example, as discussed in Nicosia et al. 2013) can be computed, such as node-level metrics, including centrality, page rank, etc.; and network-level metrics, such as diameter, density, etc. In addition, based on the network properties, predictions can also be made about future network evolution. The example in Figure 2.4 illustrates one such task in a sample traffic data.

---

[2] www.smrfoundation.org/nodexl/.

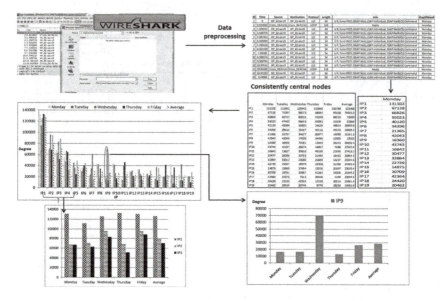

Figure 2.4 Exploratory analysis using Degree Centralities.

Data from network traffic is collected through packet sniffers such as Wireshark. To find communication behaviors of IP addresses along with anomalous fluctuations, exploratory analysis is performed on these data. The data from the network traffic need to be preprocessed, and this preprocessing will change with the task being performed. For instance, if in this example we wish to perform analysis by day of the week, the traffic data are sorted by the day of the week to get patterns by day, such as all Mondays or all Tuesdays. We can then compute the degree (i.e., number of edges incident on a vertex) of each node by day of the week. This can be performed for specific dates also; however, in this particular example we are interested to see behavior on certain days of the week by each of the IP addresses. We can sort the IP addresses by their degrees across days of the week, and the top ones appear to be consistently present in the traffic. Similarly, nodes with low degrees can also be identified. In such a scenario, it would be interesting to find a node, which is generally highly consistent as a high-degree node, to appear in the list of nodes with a lower degree, indicating a shift in the traffic pattern. Now let us consider the bar chart of the degrees for each IP address across each day of the week. We can observe that some IP addresses are consistently higher degree across all days of the week, which is further illustrated by the plot for IP1, IP2, and

IP3 across all days of the week. We can also see that the degrees of IP9 and IP7 seem to be higher on some days but lower on other days. This is further clarified by the plot for IP9, which shows Wednesday as a day where IP9 has inconsistent behavior.

Thus, through such exploratory analysis it is not only possible to identify nodes that are inconsistent but also time points where the behavior is inconsistent. Alternatively, this method can also be used to identify highly connected nodes (such as nodes receiving higher than normal connections during a breach) or least connected nodes (perhaps nodes that are impacted by a breach and lose connectivity). This type of consistency and inconsistency can be identified at the node level and at the graph level as discussed in Namayanja and Janeja (2015 and 2017)

Another study (Massicotte et al. 2003) introduces a prototype network mapping framework that uses freely available network scanners (nmap, Xprobe) on built-in network protocols (ICMP, ARP, NetBIOS, DNS, SNMP, etc.) to create a real-time network topology mapping with the help of intelligence databases. It must be used in tandem with an intrusion detection system. Studies discussed earlier for graph metrics can be applied to such works as well after the topology is discovered.

2.2.4 User System Data

Figure 2.5 outlines several key features that can be extracted to monitor unusual activities at the individual system level. Example features include active process resident memory usage, which is available for all operating systems (OS) and allows for building a profile on the normal memory usage of a process over time. As an example, an abnormal spike in memory usage can be attributed to processing a large volume of data. This might be useful in detecting a potential insider threat, especially when integrated with other user behavioral data from sensors monitoring user stress levels or integrating with other log datasets. Similarly, CPU time utilization can be used for measuring system usage. Several OS-specific features, such as kernel modules and changes in registry values, are also identified in Figure 2.5. However, it is important to use multiple signatures over time from several of the features to eliminate the regular spikes of day-to-day operations. This is the key differentiator for a robust analysis where we do not simply rely on one or two features but multiple features and their stable signatures (as compared to historical data) to distinguish alerts. Tools such as OSQuery

Feature name	OS specific
Active process name, active process filesystem path, active process ports and sockets, active process file access, active process resident memory usage, active process CPU time utilization, active process system calls, active process priority value, active process owner and group information, loaded peripherals drivers, key-store access patterns	All OS
Loaded kernel modules	Linux/Unix
Loaded kernel extensions	Mac OSX
Change in registry values	Windows
File system journaling (metadata) information	All major file systems (NTFS, ext4, HFS+)
Network routing tables	All major OS
Network firewall rules	All major firewall implementations
System-level sensors (current, voltage in different bus inside PC, CPU/GPU fan speed, etc.)	Almost all peripherals

Figure 2.5 OS-specific variables for CPU processing.

(OSQuery 2016) and Snare (SNARE 2016) can facilitate capture of these features.

Stephens and Maloof (2014) provide a very general framework for insider threat detection by gathering information from file read/write activities, printing, emailing, and search queries, then building a probabilistic Bayesian belief network from the sensor and context data, such as a user behavior profile from past actions. Van Meigham (2016) focuses on macOS malware detection using a kernel module to intercept system calls and generating a heat map analysis on the results.

2.2.5 Other Datasets

In addition to the datasets discussed, there are additional datasets that can be utilized to leverage knowledge about cyberattacks.

Access control data: These data can help better understand usage of the assets that need to be protected. Role mining (Vaidya et al. 2007, Mitra et al. 2016) from access control data can help shape and create better and more robust roles.

Eye tracker data: A user's behavior can be judged by the interactions of the user with the system being used. One such mode of input is the screen. Data collected from the user's eye gaze, captured through an eye tracker, can help analyze the user's level of engagement with a system and user preferences or positioning important items on the screen (such as those discussed in

Darwish and Bataineh 2012) to evaluate browser security indicators. The data collected through the eye tracker can be mined for patterns such as associations between security cue locations on the screen and number of views or clicks. Clustering can be performed on eye gaze data to identify presence or absence of clusters around security cues. Associations can be analyzed between user's perception of security, backgrounds, and demographics to different zones of eye gaze foci in a stratified manner. If users perceive disclosing important information through emails as a low-risk activity, they are less likely to see the security cues. Similarly, if they see the security cues, their perceived risk of responding will be high. Studies have hypothesized that user education can change user's perception of security and help them to better see these security cues, increasing the likelihood of threat detection or identifying threats through visual cues such as in the case of phishing.

Vulnerability data: Software vulnerability is a defect in the system (such as a software bug) that allows an attacker to exploit the system and potentially pose a security threat. Vulnerabilities can be investigated, and trends can be discovered in various operating systems to determine levels of strength or defense against cyberattacks (Frei et al. 2006). Using the National Vulnerability Database from the National Institute of Standards and Technology (NIST) (NIST 2017), trends can be analyzed for several years and across major releases for operating systems to reinforce knowledge of choices for critical infrastructural or network projects.

NVD is built on the concept of Common Vulnerabilities and Exposures (CVE),[3] which is a dictionary of publicly known vulnerabilities and exposures. CVEs allow the standardization of vulnerabilities across products around the world. NVD scores every vulnerability using the Common Vulnerability Scoring System (CVSS).[4] CVSS is comprised of several submetrics, including (a) base, (b) temporal, and (c) environmental metrics. Each of these metrics quantifies some type of feature of a vulnerability. For example, base metrics capture characteristics of a vulnerability constant across time and user environments, such as complexity, privilege required, etc. The environmental metrics, on the other hand, are the modified base metrics reevaluated based on organization infrastructure. NVD allows searches based on subcomponents of these metrics and also based on the basic security policies of confidentiality, integrity, and availability. These searches can provide data for analysis to identify trends and behaviors of vulnerabilities across operating systems or other software for different types of industries.

---

[3] http://cve.mitre.org/.   [4] https://nvd.nist.gov/cvss.cfm; www.first.org/cvss.

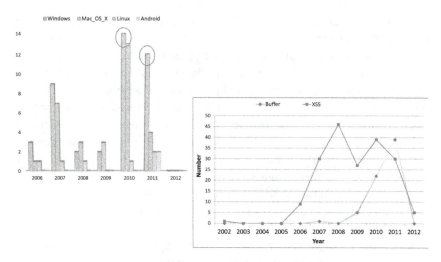

Figure 2.6 Comparison of vulnerabilities over operating systems.

Let us consider cross-site scripting vulnerability.[5] When data regarding the number of vulnerabilities are pulled from NVD across 2006 to 2012, we can see the trends of operating systems that are most impacted by this vulnerability, as shown in Figure 2.6. In addition, we can also compare the occurrences of different types of vulnerabilities such as cross-site scripting and buffer overflow. While this is a straightforward plotting of number of vulnerabilities across years, it provides insights into the robustness of operating systems for different types of vulnerabilities and across different CVSS metrics. Such analyses can be an important feed into decision making before choices for adopting software are made from a security point of view in organizational applications.

2.3 Integrated Use of Multiple Datasets

Let us consider a scenario where multiple datasets can be utilized to study potential cyberattacks. Cyberattacks are rare compared to the day-to-day traffic in a computer network; therefore, they appear in datasets as anomalies. Anomalies are essentially data points or patterns that are unusual with respect to the normal. It is clear that there needs to be a frame of reference that is

---

[5] https://tools.cisco.com/security/center/viewAlert.x?alertId=35601, Adobe Flash Player Cross-Site Scripting Vulnerability.

"normal" compared to which something is deemed an "anomaly." A single dataset such as any of the ones discussed so far can be used for anomaly detection, but it is important to note that if multiple datasets result in similar types of anomalies, then the credibility of labeling an anomaly is higher.

One such integrated evaluation would be to discover anomalies in network traffic data with a temporal, spatial, and human behavioral perspective. Studying how network traffic changes over time, which locations are the sources, where is it headed, and how are people generating this traffic – all these aspects become very critical in distinguishing the normal from the abnormal in the domain of cybersecurity. This requires shifting gears to view cybersecurity as a holistic people problem rather than a hardened defense problem. By utilizing some of the datasets discussed in this chapter, we can answer the following important questions in studying these aspects:

Firstly, computer networks evolve over time, and communication patterns change over time. Can we identify these key changes that are deviant from the normal changes in a communication pattern and associate them with anomalies in the network traffic?

Secondly, as attacks may have a spatial pattern, sources and destinations in certain geolocations can be more important for monitoring and preventing an attack. Therefore, can key geolocations that are sources of attacks, or key geolocations that are destinations of attacks, be identified? Moreover, can IP spoofing be mitigated by looking at multiple data sources to supplement the knowledge of a geospatial traffic pattern?

Thirdly, any type of an attack has common underpinnings of how it is carried out; this has not changed from physical security breaches to computer security breaches. Can this knowledge be leveraged to identify behavioral models of anomalies where we can see patterns of misuse?

Recent work highlights some of these questions in discovering anomalies utilizing network data to study human behavioral models such as Chen et al.) 2014) and Quader and Janeja (2014). These will be discussed further in Chapter 10.

2.4 Summary of Sources of Cybersecurity Data

Through this chapter, multiple types of sources of cybersecurity data have been discussed. Table 2.1 summarizes these data under the following: (a) data source, (b) literature study examples, and (c) type of detection it can be used for.

Table 2.1 *Summary of sources of cybersecurity data*

Source of cybersecurity data	Literature study examples	Type of detection it can be used for
Keystroke logging	Heron 2007, Cai and Hao 2011, Gupta et al. 2016, Hussain et al. 2016	User behavior, malicious use to detect user credentials
IDS log data	Abad et al. 2003, Koike and Ohno 2004, Vaarandi and Podiņš 2010, Deokar and Hazarnis 2012, Chen et al. 2014, Janeja et al. 2014, Quader and Janeja 2014, 2015	Association rule mining, human behavior modeling, log visualization, temporal analysis, anomaly detection
Router connectivity and log data	Tsuchiya 1988, Sklower 1991, Qiu 2007, Geocoding Infosec 2013, Kim Zetter Security 2013	Suspicious rerouting, traffic hijacking, bogus routes
Firewall log data	Golnabi et al. 2006, Abedin et al. 2010	Generate efficient rule sets, anomaly detection in policy rules
Raw payload data	Wang and Stolfo 2004, Parekh et al. 2006, Limmer and Dressler 2010, Kim et al. 2014, Roy 2014	Malware detection, embedded malware, user behavior
Network topology	Massicotte et al. 2003, Nicosia 2013, Namayanja and Janeja 2015, 2017	Consistent and inconsistent nodes, time points corresponding to anomalous activity
User system data	Stephens and Maloof 2014, Van Meigham 2016	User profiles, user behavior data, insider threats
Access control data	Vaidya et al. 2007, Mitra et al. 2016	Generate efficient access control roles
Eye tracker data	Darwish and Bataineh 2012	Browser security indicators, security cues, user behavior
Vulnerability data	Frei et al. 2006	Vulnerability trend discovery

3

Introduction to Data Mining

Clustering, Classification, and Association Rule Mining

3.1 Knowledge Discovery and Data Mining Process Models

Data mining (DM) is the discovery of hidden and nontrivial patterns in very large datasets. The discovered patterns are potentially actionable and beneficial to study the problem at hand.

There are several steps involved in this process as proposed initially by Fayyad and Shapiro (1996). Figure 3.1 depicts the goals of knowledge discovery (KD) and components of data mining methods they discussed. These goals of KD include the discovery of new patterns or verifying a hypothesis that the users generally accept or are interested in evaluating, such as prediction of future events or explanation to the user in the form of understandable and intuitive knowledge discovered. Increasingly, as data are becoming very large, data mining fits into the core analytics of any big data solution. In such scenarios, the core functionality of the mining algorithms does not change drastically; however, the infrastructure managing the parallelization is a key distinguishing factor in a big data environment. We further discuss the big data perspective to data mining in Chapter 4.

A data mining method that is used for the knowledge discovery will generally comprise multiple components, including the following:

(a) The model being used and its representation. This refers to the language used to describe the patterns along with any representational assumptions.
(b) A method to evaluate the model. DM algorithms have an expected output, and quality of results based on this can be quantified through an evaluation metric (such as accuracy and error metrics).

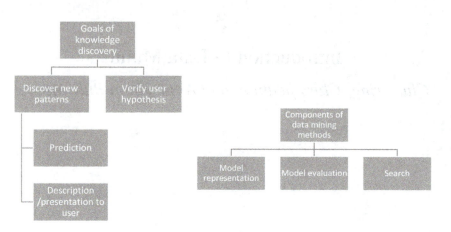

Figure 3.1 Goals of knowledge discovery and components of data mining methods.

DM method	Example evaluation criteria
Classification	Accuracy, precision, recall, F-measure
Clustering	Sum of Squared Error, silhouette coefficient
Association rule mining	Confidence, support, lift

Figure 3.2 DM method example evaluation criteria.

(c) A search component. This involves a parameter search and model search. This component allows for finding the optimal fit of both the model and parameter to use based on maximizing the evaluation criteria.

Some example methods and their evaluation criteria are shown in Figure 3.2. These will be discussed further in the following sections.

Figure 3.3 summarizes the steps for a standard knowledge discovery process. The process starts with large and potentially heterogeneous data sources. Through user input, data need to be identified and selected based on the task being addressed. As discussed in some models (such as Cross Industry Standard Process for DM [CRISP-DM]; see Chapman et al. 2000, Shearer 2000), it is important to have user input at this stage to clearly understand the business or user requirements that can facilitate better and more targeted data selection. Once the right data sources are identified, integrated data

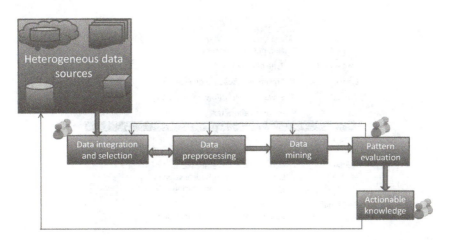

Figure 3.3 KDD process.

preprocessing is performed on these data sources. Data preprocessing tasks can include filling missing values, semantic mapping, removing redundancy in the data through correlation, noise removal, smoothing of the data, data volume reduction, and feature selection, among others. A large amount of preprocessing can done while integrating the data to resolve data inconsistencies. Data preprocessing generally takes up a majority of time, up to 80%, in any data mining project. A good preprocessing leads to good data mining. Data that have not been sufficiently preprocessed may lead to frivolous and random results. Thus, sufficient time should be allocated to the preprocessing tasks.

Once the data have been processed, then the relevant data mining task can be applied. Then the results need to be evaluated, and once this evaluation is quantified any patterns found can become actionable knowledge. It is clearly possible that any stage can send the process back to any of the preceding steps. In addition, once actionable patterns have been tested or examined by the end users, changes can be made to how and what data are collected for better knowledge discovery. All these steps are further described in the following sections. A detailed comparison of multiple DM process models is provided by Kurgan and Musilek (2006), which discusses a step-by-step comparison of over six such models.

3.2 Data Preprocessing

Data in the real world tend to be messy. This can be caused by device malfunction, data entry errors, or data integration from heterogeneous sources.

Attribute data type	Example
Numeric	Number of bytes sent
Categorical	Type of attack
Binary	Presence or absence of virus
Ordinal	Severity of alert (low, medium, high)
Text	Intrusion alarm text
Complex Types of Datasets	**Example**
Unstructured text	Spam email Intrusion log data
Spatial data	Geographical server locations Locations of cyberphysical sensors Locations of spam origination
Graph data	IP communication graph Routing paths for communication

Figure 3.4 Examples of some data types.

To get high-quality mining results that are actionable and beneficial, it is important to clean up the messy data. Data can be very large in terms of size and number of attributes, meaning that important patterns get hidden in the subspaces. It is important to focus on the right portions of the data both in terms of the volume and the attributes. Data preprocessing such as data cleaning, data transformation, and data reduction, as well as careful data integration, prepares the data for mining.

These tasks will vary based on the data types and the complexity of the data. Data can be of different types, including text, numeric (discrete or continuous), ordinal (order or ranked data, such as severity scores, which have an inherent order to them), binary data (with only two possible outcomes), and categorical data (with multiple categories). Various data types and types of complex datasets are shown in Figure 3.4, along with brief descriptions and examples of relevant datasets of these types. Some complex datasets may consists of multiple types of attributes in them; for example, intrusion log data will consist of text, categorical, and numeric data attributes.

The preprocessing tasks to apply are selected based on the complexity of the data and the attribute types. For example, similarity in the data is defined differently for numeric attributes versus binary valued attributes. Similarly, for complexity of the data, for example, spatial data, would require additional steps such as discovering spatial proximity, such that the mining task can be separated by spatial neighborhoods.

Data preprocessing includes several tasks as discussed in the following subsections.

3.2.1 Data Cleaning

Many times in network traffic data we might see missing data values due to dropped packets, traffic fluctuations over different time periods, and generally redundancies in network communication data. This step addresses the general cleanup of messy data, including (a) missing data values, (b) fluctuations in the data, and (c) inconsistencies and redundancies in the data.

Missing data: To address the missing values, the mean of the attribute (a) if numerical or mode if categorical, can be used to replace the missing values (see Figure 3.5). However, if the dataset is large or has multiple classes/groups, a fairly simple way to deal with missing values is to use the mean of the group to replace the missing values in that particular group (Luengo et al. 2012). This is a fairly intuitive and simple way to deal with missing values. Other more involved methods can be used to predict the missing values by training based on the records that have the complete data.

How much missing data can be replaced? A rule of thumb is that if roughly 5% of the data are missing, then it is feasible to replace it. One could also

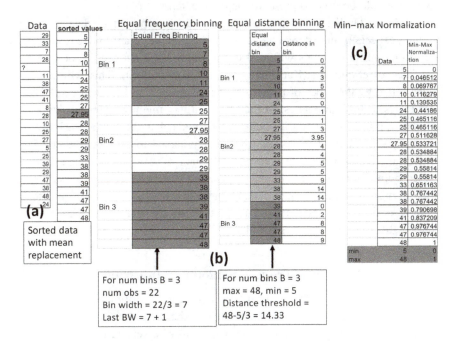

Figure 3.5 Example data preprocessing.

consult with a domain expert or utilize domain heuristics to decide if data should be discarded or filled in to impute the missing data.

Noisy data: Fluctuations in the data, when taken together in similarity or distance-based methods, can cause results to be messy. Thus, it is useful to clean the noise by smoothing out the data to provide simpler and more refined representations. If the data can be divided into small groups and the mean behavior of the groups can be used to represent all the data in the group, then the data will be much smoother.

Small groups can be created by creating small bins or buckets in the data, and the mean or mode of the data can replace all the values in each bin. Binning is essentially an unsupervised splitting-based discretization method of the data. Several discretization techniques are discussed in by Liu et al. (2002) and Garcia et al. (2013). Equal frequency binning roughly deposits an equal number of points are across a fixed number of bins as shown in Figure 3.5b. Similarly, equal distance binning distributes an equal distance across a fixed number of bins (Figure 3.5b).

Clustering where similar data points are grouped together and the mean or centroid of the cluster can be used to replace the other values can also create a smooth dataset. In both of binning and clustering, a relatively large number of groups should be used to preserve the data patterns.

Outliers: Outliers in the data can drastically alter data mining output, especially in distance-based methods. It is important to decide before-hand through discussions with end users whether outliers need to be accom-modated or eliminated (Kauffman and Rousseeuw 1990). This will also be determined by the types of patterns being discovered. If the main task of the mining is to find anomalies, in that case outliers might be kept in the data; however, if the mining task is finding the normal behavior, such as the baseline network signatures, then it might be more practical to remove outliers. For univariate data, several statistical methods such as interquartile range (IQR)–based outlier detection, discordancy tests, and standard deviation–based tests can be used. For multivariate data, distance-based outlier detection methods can be utilized. Outlier detection as part of the anomaly detection tasks is further discussed in Chapters 6 and 7.

3.2.2 Data Transformation and Integration

When data are merged from multiple sources, the resolution of the data may be different; for example, it could be years rather than days. In addition, the attribute ranges may vary, and these ranges may be very large. In these and other scenarios, the data will need to be transformed such that the traditional data mining algorithms can be uniformly applied. Other data integration steps such as mapping the structure and content also need to be performed.

Normalization: Many normalization methods have been presented in the traditional statistical literature. One common method of normalization is the min–max normalization (as shown in 3.1) or feature scaling such that d' is the transformed value and d is the original value in an attribute 'D'. An example is shown in Figure 3.5c:

$$d' = \frac{d - minD}{maxD - minD} \left(new_{maxD} - new_{minD}\right) + new_{minD} \qquad (3.1)$$

In this method, a new range, for example 0–1, is created for the data such that the old min becomes 0 and the old max becomes 1 so that all the data are within this range. This allows for a rescaling of the data to a new well-defined range. Other measures such as z-score normalization work well when the data are normally distributed and the mean is well defined. A comparison of normalization methods, including min–max, z-score, and decimal scaling, is provided by al Shalabi et al. (2006).

3.2.3 Data Reduction

Data mining is inherently useful when patterns need to be discovered in very large amounts of data. For example, network traffic data from Wireshark can become terabytes of data even within a few seconds depending on the network size. Similarly, source and destination-based communication graph can be a massive dataset. In such cases data reduction is an important strategy to help reduce the volume and attribute set of the data.

One important step in performing data mining on such massive datasets is reducing the dimensions that may not have sufficient data to begin with or may not be representative of the patterns to be found. For example, in the Wireshark data capture, we might mainly be interested in looking at just the source and destination to generate a communication graph and annotate the graph with packet size. In such scenarios, it is useful to reduce the volume and dimensionality of the data. Moreover, in sparse datasets, data reduction helps identify the key subspaces of the data. Data reduction, particularly volume reduction, is also related to the smoothing techniques mentioned in the previous sections, because the central measures of the smoothed data can be used instead of all the data points.

Methods such as feature selection can be used to identify the relevant features for performing data mining (Molina et al. 2002, Chandrashekar and

Sahin 2014). Feature selection methods can be ranking-based methods that use entropy measures to quantify how much data are useful in each of the attributes. Methods such as singular-value decomposition and principal component analysis (Fodor 2002 and Wall et al. 2003) work on the common principal to transform the data such that a combination of the features can be used as transformed features.

3.3 Data Mining

Data in security applications are heterogeneous, high-dimensional, and often complex. In this section, we consider three key groups of methods, namely clustering, classification, and association rule mining. The supervised methods are also referred to as machine learning, where historic data help train the algorithm to make predictions. Additional methods such as deep learning are discussed in Chapter 11.

Each of these methods also feeds into the discovery of anomalies or unusual patterns, which is particularly relevant to cybersecurity (see Figure 3.6). In particular, anomaly detection deals with finding individual objects and rare

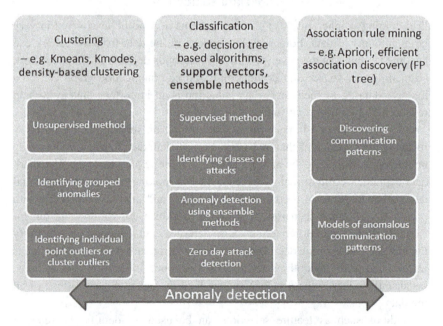

Figure 3.6 Data mining methods.

combinations of objects that are unusual (anomalous) with respect to other "normal" data points. Often the normal is a cluster or a set of clusters and the anomalies are the outlier data points.

We start by introducing measures of similarity, which are essential for clustering and various metrics for evaluation of the results of data mining.

3.3.1 Measures of Similarity

3.3.1.1 Distance Measures

If we want to identify a network traffic data point that looks deviant compared to others, the fundamental way to do that is to see how similar or dissimilar it is to other data points in the network traffic. We use these measures when we identify clusters as discussed later in this chapter and also when we identify distance-based outliers, discussed in Chapter 7.

The similarity or dissimilarity between two objects can be interpreted as the distance between them. A nonnegative function $d(x,y)$, measuring distance between objects x and y is a metric if it satisfies the following:

- The identity property, $d(x,x) = 0$
- The symmetry property, $d(x,y) = d(y,x)$
- The triangle inequality, $g(x,y) + g(y,z) \geq g(x,z)$

Euclidean distance, the straight-line distance between two points in Euclidean space in terms of the attributes of each data point, is one of the most commonly used distance metrics.

Euclidean distance (ED) is computed given two n-dimensional data points $X(x_1, x_2, \ldots, x_n)$ and $Y(y_1, y_2, \ldots, y_n)$, as shown in (3.2):

$$ED(X,Y) = \sqrt{(x_1 - y_1)^2 + (x_2 - y_2)^2 + \cdots + (x_n - y_n)^2} \qquad (3.2)$$

Manhattan distance (MD) is the "city block" distance or the distance measured on each axis. MD is computed as shown in (3.3):

$$MD(X,Y) = (|x_1 - y_1| + |x_2 - y_2| + \cdots + |x_n - y_n|) \qquad (3.3)$$

The *Minkowski distance (MnD)* is the generalizable distance from which both Euclidean and Manhattan distance are derived. MnD is computed as shown in (3.4):

$$MnD(X,Y) = \sqrt[p]{(x_1 - y_1)^p + (x_2 - y_2)^p + \cdots + (x_n - y_n)^p} \qquad (3.4)$$

For $p = 2$, the Minkowski distance generalizes to Euclidean distance.

Distance metric	Formula
Minkowski	$MnD(X,Y) = \sqrt[p]{(x_1 - y_1)^p + (x_2 - y_2)^p + \cdots + (x_n - y_n)^p}$
Manhattan	$MD(X,Y) = (|x_1 - y_1| + |x_2 - y_2| + \cdots + |x_n - y_n|)$
Euclidean	$ED(X,Y) = \sqrt{(x_1 - y_1)^2 + (x_2 - y_2)^2 + \cdots + (x_n - y_n)^2}$

Figure 3.7 Example distance metrics.

Hausdorff distance (HD) is the maximum distance of a set to the nearest point in the other set. Hausdorff distance is a distance metric that finds the distances between two points considering the contribution of each dimension. It is defined as follows: Given two n-dimensional objects $X(x_1, x_2, \ldots, x_n)$ and $Y(y_1, y_2, \ldots, y_n)$,

$$HD(X,Y) = \text{Max}\,\{h(X,Y), h(Y,X)\},$$
$$\text{where } h(X,Y)' = \text{max}\,(\text{min}\,(x_i - y_i))$$
$$\text{and } h(Y,X) = \text{max}\,(\text{min}\,(y_i - x_i)).$$

This distance takes each dimension into account while calculating the distance between two points, thus bringing out the stark differences between the specific dimensions. HD has been used in image processing literature to discover difference between images. As deep fakes in video and imaging data become prevalent, distance measures such as Hausdorff distance can be quite useful.

Some of the distance measures are summarized in Figure 3.7.

3.3.1.2 Similarity in Binary-Valued Variables

Consider two vulnerabilities where you are trying to identify vulnerabilities that are similar to each other. We can extract keywords from all vulnerability descriptions and produce a binary feature vector for each vulnerability with a presence of a keyword (1) or absence of a keyword (0). We can use similarity measures on these binary-valued feature vectors to find vulnerabilities that are similar to each other.

When computing a similarity coefficient matrix for binary-valued attributes, such as in the preceding example and as illustrated in Figure 3.8, we start with the data matrix comprised of feature vectors for each object. The data matrix is thus an $n \times m$ matrix consisting of n objects each with a feature vector of m features. The first step is to determine the contingency matrix of this data matrix, which essentially is the values of **a, b, c,** and **d**. Here, **a** is the number of positive matches for each object pair where objects o_i and o_j both have a value of **1**, **b** is the number of mismatches where o_i has a value of **1** and o_j has a value of **0**, **c** is the number of mismatches such that o_i has a value of **0** and o_j

(a)

Data matrix

O1	1	1	0	0
O2	1	1	1	0
O3	0	0	0	1

(b)
Contingency matrix

	a (1-1)	b (1-0)	c (0-1)	d (0-0)
S(O1,O2)	2	0	1	1
S(O1,O3)	0	1	1	2
S(O2,O3)	0	3	1	0

(c)
Similarity matrix (Jaccard coefficient)

	O1	O2	O3
O1	1	0.5	0
O2		1	0
O3			1

Figure 3.8 Process of similarity computation.

has a value of **1**, and **d** equals the number of negative matches such that o_i and o_j both have a value of **0**. Once these values are computed, they can be used to compute the similarity using different types of similarity coefficients such as the Jaccard coefficient **(a/a + b + c)**. The output is a $n \times n$ triangular matrix with the computed similarity between each object pair.

The *Jaccard coefficient* is an asymmetric coefficient that ignores negative matches. Asymmetric coefficients should be applied to data where absences (0s) are thought to carry no information. For example, if we would like to study attacks, then a system that did not have a set of attacks is not a relevant question so features with a **0–0** match (i.e., the system has not had an attack) is not relevant. Therefore, asymmetric coefficient is useful to employ. Symmetric coefficients acknowledge negative matches and should therefore be applied to data where absences are thought to carry information. An example is the *simple matching coefficient (SMC)*. For example, if we are studying impact of a vulnerability patch on a software, then if in two types of applications there was no impact of the patch, then this is pertinent information we want to capture. Thus, in this scenario we would use a symmetric coefficient. There are some other types of coefficients, called hybrids, that include the **0–0** match in either the numerator or denominator but not both. Several different types of similarity coefficients are proposed and evaluated (Lewis and Janeja 2011), and some examples are shown in Figure 3.9.

Asymmetric	
Coefficient	Expression
Anderberg (range 0–1)	$\dfrac{a}{a + 2(b + c)}$
Jaccard–Tanimoto (range 0–1)	$\dfrac{a}{a + b + c}$
Kulczynski (range 0–1)	$\dfrac{1}{2}\left(\dfrac{a}{a + b} + \dfrac{a}{a + c}\right)$
Ochiai–Cosine (range 0–1)	$\dfrac{a}{\sqrt{(a + b)(a + c)}}$
Sorensen–Dice (range 0–1)	$\dfrac{2a}{2a + b + c}$
Symmetric	
Baulieu (range –1 to 1)	$\dfrac{4(ad - bc)}{(a + b + c + d)^2}$
Simple matching (range 0–1)	$\dfrac{a + d}{a + b + c + d}$
Russel–Rao (hybrid, range 0–1)	$\dfrac{a}{a + b + c + d}$

Figure 3.9 Example types of similarity coefficients.

3.3.2 Measures of Evaluation

Every data mining method needs to have a way to evaluate the results to ensure quality of results from an algorithmic perspective as well as usefulness, ground truth evaluation, and business evaluation.

For *classification approaches* where the accuracy of predicted labels is being evaluated, measures such as accuracy, precision, recall, and F-measure are used. These are based on validating the results against real-world or known class labels. We compare the experimental finding with the labeled ground truth for class 1 and class 2, for example anomaly or not an anomaly, to measure the accuracy of the approach. These measures are based on true positive (TP), which indicates that the label is classified correctly as an anomaly; the true negative (TN), which indicates if the label is classified correctly as not an anomaly; false positive (FP), which indicates that the node is misclassified as an anomaly; and false negative (FN), which indicates that

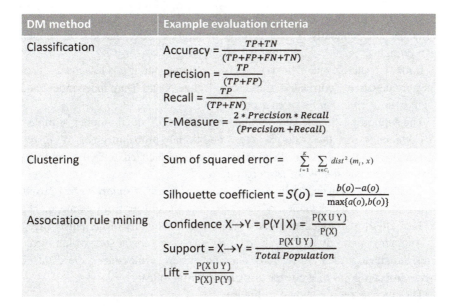

DM method	Example evaluation criteria
Classification	Accuracy = $\frac{TP+TN}{(TP+FP+FN+TN)}$ Precision = $\frac{TP}{(TP+FP)}$ Recall = $\frac{TP}{(TP+FN)}$ F-Measure = $\frac{2*Precision*Recall}{(Precision+Recall)}$
Clustering	Sum of squared error = $\sum_{i=1}^{K}\sum_{x\in C_i} dist^2(m_i,x)$ Silhouette coefficient = $S(o) = \frac{b(o)-a(o)}{\max\{a(o),b(o)\}}$
Association rule mining	Confidence X→Y = P(Y|X) = $\frac{P(X\cup Y)}{P(X)}$ Support = X→Y = $\frac{P(X\cup Y)}{Total\ Population}$ Lift = $\frac{P(X\cup Y)}{P(X)\ P(Y)}$

Figure 3.10 Example measures of evaluation.

the anomaly is misclassified as not an anomaly. There are several performance measures that can be calculated based on the labeled anomalies as shown in Figure 3.10.

There are additional measures that can be used, such as (1) true positive rate = *TP/(TP + FN)*, which shows the percentage of positive instances correctly classified; (2) true negative rate = *TN/(TN + FP)*, which shows the percentage of the negative instances correctly classified; (3) false positive rate = *FP/(TN + FP)*; and (4) false negative rate = *FN/(FN + TP)*. Overall accuracy is a commonly accepted performance measure for classification performance. However, accuracy alone can be misleading, for example in a setting where anomalies are small percentage in the data. In such instances, a combination of precision and recall in the form of F-measure can be used. The additional measures allow us to validate the results from multiple perspectives.

In case of *association rule mining*, measures such as lift, confidence, and support are used to measure the quality of results of association rules of the form X→Y.

Lift is a correlation measure that assesses the degree to which the occurrences of one lifts the occurrences of the other. The lift between the occurrences of X and Y items in a transaction can be measured as lift(X→Y) = P(X∪Y)/P(X)P(Y), where numerator defines the occurrences of the X and

Y instances together and the denominator indicates the occurrences of the instances independently. The preceding equation can be extended to more than two domains.

If lift > 1, then X and Y are positively correlated, and if it is less than 1, then they are negatively correlated. If the lift $= 1$, then X and Y are independent and there is no correlation between them.

The support of the rule is the probability of P(X∪Y)/total number of tuples.

Confidence of the rule is the conditional probability of Y given X (i.e., P(Y|X)) = P(X∪Y)/P(X). Each rule is associated with a confidence that measures the degree of association.

Clustering quality can be measured through the *sum of squared error (SSE)*, which measures the deviation of every point in the cluster from its mean. The SSE of all clusters together gives a measure of the quality of the clustering.

Another commonly used measure is the *silhouette coefficient*, which measures the shadow of a cluster over another cluster by measuring the distance between each point of a cluster to its neighboring clusters.

These measures are shown in Figure 3.10.

3.3.3 Clustering Algorithms

Clustering is a technique used for finding similarly behaving groups in data or to identify preexisting structure in the data. Ideally, a clustering method should lead to a crisp demarcation of the data such that objects in the same group are highly similar to each other and objects in different groups are very dissimilar to each other, that is, intercluster distance should be maximized and intracluster distance should be minimized.

In addition to distinguishing between various types of objects, clustering can be used as an exploratory process and as a precursor to another mining task such as anomaly detection. When a cluster is discovered, the objects outside of this structure could be of interest (e.g., anomaly detection). In other cases, the cluster itself could be of interest.

Clustering has been a well-studied problem in the statistical literature, and there exist several well-developed algorithms already tried and tested (Kotsiantis and Pintelas 2004, Jain 2010). Clustering approaches can be roughly divided into several subclasses of algorithms, as shown in Figure 3.11. *Partitioning approaches* divide the data into partitions with optimal partitions being defined based on some heuristics as in the case of K-Means. Hierarchical algorithms divide the data into a hierarchy starting from all data points into one cluster and dividing up the data points such that each data point is in its own cluster. Density-based approaches divide the data

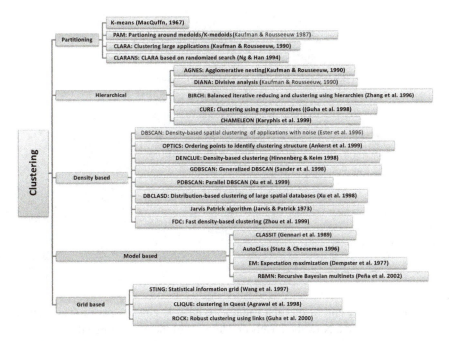

Figure 3.11 Clustering approaches.

into groups based on density of the data points in a user-defined neighborhood range, such as density-based spatial clustering of applications with noise (DBSCAN). We focus on a few selected and well-used algorithms to illustrate the concepts of clustering across some of these types of approaches.

3.3.3.1 Partitioning Algorithms: K-Means

The primary approach of partitioning algorithms, such as K-means, is to form subgroups of the entire set of data, by making K partitions, based on a similarity criterion. The data in the subgroups are grouped around a central object such as a mean or medoid. However, they differ in the way that they define the similarity criterion, central object, and convergence of clusters. K-means (MacQueen 1967) is based on finding partitions in the data by evaluating the distance of objects in the cluster to the centroid, which is the mean of the data in the cluster. The algorithm, depicted in the example in Figure 3.12, starts with a set of points and a K value for number of clusters to form and seed centroids that can be selected from the data or randomly generated. The algorithm begins by partitioning points around the seed centroids such that the point is allocated to the centroid to which its distance is

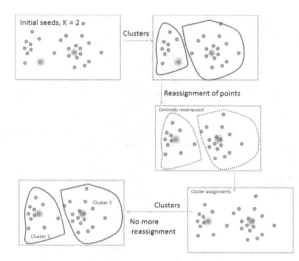

Figure 3.12 K-means clustering.

smallest. At the end of the first round, we have K clusters partitioned around the seed centroids. Now the means or centroids of the newly formed clusters are computed and the process is repeated to align the points to the newly computed centroids. This process is iterated until there is no more reassignment of the points moving from one cluster to the other. Thus, K-means works on a heuristic-based partitioning rather than an optimal partitioning. The quality of clusters can be evaluated using the sum of squared errors (Figure 3.10), which computes the distance of every point in the cluster to its centroid. Intuitively, the bigger the error, the more spread out the points are around the mean. However, if we plot the SSE for K = 1 to K = n (n number of points), then SSE ranges from a very large value (all points in one cluster) to 0 (every point in its own cluster). The elbow of this plot provides an ideal value of K.

K-means has been a well-used and well-accepted clustering algorithm due to its intuitive approach and interpretable output. However, K-means does not work very well in the presence of outliers and does not form nonspherical or free-form clusters.

3.3.3.2 Partitioning Algorithms: CLARANS

Clustering large applications with randomized search (CLARANS), proposed by Ng and Han (1994), is a type of partitioning approach. It extends the ideas proposed in partitioning around medoids (PAM-K-medoid) and clustering large applications (CLARA) proposed by Kaufman and Rousseeuw (1987, 1990). This algorithm draws samples with randomness at each step of the

Let us say our data is : 2   3   5   8   9   12

Input parameters:
NumLocal = number of local minimas (# of iterations)
MaxNeighbors = number of cost comparisons in each iteration
Eg: NumLocal = 4; MaxNeighbor = 5

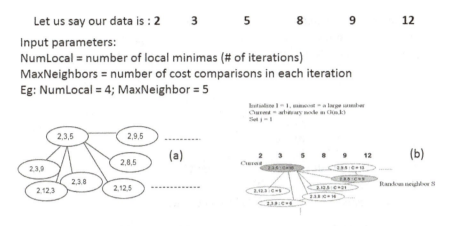

Figure 3.13 CLARANS process.

process. The quality of clustering is dependent on the sampling technique being used. Similar to other partitioning techniques, K is fixed. Each cluster is represented as a graph node containing the solution of clustering in terms of medoids or the central representative object around which other objects are clustered. The neighboring node differs by one object from its neighbor, and they are connected by an edge. For example, a node with objects 2, 3, and 4 and a node with objects 3, 4, and 5 differ in only one object so they are neighbors and are joined by an edge. It selects a sample of neighbors unlike CLARA, which selects a sample of the original data. For each node selected, the squared error is calculated. CLARANS also uses the technique to determine the natural clustering using the silhouette coefficient (Kauffman and Rousseeuw 1990).

The algorithm works as shown in Figure 3.13.

The edge graph looks as shown in Figure 3.13a. It starts by setting parameter Current to an arbitrary node and set S to a random neighbor of Current. It finds the cost difference between *Current and S*. If S has a lower cost, then it sets *Current* to S and resets $j = 1$. Now if S has cost more than *Current*, then a counter is incremented. If J is less than the parameter *maxneighbors*, then the algorithm finds a new random neighbor of Current; otherwise, it compares the cost of current with *minCost* threshold; if it is less than *mincost*, then it sets a flag for *bestnode* to *current*. If threshold for number of iterations is met, then *bestnode* is output; otherwise, a new random current node is selected to repeat the process.

Silhouette Coefficient CLARANS uses the silhouette coefficient (proposed in Kaufman and Rousseeuw 1987) to identify the quality of clustering results in terms of structure and its silhouette or shadow on other clusters.

Given object o in a cluster A, then $a(o)$ is the average distance between the object o and the objects in cluster A. $b(o)$ is the average distance between the object o and the objects in the second-closest cluster B. The silhouette of o is then defined as

$$S(o) = \frac{b(o) - a(o)}{\max\{a(o), b(o)\}}$$

where

$S(o) = -1$: not well assigned, on average closer to members of B
$S(o) = 0$: in between A and B
$S(o) = 1$: good assignment of "o" to its cluster A

The silhouette coefficient of a clustering is thus the average silhouette of all the objects in the cluster.

CLARANS provides an efficient way to deal with the issues related to PAM (K-Medoids) that involves a large number of swapping operations, leading to very high complexity. It also improves upon CLARA. CLARANS is similar to CLARA in terms of sampling, but here the sampling is done at every step. However, objects are stored in main memory and the focus on representative objects is missing. This issue has been addressed using spatial data structures such as R* trees and focusing techniques. Although CLARANS enables outlier detection, it is not primarily geared toward the process of detecting anomalies.

3.3.3.3 Density-Based Algorithms: DBSCAN

Density-based algorithms can be useful for traditional cybersecurity data, such as network traffic data, to identify dense clusters in Euclidean space. In addition, they are also very useful for geospatial datasets. For example, in studying threats over a geospatial region, this could be a useful method. Similarly, for sensor networks that rely a lot on the spatial layouts, it may be useful to identify similarly behaving dense clusters and potential anomalies that stand apart from sensors in proximity.

Density-based algorithm for discovering clusters in large spatial databases with noise, proposed by Ester et al. (1996), is the foundation of several other density-based clustering algorithms. The basic idea is that we see clusters as dense or sparse regions based on the number of points in the neighborhood region of a point under consideration. They formalize these ideas with a certain radius and a minimum number of points in the region (parameters: ε, MinPts). The minimum number of points in a radius of ε facilitates the measurement of density in that neighborhood. ε Neighborhood (in Euclidean point space) is the neighborhood of a point that contains the (minPts) points. Variations of

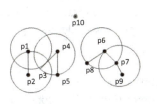

Example: MinPts=3, ε=1   (b)
Core Points: p2, p4, p6, and p7
p1 is directly density reachable from p2
p3 is directly density reachable from p4
p5 is directly density reachable from p6
p6 is directly density reachable from p7

p8 is indirectly density reachable from p7 as p8
DDR from p6 and p6 DDR from p7 so by
transitivity p8 is indirectly density reachable
from p7
p1, p3, and p5 are all density connected points
p10 is an outlier

(a)

Figure 3.14 DBSCAN process.

DBSCAN identify ε through computing K distance for every point, i.e., if $k = 2$, the distance between the point and its second-nearest neighbor, and sort this in descending order. The K-Distance is plotted and a valley or dip in the K-distance plot along with a user input of the expected noise determines the ε neighborhood. The algorithm defines density in terms of core points. A core point is an object that has the minimum points in its neighborhood defined by ε.

The algorithm works as shown in Figure 3.14. The algorithm begins by identifying core points and forming clusters through directly density reachable points from this core point. It then merges the cluster with such points. The process terminates when no new point can be added.

Thus, a density-based cluster is a set of density-connected objects. Every object not contained in any cluster is considered to be noise.

This approach identifies connected cluster structures, which can identify arbitrarily shaped clusters unlike the other partitioning algorithms. It takes into consideration a neighborhood of an object based on the distance and count of the objects in the neighborhood. The initial ε distance is calculated using the K nearest neighbor (K-NN) query with some level of user input. Once the clusters start emerging, they can be merged using the concepts of density connectivity and density reachability. However, this may lead to forming of big global clusters (single link effect) without identifying local cluster structures. This does not truly reflect the density of the cluster in terms of the local density structure. This algorithm is also sensitive to input parameters such as the minimum objects in the neighborhood and the value of K for the K-NN query. Moreover, this is approach is not well suited to high-dimensional datasets since the density connectedness is not directly applicable and intuitive for all the dimensions. It could be possible that objects in some dimensions are similar, but very dissimilar in some other dimensions. Several variations of DBSCAN, as shown in Figure 3.11, have been proposed addressing these limitations.

3.3.3.4 Density-Based Algorithms: OPTICS

Ordering points to identify the clustering structure (OPTICS), proposed by Ankerst et al. (1999), is a density-based algorithm. Many real-time datasets cannot be characterized by global density parameters. Different local densities may be needed to identify clusters in different regions of the data space. Mostly the clusters that are formed are large without any segregation of smaller clusters that may be contained in these.

Density-based clustering may miss detecting these smaller structures within a dense cluster as there can be several possible parameter values that can be used. For a constant MinPts value, density-based clusters with respect to higher density (or low radius) are completely contained in density-connected sets with respect to a lower density (or high radius).

OPTICS extends the DBSCAN algorithm to generate clusters with multiple densities simultaneously. Moreover, a specific order is followed in which objects are processed. More dense clusters (low radius) are processed first. It does not assign cluster memberships but just stores the order in which objects are processed. This information is later used to assign memberships and is provided as two values: core distance and reachability distance. *Core distance* is the smallest distance ε' between a point p and an object in its ε-neighborhood, such that p would be a core object with respect to ε'. In Figure 3.15, distance *core (o)* makes o a core object. This distance in the example is less than the ε neighborhood. *Reachability distance* of an object p with respect to another object o is the smallest distance such that p is directly density reachable from o if o is a core object. The reachability distance cannot be smaller

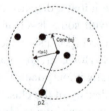

Core distance (o) reachability distance
(p1,o), r(p2,o) for minpts = 3

Figure 3.15 Core and reachability distance.

than the core distance of 'o'. The reachability distance of p depends on the core object with respect to which it is calculated.

A low reachability indicates an object within a cluster; high reachability indicates a noise object or a jump from one cluster to another. Ankerst et al. (1999) propose a technique to view the cluster structure graphically using the reachability plot. This is a graph of the reachability distances for each object in the cluster ordering. This cluster ordering is facilitated by a data structure, namely the access control list. An object p1 is selected and the core distance is selected around p1. This leads to the identification of objects in this neighborhood, and their reachability distances are measured and stored in the access control list. This process is performed iteratively in the neighboring objects as well. Subsequently, the distance is plotted on the reachability plot.

OPTICS addresses the issue of not only traditional clustering but also intrinsic clustering structure, which other clustering techniques ignore (single-link effect). Many clustering techniques have global parameters producing uniform structures, and many times the smaller clusters are merged in the nearby clusters connected by few points into one big cluster. Thus, OPTICS addresses this issue of intrinsic clusters that helps in identifying dispersion of data and correlation of the data. However, this approach is still somewhat sensitive to input parameters such as minpts in a neighborhood K value for the KNN query. There could be a scenario when a small cluster itself could be outlying with respect to a global structure. This book does not address such a scenario.

3.3.4 Classification

Given a collection of records, the goal of classification is to derive a model that can assign a record to a class as accurately as possible. A class is often referred to as a label; for example, a data point is anomaly or not. For example, Anomaly and Not an anomaly can be two classes. Objects can also be classified as belonging to multiple classes. Classification is a supervised method that is based on a well-formed training set, i.e., prelabeled data with samples of both classes, to create a classifier model that identifies previously unseen observations in the test set for labeling each instance with a label based on the model's prediction. The overall process of classification is shown in Figure 3.16. In general, the labeled data, which is a set of database tuples with their corresponding class labels, can be divided into training and test data. In the training phase, a classification algorithm builds a classifier (set of rules) for each class using features or attributes in the data. In the testing phase, a set of data tuples that are not overlapping with the training tuples is selected. Each

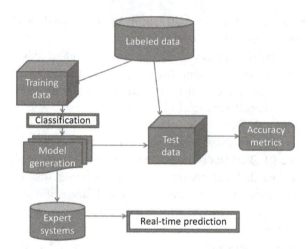

Figure 3.16 Classification process.

test tuple is compared with the classification rules to determine its class. The labels of the test tuples are reported along with percentage of correctly classified labels to evaluate the accuracy of the model in previously unseen (labels in the) data. As the model accuracy is evaluated and rules are perfected for labeling previously unseen instances, these rules can be used for future predictions. One way to do that is to maintain a knowledge base or expert system with these discovered rules, and as incoming data are observed to match these rules, the labels for them are predicted.

Several classification algorithms have been proposed that approach the classification modeling using different mechanisms (see Figure 3.17 and Kotsiantis et al. 2006). For example, the decision tree algorithms provide a set of rules in the form of a decision tree to provide labels based on conditions in the tree branches. Bayesian models provide a probability value of an instance belonging to a class. Function-based methods provide functions for demarcations in the data such that the data are clearly divided between classes. In addition to some of the basic methods there are also classifier combinations, namely ensemble methods, which combine the classifiers across multiple samples of the training data. These methods are designed to increase the accuracy of the classification task by training several different classifiers and combining their results to output a class label. A good analogy is when humans seek the input of several experts before making an important decision. There are several studies suggesting that diversity among classifier models is a required condition for having a good ensemble classifier (Li 2008, Garcia-Teodoro et al. 2009). These studies also suggest that the base classifier in the

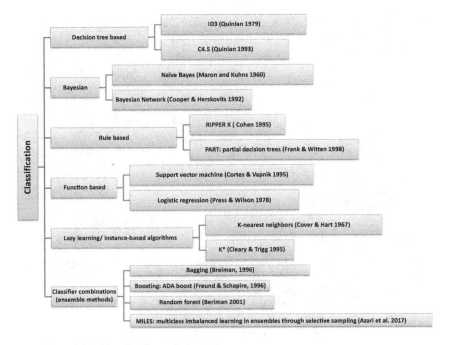

Figure 3.17 Classification techniques.

ensemble should be a weak learner in order to get the best results out of an ensemble. A classification algorithm is called a weak learner if a small change in the training data produces big difference in the induced classifier mapping.

We next discuss a few relevant classification methods.

3.3.4.1 Decision Tree Based: C4.5

Proposed by Quinlan (1993), C4.5 is a well-accepted classification method that provides an intuitive model in the form of a decision tree based on the training set.

Let us consider a small internet trace data, shown in Figure 3.18a, including attributes such as day of the week, average size of packets, and average size of the flows, and labeled with attack information as to whether such traces contained attacks or not. The task would be to classify whether there will be an attack or not given the type of trace data.

The C4.5 decision tree algorithm starts by evaluating attributes to identify the attribute that gives the most information for making a decision for labeling with the class. The decision tree provides a series of rules to identify which attribute should be evaluated to come up with the label for a record where the

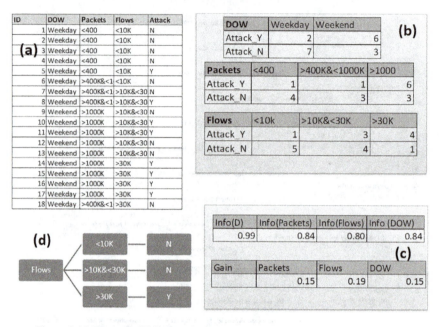

Figure 3.18 Example C4.5 execution.

label is unknown. These rules form the branches in the decision tree. The purity of the attributes to make a decision split in the tree is computed using measures such as entropy. The entropy of a particular node, $Info_A$ (corresponding to an attribute), in a tree is the sum, over all classes represented in the node, of the proportion of records belonging to a particular class. The entropy computation of the data, $Info_D$ and attribute, $Info_A$ (e.g., Info (packets)) is shown in Figure 3.19. When entropy reduction is chosen as a splitting criterion, the algorithm searches for the split that reduces entropy or equivalently the split that increases information, learned from that attribute, by the greatest amount. If a leaf in a decision tree is entirely pure, then classes in the leaf can be clearly described, that is, they all fall in the same class. If a leaf is highly impure, then describing it is much more complex. Entropy helps us quantify the concept of purity of the node. The best split is one that does the best job of separating the records into groups where a single class predominates the group of records in that branch.

The attribute that reduces the entropy or maximizes the gain ($Gain_A = Info_D - Info_A$) is selected as a splitting attribute. Once the first splitting attribute is decided, then recursively the process is repeated in all the attributes of the subset of the data remaining, resulting in a decision tree such as is shown

Expected information needed to classify a tuple in a dataset

$$Info(D) = -\sum_{i=1}^{m} p_i \log_2(p_i)$$

$$Info(D) = I(8,10) = -\frac{8}{18}\log_2(\frac{8}{18}) - \frac{10}{18}\log_2(\frac{10}{18}) = 0.99$$

How much more info would you still need (after partitioning) to get exact classification?

$$Info_A(D) = \sum_{j=1}^{v} \frac{|D_j|}{|D|} \times I(D_j)$$

$$Info_{packets}(D) = \frac{5}{18}I(1,4) + \frac{4}{18}I(1,3)$$

$$+ \frac{9}{18}I(6,3) = 0.83$$

$$Info_{packets}(D) = \frac{5}{18}(-\frac{1}{5}\log_2\frac{1}{5} - \frac{4}{5}\log_2\frac{4}{5}) + \frac{4}{18}(-\frac{1}{4}\log_2\frac{1}{4} - \frac{3}{4}\log_2\frac{3}{4})$$

$$+ \frac{9}{18}(-\frac{6}{9}\log_2\frac{6}{9} - \frac{3}{9}\log_2\frac{3}{9}) = 0.83$$

How much would be gained by partitioning on this attribute?

$$Gain(packets) = Info(D) - Info_{packets}(D) = 0.15$$

Expected reduction in the information requirement caused by knowing the value of this attribute.

Figure 3.19 Entropy computation for a data set and attributes.

in Figure 3.18d. Several other measures for attribute selection measures can be used (such as evaluated by Dash and Liu 1997).

3.3.4.2 Classifier Combinations: MILES

In massive datasets, patterns can often be hidden and hard to discern with individual classifiers. Moreover, if different parts of the data can contribute to a different aspect of the pattern, a single classifier may not be useful. Let us consider an example of phishing detection (Azari et al. 2020). If we look at email messages to predict whether an email could be phishing or not, we can look at the header information or the body of the email to get different elements of potential phishing. Moreover, the data may have imbalance in terms of phishing emails and normal emails. In this case, using an ensemble-based method, which can handle class imbalance, can be very useful to consider different parts of the email to flag a phishing message.

Multiclass imbalanced learning in ensembles through selective sampling (MILES) (Azari and Janeja 2017) is an approach that comprises the following three components: (i) creating training sets using clustering-based selective sampling, (ii) rebalancing the training sets, and (iii) combining the classifiers and forming the ensemble. In ensemble learning, it is important to form

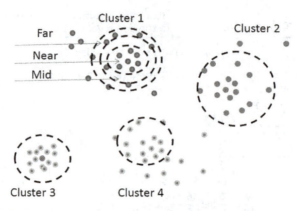

Figure 3.20 Selection of training sets in MILES.

learning sets from different regions in the feature space. This is particularly
important if the data are imbalanced and have distribution of multiple classes
with some majority and minority classes in the feature space. Learning sets that
are dissimilar can produce more diverse results. MILES adopts clustering as a
stratified sampling approach to form a set of learning sets that are different
from each other, and at the same time each one of them is representative of the
original learning set D. It uses K cluster sets to selectively choose the training
samples. It utilizes the concept of split ratio (SR) to split the examples in
clusters into three strata (near, far, and mid) around the cluster centroids as
shown in Figure 3.20.

First, a base classifier H is selected. Here H can be decision tree classifier
such as C4.5, described earlier. Next, the base classifier is trained with training
sets N, F, and M in order to form a set of learned classifiers
$\pi = \{H_N, H_M, H_F\}$. Then the maximum vote rule is used to combine the
votes of the classifiers and build the ensemble $\bar{H}$. $\bar{H}$ is the original ensemble
MILES, which is created by combining the votes that come from
$\{H_N, H_M, H_F\}$. The $\bar{H}^{Under}$ is the variation of MILES combined with random
undersampling, where $\{N_{Under}, M_{Under}, F_{Under}\}$ are utilized, and $\bar{H}^{Over}$ is the
variation of MILES combined with random oversampling, where
$\{N_{over}, M_{over}, F_{over}\}$ are utilized. Undersampling is useful when there are too
many instances of a class, and oversampling is useful when there are too few
samples of the class.

The training examples could potentially be selected into more than three
training sets, however: (1) If the number of splits is increased to very highly
granular demarcations, then there will be splitting of already identified similar
groups so the diversity of the training set will go down. (2) An ensemble

requires at least three classifiers to form a maximum vote combination rule, so a minimum of three sets can be sufficient. (3) A smaller ensemble is faster and more efficient because there are fewer classifiers to train. Results with MILES have shown a size of three produces the highest diversity in terms of a diversity statistic (Q statistic) and also the best classification performance for the proposed ensemble.

3.3.4.3 Other Approaches

Bayesian methods, such as naive Bayes (Maron and Kuhns 1960), provide a probabilistic label for a tuple of the test data based on the training set. The naïve Bayes classifier considers each attribute and class as a random variable. Now given a tuple with attribute values, the goal is to predict probability of class label C. Specifically, it is based on finding the class probability given the attribute values that can be framed as a conditional probability P(C|Attributes). The naïve Bayes algorithm assumes independence of attributes such that the P(C|Attributes) becomes $P(C|A1) * P(C|A2) * \cdots * P(C|An)$. The idea is to find class C, which maximizes this probability. While this is a relatively intuitive method, it relies on the independence assumption. Bayesian networks, on the other hand, represents dependency among attributes.

Another popular function-based method is support vector machines (SVM) (Cortes and Vapnik 1995). SVM relies on the identification of support vectors that linearly partition the data based on the class labels. It looks for a maximal marginal hyperplane, which maximizes this separation. If the data are not linearly separable, such that the decision boundary is not clearly defined, it uses a nonlinear mapping of attributes to transform the original training data attributes to a higher dimensional space for a well-defined classification.

3.3.5 Pattern Mining: Association Rule Mining

Pattern essentially refers to occurrence of multiple objects in a certain combination that could lead to discovery of an implicit interaction. A frequent pattern refers to frequently co-occurring objects. A rare pattern essentially refers to a combination of objects not normally occurring and that could lead to identification of a possible unusual interaction between the objects.

Events become relevant when they occur together in a sequence or as groups. Some approaches deal with this as a causal problem and therefore rely on conditional probability of events to determine the occurrence. If events are seen as itemsets in transactions, focus has been put on finding conditional relationships such that presence of A causes B with a certain probability. However, there might be events where there might be no implied causal

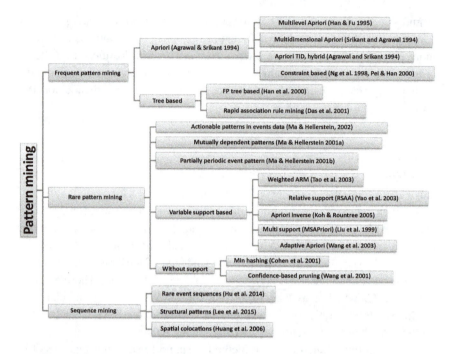

Figure 3.21 Pattern mining approaches.

relationships between them, but the relationship is based purely on co-occurrence. For example, events might have no implied or evident causal relationship but a co-occurrence relationship based on frequency of occurrence
(Agrawal et al. 1994) based on a certain degree of support or confidence
defining the probability of one event given the other. A categorization of the
various pattern mining approaches is shown in Figure 3.21. Several surveys of
patterns such as associations (Zhao and Bhowmick 2003) and rare patterns
(Koh and Ravana 2016) provide an overview of these approaches.

  We discuss two approaches to show a contrast between the discovery of
patterns based on frequency of occurrence versus the discovery of patterns
where the frequency of events is very less and thus will require other information for discovery of the rare pattern.

3.3.5.1 Frequent Pattern Mining: Apriori

The Apriori algorithm (Agarwal and Srikant 1994) is one of the most well-
established data mining algorithms and the basis for the work of several
frequent pattern mining approaches. It provides the approach to discover
association rules. It is used to identify relationships among a set of items in a

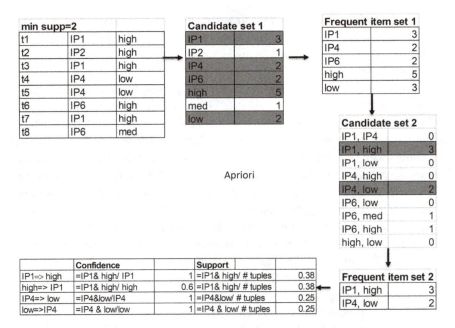

Figure 3.22 Example run for the Apriori algorithm.

database. An example is shown in Figure 3.22, with a set of transactions containing IP addresses and levels of alerts raised in an IDS (high, med, and low). Now given a set of transactions in the database, if IP1 and high are two items, the association rule IP1 → high means that whenever an item IP1 occurs in a transaction, then high also occurs with a quantified probability. The probability or confidence threshold can be defined as the percentage of transactions containing high and IP1 with respect to the percentage of transactions containing just IP1. This can be seen in terms of conditional probability where P(high|IP1) = P(IP1 ∪ high) / P(IP1).

The strength of the rule can also be quantified in terms of support, where support is the number of transactions that contain a certain item; therefore, support of X is the percentage of transactions containing X in the entire set of transactions. Confidence is determined as Support (IP1 ∪ high) / Support (IP1), which gives the confidence and support for the rule for IP1 → high. The rule IP1 → high is not the same as high → IP1 as the confidence will change.

The Apriori algorithm is based on finding frequent itemsets and then discovering and quantifying the association rules. One major contribution of the Apriori algorithm is that it provides an efficient mechanism of discovering frequent itemsets. A subset of a frequent itemset must also be a frequent itemset, i.e., if {IP1, high} is a frequent itemset, both {IP1} and {high} should be a frequent itemset. It iteratively finds frequent itemsets with cardinality from 1 to k (k-itemset).

Apriori generates the candidate itemsets by joining the itemsets with large support from the previous pass and deleting the subsets that have small support from the previous pass. By only considering the itemsets with large support, the number of candidate itemsets is significantly reduced. In the first pass, itemsets with only one item are counted. The itemsets with higher support are used to generate the candidate sets of the second pass. Once the candidate itemsets are found, their supports are calculated to discover the items sets of size two with large support, and so on. This process terminates when no new itemsets are found with large support. Here min support is predetermined as a user-defined threshold. Similarly, a confidence threshold is predetermined by the user. For example, in Figure 3.22, the min support is 0.25, and min confidence is 0.6. The rule IP1 → high has confidence 1 and support 0.38 and is thus a strong rule.

The Apriori algorithm proposes a highly intuitive technique for identifying association rules. Several variations, as shown in Figure 3.21, with efficient versions are proposed, such as FP tree and Rapid ARM. For example, multi-level associations (Han and Fu 1995) deal with levels of items (such as the alert level high may have subtypes), and multidimensional associations (Srikant and Agarwal 1996) discover rules in multidimensional datasets with different types of discretization for the attributes. Constraint-based rules (Ng et al. 1998) discuss imposing constraints through user input on the rules and pruning-based rules on constraints. Spatial colocations (Huang et al. 2006) discovers rules in spatial datasets that identify colocations of different itemsets in space

Apriori does not address discovery of rare patterns. If we wish to identify the rare patterns, they would be ones with very low support, leading to an extremely large number of meaningless rules. There is a whole class of algorithms proposed for rare pattern mining (as shown in Figure 3.21) that devise variations of the support constraints for rare pattern mining.

3.3.5.2 Rare Pattern Mining: Mining Mutually Dependent Patterns
Mining mutually dependent patterns (proposed by Ma and Hellerstein 2001a) introduces data mining for event bursts, periodicities, and mutually dependent events based on event management used in computer and communication systems. The main focus is on the mutually dependent patterns. Mutual dependencies are discovered as M-patterns or mutually dependent patterns

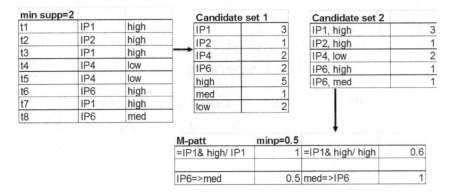

Figure 3.23 M-pattern example.

for mining events that occur together and are mutually dependent. Thus, occurrence of one event is also an indication of the occurrence of the other event by a certain probability. The detection of M-patterns can be illustrated using the example shown in Figure 3.23. Let us say we have event dataset (transactional data) from IDS logs indicating IP address and alarm text (high, med, and low).

The algorithm IsMPattern is initiated with the value for minimum dependence threshold, such that $0 \leq minp \leq 1$. An expression E (such as IP1, high) is evaluated in terms of individual supports of both directional rules (IP1 $\rightarrow$ high and high $\rightarrow$ IP1). M-pattern relies on a strong bidirectional dependence; thus it enables the algorithm to discover items even if the supports are low. However, when generalized for larger minp, the algorithm also discovers frequent patterns similar to association rule mining. The itemsets considered for mining for such event sets or patterns do not eliminate low-support items (nonzero). However, they do eliminate itemsets that may not be m-patterns, as shown in Figure 3.23. Now, given the itemsets, let us consider E = IP1 & high, then P(IP1 $\rightarrow$ high) = 1 and (high $\rightarrow$ IP1) = 0.6. If the minp threshold is 0.5, this set is an m-pattern. Similar to the example shown in Figure 3.22 (min support threshold = 0.25, and min confidence = 0.6), this is also a strong confidence rule. However, when we look at E = (IP6, med), then this is an m-pattern but not a strong confidence rule.

The process of identification of rare patterns is based on a probability level. Thus, even if the supports are low it can identify the rarity of the pattern. It also discovers rare patterns such that if an expression is an m-pattern, then the subsets of the expressions are also m-patterns.

4

Big Data Analytics and Its Need for Cybersecurity

Advanced DM and Complex Data Types from Cybersecurity Perspective

4.1 What Is Big Data?

The global internet population has grown from 2.1 billion in 2012 to 4.6 billion in 2021 (Statista 2021). These users are generating myriad datasets along with the network traffic to move these data on the internet. We produce 2.5 quintillion of data every day (Domo 2017), and $2 trillion is projected to be spent in e-commerce is 2020 (Statista 2020). The nature of big data comes from the complexity of the data and the mechanisms required to bus, analyze, and find insights from the data. Several initiatives have been established to define what we mean by big data (such as Bayer and Laney 2012, Ward and Barker 2013, and NIST 2015). Based on the different types of definitions, there are three or more of the qualities of the big data also referred to as V's, as shown in Figure 4.1. The most known qualities of big data are the volume, velocity, and variety of the data.

One thing that is clear that big data does not just refer to the volume or size of the data. Data can be complex and have the following qualities:

- Velocity: data generated at a rapid pace
- Variety: data consisting of multiple types of heterogeneous data
- Veracity: data that provide trustworthy insights into the domain function
- Value: data that may be able to generate revenue or provide other benefits
- Venue: data that are dynamic with respect to the location
- Volume: large amounts of data being generated
- Variability: some aspect of data changing over time

Big data are the dataset that has a combination of these qualities. In some cases, data that may not be particularly large but has many of these other qualities, such

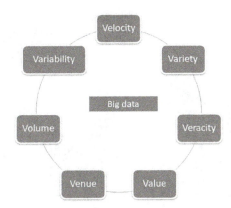

Figure 4.1 The V's of big data.

as variability, variety, and value, may also be considered big data. The term "big" may refer to the big aspect of the overall complexity of the data. If a dataset is highly unusual in terms of its complexity, it may qualify as big data under one of the big data qualities.

In the cybersecurity domain, there are several applications that qualify as big data. If we consider network data traffic, it is massive; for example, in a midsize organization, it can range into petabytes per second. If we consider Internet of Things (IoT), the complexity of data is based on the velocity and variety and in some cases also the volume. A wireless sensor network or a network of IoT monitored through distributed IDS (Otoum et al. 2019) can generate a constant stream of data originating from multiple sensors over time, producing high variability in the data. This provides a complex and rich dataset.

The value from these big datasets can be derived by sifting through these complex datasets to derive insightful patterns.

4.2 Big Data in Cybersecurity

According to the World Fact Book maintained by the CIA (2021), the number of internet users is now in the billions. Figure 4.2 shows the top 25 countries in terms of internet users.

It is clear that a vast number of users on the internet are generating traffic from computers, mobile devices, and other things or devices. If we try to quantify this network traffic data, it is truly complex in terms of the variety of the data generated, volume of the data, and velocity at which it is generated. In addition to the individual users, there are also organizations generating the data and network traffic.

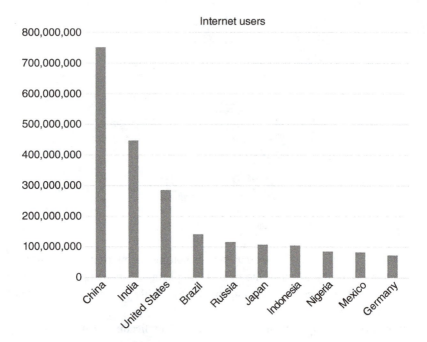

Figure 4.2 Number of internet users by country est. 2018.

Interestingly, the number of attacks (for example, the web attacks discussed in Akamai 2016) sourced worldwide paints a slightly different picture, as shown in Figure 4.3.

While majority of the attackers may come from countries with more internet users, in addition they may also come from the countries with fewer internet users. For example, the number of internet users in Lithuania in 2018 was a fraction of that of the United States and is 116th in the list of countries ranked by the number of internet users. Despite this, Lithuania was placed eighth in terms of the countries sourcing web application attacks. Similarly, more recent reports (Akamai 2019) have listed other countries in the top sources of web attacks even as they do not appear to be a country with highest number of internet users.

The amount of internet traffic generated may not be an indicator of attack traffic. There are other factors at play in identifying cyberattacks on the larger world stage taking into account not only the number of internet users but sociopolitical factors, crime rates, and other cyberattacks. For example, a simple search of Lithuania and cyberattacks reveals that Lithuania is also at the receiving end of many major cyberattacks. Lithuania led a cyber shield

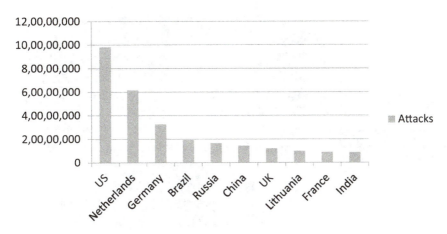

Figure 4.3 Sources of web attacks from countries (2016).

exercise to practice procedures for protecting the cyber infrastructure (L24, 2016). Thus, it is not clear whether the sourced attacks, where Lithuania ranked eighth across countries in the fourth quarter of 2016, are more defensive or offensive.

It is clear that a deeper dive can reveal many more insights into the real state of affairs on the internet. If we consider an organization and study trends of usage and simple rules to analyze traffic, we may miss insights of potential advanced persistent threats. Such threats can be evaluated by not just looking at data in isolation but in combination with user behaviors, sociopolitical factors, context of time, and potentially many other contextual features. This is truly a big data problem as it brings in the volume, velocity, variety, variability, and venue and can lead to great value with high veracity of the results. Here testing the veracity is equally important to generating value.

The challenge is to sift through the internet traffic and identify attacks. This can be at the device level, user level, or the network level at large.

4.3 Landscape of Big Data Technologies

Big data technologies can be selected based on criteria that fit a business need (as highlighted in Cloud Security Alliance 2014). The set of criteria is shown in Figure 4.4.

These criteria include the latency in response time, whether the data are structured, if a SQL-like environment is required, types of analytics required, specific types of visualizations that may be needed, and the security and

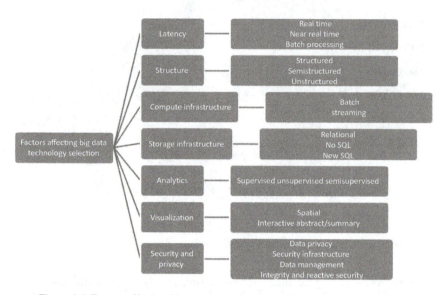

Figure 4.4 Factors affecting big data technology selection.

privacy needs of the business. Several big data technologies can be selected based on these criteria. A pictorial representation of some of these technologies is shown in Figure 4.5 (Grover et al. 2015 and Roman 2017). For example, if the need of the business is low latency and SQL-like processing, then the business can select tools that have a quick turnaround time for queries in massive datasets. Of the several big data analytics frameworks present in the market, the business can select the tools that provide massively parallel processing (MPP), such as engines on top of Hadoop that have high SQL-like functionality and portability, such as Apache Hive, Facebook Presto, Apache Drill, and Apache Spark. Out of these, Presto and Spark have been shown (Grover et al. 2015) to produce better outcomes for SQL-like processing.

4.4 Mahout and Spark Comparative Analysis

Of the big data technologies, Mahout, which powered several machine learning applications,[1] and Spark have been identified as a major big data technologies (Meng et al. 2016). For massive cybersecurity datasets such as traffic data

---

[1] https://mahout.apache.org/general/powered-by-mahout.html.

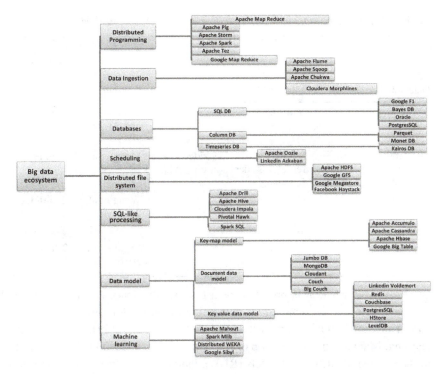

Figure 4.5 The big data technology ecosystem.

or sensor network data, even small differences in speedup can mean the difference in millions of dollars. Thus, in selecting a big data technology, it is also essential to study the scale-ups with the type of technology used.

Let us consider these two big data technologies, which are used for machine learning and data mining. Apache Mahout[2] works on top of the Hadoop map reduce framework to provide a data analytics library. Spark provides its own map reduce framework and provides an integrated Spark machine learning library (MLLib) for machine learning and analytics tasks.

Hadoop is an open-source mechanism for parallel computation in massive datasets. It provides the Hadoop File System (HDFS) and the map reduce framework, which provides the mechanism for parallel processing, as will be discussed in an example case study for change detection. The key steps require breaking down the data and processing the data in parallel through mappers that work on key and value pairs. The pairs are then reduced and the

---

[2] http://mahout.apache.org/.

Table 4.1 *Sample comparisons of speedup between Spark and Mahout*

Data size	Nodes	Method	Citation	Spark over Mahout speedup achieved
62 MB–1,240 MB	1–2	K-means	Gopalani and Arora 2015	2 times
200–1,000 mil data points	16	Logistic regression, ridge regression, decision tree, ALS K-means	Meng et al. 2016	3 times
50K–50 mil points	10	C4.5 K-means	Wang et al. 2014	2–5 times
Upto 7.5 GB	1	Word count		3–5 times
0.5–4 GB	4	K-means	Misal et al. 2016	2 times

aggregated information is produced as a final result. Spark provides its own implementation of the map reduce processing but also additional inbuilt SQL and machine learning library (MLLib). For Hadoop to perform the machine learning, Mahout can work on top of Hadoop. The key speedup in Spark is due to the resilient distributed datasets (RDD), which are stored in memory; they are also resilient to loss, as they can rebuild lost data based on where they originate from. Spark also allows for machine learning algorithms to retrieve the data from memory iteratively.

Comparative performance of data mining and machine learning algorithms on Spark and Mahout with Spark have shown several orders in speedup. For example (Gopalani and Arora 2015), Spark has been shown to have roughly two times greater speedup over Mahout. Table 4.1 outlines some comparative analysis found in the literature. In general, Spark achieved a speed up of about two times greater than Mahout across various datasets and techniques. This is just one type of comparison when low latency and speedup are desired; there may be other comparisons that need to be evaluated when other analysis attributes are relevant, as shown in Figure 4.4. In mission-critical systems where dependable real-time responses are needed, these speedups can translate to real-world impacts in analyzing anomalies in massive network traffic datasets (Kato and Klyuev 2017).

4.5 Complex Nature of Data

The premise of achieving a high level of analysis and mining in big data is a good understanding of the nature and complexity of the data. The mining in large heterogeneous data is increasingly becoming challenging due to the complexity of the data. Many data mining algorithms have been proposed for traditional (numeric, categorical) datasets. However, the nature of the data itself renders a challenge to the data mining. Mainly such problems can be exemplified in the mining of high-dimensional datasets. The quality of the mining results is affected adversely as the number of dimensions increases. Here dimension refers to the attributes of an object. This is especially true in outlier detection, i.e., the identification of anomalous objects. In higher dimensions, data become sparse, and points tend to become equidistant. This adversely affects the methods based on density of points, unless data follow certain simple distributions. Thus, the outliers could be hidden in high dimensions. Another fact is that for outlier detection a subset of the entire attribute set could be used to detect or indicate the outliers. In addition, the nature of the data – whether it is spatial, temporal, graph, or unstructured data – can also make the mining process fairly complex. In each of these types of complex datasets, the data preprocessing, which is already the most intensive part of any data mining project, can become even more involved and challenging.

4.5.1 Nature of Data: Spatial Data

Spatial data mining deals with identification of nontrivial and useful knowledge discovery in a spatial database, where spatial (point, lines, polygons, location, pixel data) and nonspatial data (e.g., population count) are stored. Unlike traditional data mining, it is important to address the nature of spatial data, which renders new challenges in the inherent spatial autocorrelation and heterogeneity in the data. Spatial data are seen in the cybersecurity domain in sensor networks placed in a region. These are particularly relevant to cyber-physical systems (Tan et al. 2009), which have interactions with several physical sensors that are impacted by the regional variables and also nonspatial elements, such as the computer networks involved in the communication and analysis of the data. CPS provides a very comprehensive example of how the cyber elements interact with the physical elements such that to perform any type of knowledge discovery, the physical elements along with the environmental variables impacting the physical locations need to be modeled correctly.

Thus, understanding the nature of data is even more important for spatial data mining because of the inherent complexities of the spatial data themselves. Spatial data consist pixel data, data pertaining to space-multidimensional points, lines, rectangles, polygons, cubes, and other geometric objects. The data are in very large volumes; it would essentially take an infinitely large database to capture the real world precisely. Spatial data pose more of a challenge due to the type of data, volume of data, and the fact that there is a correlation between the objects and their neighbor or neighborhood. There can be relationships between spatial objects such as topological relationships, direction relationships, metric relationships, or complex relationships, which are based on these basic relationships. Moreover, the data could depict temporal changes, which is inherent in the data themselves. The same spatial data can also be represented in different ways, i.e., raster and vector format. For example, georeferenced data include spatial location in terms of latitude, longitude and other information about spatial and nonspatial attributes. This essentially means that there is some preprocessing on the raw data such as satellite imagery or tiger files to extract the georeferenced attributes and some other nonspatial attributes such as vegetation type, land-use type, etc.

Another view where spatial data can benefit cybersecurity applications is in characterization of the region with socioeconomic data and cybercrime data. The approach proposed by Keivan and Koochakzadeh (2012) first creates a characterization to determine which cities, areas, or countries may be more likely to send a malicious request. This is based on the *number of complaints received at each location* for different types of cybercrimes. Locations with a number of complaints above the median are classified as "critical," while locations with a number of complaints below the median are classified as "safe." In addition, demographic data such as housing (occupied, vacant, owned/rented, etc.), population (gender, age, etc.) are also used in the characterization. Based on the complaints by location and the demographic information, they predict the potential of a location as a cybercrime origin.

Ferebee et al. (2012) utilize spatial data to produce a cybersecurity storm map that combines several data streams and provides a geospatial interface to visualize the location of cyber activity. This concept has been studied at length in other types of disaster recovery domains but not so much in cybersecurity.

Banerjee et al. (2012) highlights the importance of looking at the cyberattacks and their impact and interaction with the physical environment. Since CPS is not limited to sophisticated users, usability is also a big consideration, and this can impact the value of the system and eventually the veracity of the findings if the usability and interpretability of the systems is low. This work builds on the cyberphysical security (CypSec) concepts that discuss the mapping of the cyber and physical components to provide an environmentally coupled solution (Venkatasubramanian et al. 2011). Additional examples of using spatial data are described in Chapter 11.

4.5.2 Nature of Data: Graph Data

Graphs represent a set of nodes and links between the nodes. Here nodes can be IP addresses (source and destination) and the links can be the packets or communication sent between the two IP addresses. Another type of graph could be a router network, where the nodes are routers, and links are the possible paths from the router table. Graphs have been a well-studied area. With the proliferation of computer network data, graphs are becoming massive in size and are constantly evolving. This is an example where big data techniques can facilitate the discovery of novel insights. For example, how does a graph for computer network traffic change over time in terms of node level? How can graph-level properties (Namayanja and Janeja 2014) help determine potential events? Thus, if a node is highly connected, it is an important node. Similarly, we can study the behavior of the network data whether it increases the diameter of a graph or density of the graph (Leskovec et al. 2005). These properties have direct implications on managing the networks, identifying critical events such as cyberattacks, and evaluating the impact of events on the graphs.

4.5.3 Nature of Data: Other Types of Complex Data

Cybersecurity data such as network traffic data also has a *temporal* element. Later in this chapter, we discuss how traffic data evolving over time can provide novel insights. Each data point has a time stamp, and if considered sequentially, the patterns can have additional meaning in terms of the evolving patterns, such as periodicity or recurrence of patterns over time. This is particularly useful in studying advanced persistent threats (APT). Spatial and temporal data analysis for cybersecurity is further discussed in Chapter 8.

Another complex dataset is *unstructured data such as text* (for example, vulnerability descriptions in the NVD[3]). There is a lot of rich knowledge about vulnerabilities in this text description. To analyze these data, a lot of preprocessing is required to be able to discover patterns in the text within and across vulnerabilities. One example is to break down the text into keywords and translate each vulnerability into a binary-valued feature vector based on the presence or absence of the keywords. This can help identify similar or dissimilar vulnerabilities (as discussed in similarity matching in Chapter 3).

---

[3] https://nvd.nist.gov/.

Other types of complex datasets include audio, video, and image datasets, which are increasingly becoming a key data source of anomaly detection due to propagation of deep fakes (Agarwal et al. 2019).

4.6 Where Does Analytics Fit in for Cybersecurity?

Traditional cybersecurity methods looking at network traffic data focus on Intrusion detection, which aims at identifying threats of unauthorized access using signatures of unauthorized access or attacks. Data analytics can go beyond this signature-based discovery to identify complex types of attacks that may be hidden in massive datasets or may be spread out over time and multiple networks (similar to threat hunting, as mentioned in Chapter 1). Here we highlight two examples that show the need of using big data analytics in cybersecurity:

(1) Sampling based change discovery in massive networks (Namayanja and Janeja 2015)
(2) Big distributed intrusion detection system (Janeja et al. 2014)

We focus on these examples to illustrate the need for big data technologies and the complexities of the datasets involved.

4.6.1 Change Detection in Massive Traffic Datasets

Computer networks can be seen as graphs of communications between nodes, where each node is represented by an IP address. If we consider a snapshot of network traffic data, we can generate a communication graph from it. Studying these snapshots through time, we can evaluate whether there have been node-level or network-level changes in the graphs indicating potential cyberattacks, as shown in Figure 4.6 (adapted from Namayanja and Janeja 2015). Such detection of unusual time periods can be used to identify major network traffic changes due to cyber threats. Moreover, this can also help identify nodes that may have been targeted since their node connectivity changed over time. Lastly, this type of analysis can also feed into a predictive model to predict temporal patterns where periodic changes in the network may impact network performance.

Given that network communication can be massive, it is important to identify a subset of this traffic to evaluate. This can be done by targeted sampling. One way is to select the top central nodes where nodes with a very high degree of connectivity represent the major communication in the traffic data.

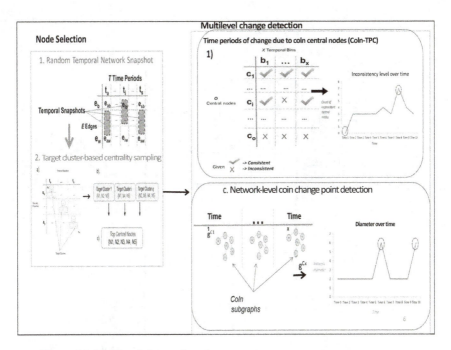

Figure 4.6 Multilevel change detection.
Source: Namayanja and Janeja (2015).

If we see these central nodes are consistent through time, represented by bins or intervals of time, then we can say that these nodes are consistent nodes. On the other hand, if these nodes are not present in all time periods, then they are inconsistent nodes.

If there are time periods where several of the central nodes become inconsistent, then this time period is a potential time point where an event affected these nodes and may require further investigation. The subgraphs for the time intervals can also be studied to evaluate graph-level properties. Thus, if the densification or diameter does not follow the network properties during time periods, it can again be an indicator of a network-level event at the time points. Cybersecurity through network and graph data is further discussed in Chapter 9.

Example

Let us consider the graphs across three time periods where the degrees of the nodes are shown in the Figure 4.7. Each graph represents a set of communication lines between the IP nodes. Note that here the degree is based on the

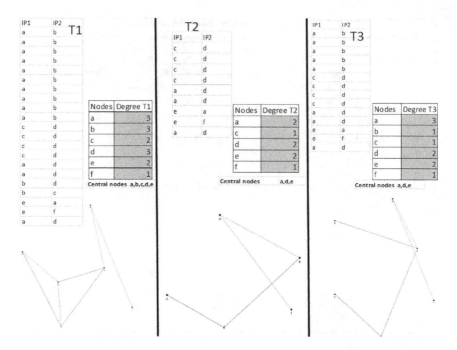

Figure 4.7 Example walkthrough for evaluating central nodes over time.

nonduplicate edges. This can be modified to a weighted degree to count for multiple times the nodes communicate with each other, for accommodating duplicate edges. Alternatively, edge weight can be added for the number of times the nodes are communicating. Here, for simplicity we only consider the nonduplicate communications. We can see that certain nodes (a, d, e) are consistently central if the degree threshold for centrality is greater than or equal to two. On the other hand, we see that node f is consistently low degree. Node b starts as a high degree but is dropped in time period T2 and again comes back as a low node degree in T3. The consistent nodes a, d, and e can be seen as the regularly used nodes if they are consistently central. If such consistent nodes get dropped after being consistent in several time periods, then this can prompt further analysis. If several nodes lose their degree in a time period, then we can also label that time period to prompt further evaluation. This process helps identify central nodes over time to evaluate any unusual changes in the communications.

Let us consider the graph analysis in parallel, through big data technologies. We depict the map reduce process for a single time period. Here the split of the data can be done within a single time period. Alternatively, the split could be

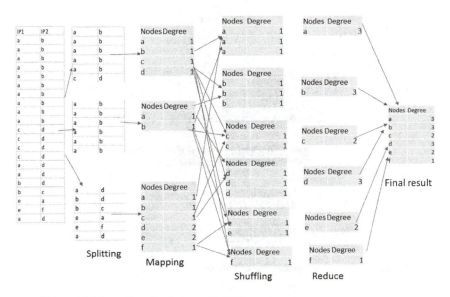

Figure 4.8 Map reduce for degree computation.

done by time period. Figure 4.8 shows the process where within a time period we split the data, and the degree count is done within those chunks where the key is the node name and the value is the degree, thus forming the key–value pair. The data are computed for each node in the shuffling and finally the values are tallied for each node in the reduce phase, producing the final result. This mechanism of map reduce is common across several big data tools. The internal workings of how the data are split and the map reduce is performed may vary.

4.6.2 Multipronged Attacks

Multipronged attacks are attacks that are spread out over time and several points in the network. Discovering such attacks becomes a challenging task particularly because the datasets become massive and heterogeneous.

A distributed intrusion detection system (dIDS) provides the infrastructure for the detection of a coordinated attack against an organization and its partners' distributed network resources. However, given the complexity of multiple attack sources and the massive amounts of data generated for such a multipronged attack, a multilevel mining framework in the form of a big distributed IDS (B-dIDS) can be utilized (as proposed in Janeja et al. 2014), as shown in Figure 4.9. This architecture utilizes IDS logs to sift through

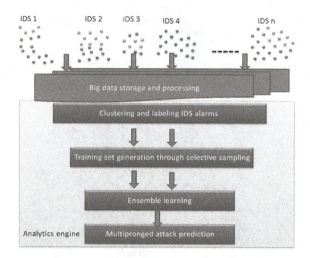

Figure 4.9 Distributed processing of IDS alerts.

alarms that may look benign individually but may indicate a critical alert in combination with other alerts.

In this distributed environment, within each subnet a dIDS agent performs local intrusion detection and generates IDS log data, as shown in the figure as IDS1... IDSn. Log data from each dIDS agent are sent to a control center, employing big data tools, where it is stored for aggregated analysis. Each signature-based agent generates a priority level associated with the alarm when an attack against a known threat is detected, and generates high, medium, and low priority alarms for "anomalous" behavior. High-priority alarms can be clearly labeled; however, the low and medium priority alarm data are very large, making it difficult for an administrator to perform manual analysis. In such a scenario, several alarms that are part of a coordinated attack will be missed. However, if we can show that the high-level alarms have similarities with low-level alarms, we can propagate the labels to the low-level alarms. Once we label them as similar to high-level alarms, we can try and study them carefully for possible breaches that are part of a coordinated attack.

There may be several alarms generated at multiple sources from multiple sensors (IDS monitors) across networks. These alarms may range from abnormal traffic, unusual port access, and unusual sources. The key idea here is to connect the anomalies using co-occurrence of alarms at specific time periods, specific location (node/computer), or similar abnormal behavior. This essentially identifies which have overlaps or similarities in terms of some of the features as shown in Figure 4.10.

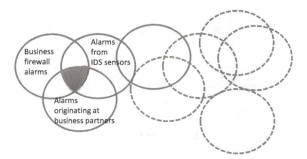

Figure 4.10 Overlapping alarms.

How do we find similarities? This can be done through clustering (as discussed in Chapter 3) the alarms together, and if alarms fall in the same cluster, then the labels from a higher-level alarm can be propagated to a lower-level alarm. Once we have these propagated labels, after domain user validation, we can use this data for future predictions as well.

Let us consider each agent to provide a training set that is generated after preprocessing the data through a clustering algorithm. Then classification in these data can be seen as a class-imbalanced learning problem. This approach uses an ensemble classification technique to automatically classify the large volume of aggregated alarm data and to alert a system administrator to a potential coordinated attack.

4.7 Privacy and Security Issues in Big Data

"Big data" has become a buzzword and a new direction for business avenues and scientific research. However, there is a trade-off to enjoying the benefits of big data.

As Figure 4.11 shows, there is a set of pros and cons to adopting big data. Big data allows the combination of several datasets in a scalable and efficient manner. It also is able to provide high value since the knowledge discovery is across multiple datasets, bringing in novel insights. However, because the data are being merged from multiple distinct datasets possibly from different domains, domain insight becomes a key to getting the value out of the big data. This can be highly subjective based on the domain experts, and as a result the interpretation of the data will have direct impact on how the data are analyzed and the results discovered. This can reduce or increase the value depending on the individual domain experts' insights and collaborative understanding in creating a combined solution.

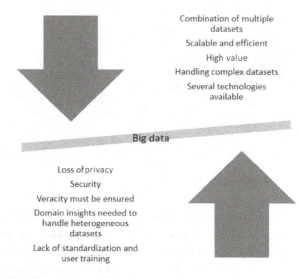

Figure 4.11 Pros and cons of big data.

Now given that a lot of data are combined in a big data solution, this can lead to novel insights, but on the other hand can also lead to loss of privacy. In today's day and age, when massive amounts of data are being collected, privacy guarantees are not possible; however, utilizing multiple datasets actually decreases the privacy. So in essence we can say that there is an inverse relationship between the utilization of big data technologies and users' autonomy over personal data.

Big data technologies are highly scalable and efficient as the data storage and processing is distributed across several nodes in a cluster computing environment. As a result such an infrastructure potentially opens up multiple access points to the data be it the network or cloud environment. This can directly impact the security of the data.

While several big data technologies are available, there is a lack of standardization in technologies, with new technologies evolving every day. As a result, portability, standardization, and adoption can be impacted.

While it is clear that big data technologies can benefit business applications, if not used appropriately they can also negatively impact the end users' experience. So is a frictionless environment, where there are no restrictions on data integration and knowledge discovery, good? Probably not. Some friction is good for getting the right information to the right people at the right time. Big data helps breach information silos; however, some balance is required to prevent privacy and security breaches. Privacy has a new challenge in big data: we might share something without realizing how it will be linked with other data, leading to privacy and security breaches somewhere in the future. The privacy concerns are also geospatial to some extent and should be evaluated as such. For example, in Norway the tax return of every individual is public (The Guardian 2016); however, the same situation would not be acceptable in the United States, where individual tax returns are private except when shared with authorization by the individual.

There is also a recent push for open data. Big data in the public domain can only be of value if more and more datasets are openly available. Thus, open data initiatives may lead to big data. However, again security and privacy must be balanced in this environment. There is indeed a high risk if open data is merged with some restrictive closed data, leading to security breaches. For example, if the social background of an individual is posted on networking sites (for example, a picture that is geo tagged or the geo history in iPhone), this when combined with other knowledge from LinkedIn and other social media sites can lead to social engineering attacks.

5

Types of Cyberattacks

This chapter summarizes a taxonomy of the different types of cyberattacks and the mechanism by which some of these attacks take place. Some of the attacks will be described in terms of the attack vector, exploit, datasets generated during the attack, and potential countermeasures for the attack. There are several types of systems and networks impacted by cyberattacks, as discussed in Chapter 1. The taxonomy described here focuses on some of the well-known types of attacks and how they relate to each other.

5.1 Types of Attacks

Several threat taxonomies are proposed, including the European Union Agency for Cybersecurity (ENISA) threat taxonomy (ENISA 16), the cyber-physical incident catalog (Miller 2014), and the Attack Vector, Operational Impact, Defense, Information Impact, and Target (AVOIDIT) cyberattack taxonomy (Simmons et al. 2009). Figure 5.1 consolidates certain categories of cyberattacks based on the general characteristics of the attacks (Quader and Janeja 2021).

Each of the major categories of attacks presents several variations, as show in the figure. Social engineering relies on understanding the social interactions of the individual and trying to gain access to user credentials. For example, through phishing an individual may be motivated to provide their username and password, which will allow a hacker to gain access to a system. Similarly, phone phishing deals with phishing but through a phone system where the user is coaxed to provide their credentials. Malware, on the other hand, deals with the class of attacks that install a malware, such as virus, spyware, Trojans, etc., on a user's system with the intent of gaining access and information from a user's system. Password attacks focus on getting user credentials either

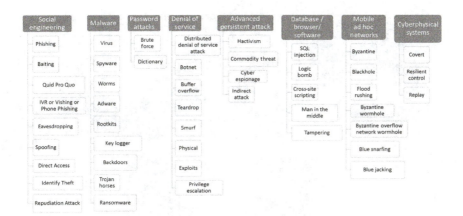

Figure 5.1 Types of attacks.

through a brute force attack or by checking the passwords against a dictionary of words. Password attack is based on a hacker trying out different passwords based on a set of passwords such as from a dictionary. To counter such attacks, complex passwords and passwords that are not repeated from one site to the next are recommended. Denial of service (DoS) attacks are caused when malicious users tend to block legitimate traffic by sending too many requests to a server. Distributed versions of these attacks cause a coordinated attack to take place, such as in the case of a botnet where several machines are carrying out these requests being sent. Advanced persistent threats persist through coordinated long-term attacks and mostly originate from organizations with long-term interest in the assets on the hacked system. These could be initiated from nation states. Database or software-based attacks are caused due to bugs in the software such as in the case of a SQL injection attack where the front-end user form can be used to initiate a query request to the back-end database to gain access to the username and password credentials. Mobile ad hoc attacks can be caused where the information flow is disrupted, such as in the case of the blackhole attack, where the network traffic is redirected and may be lost. In a cyberphysical system, there is another class of attacks such as a replay attack, where valid data are sent maliciously but repeatedly with the intent to cause delay or block the traffic. Some of these attacks are further explained in Figure 5.2, in terms of what the attack is, the mechanism of the attack, countermeasures used, and any datasets that can be harvested to study the attacks.

While we can focus on understanding each of these attacks individually, they are inherently linked by the aim of the attacker. For example, an APT is

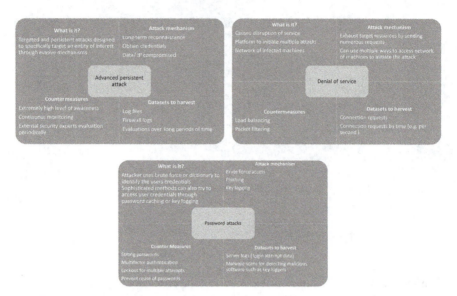

Figure 5.2 Example attack types.

generally carried out by exploiting a vulnerability or by gaining access to a system through a social engineering attack. More often than not, spear phishing is the root cause of many types of attacks. Thus, security is more than an engineering challenge, as people are an essential part of the critical infrastructure. Therefore, understanding and addressing human behavior is essential to building a security culture. Methodologies such as Cyber Kill Chain (Lockheed Martin 2015), FireEye Mandiant purple team assessment (Fireeye Mandiant 2019), and Mitre ATT&CK (MITRE 2020) provide additional insights into the mindset of the attacker and the threat method. Additional human behavioral perspectives in understanding cyberattacks are discussed in Chapter 10.

We next consider two of the attack types and describe the cyberattack and data analytics methods to discover characteristics of these attacks. We pick these two types for their complexity and multiple types of datasets that might be involved in analyzing them.

5.2 Example: Social Engineering

Social engineering is a mechanism to gain access to computer systems, and the information that resides there, in an unauthorized manner through human- or computer-mediated methods targeting the social aspects of a user's data. Compromising information about a user's credentials can be obtained through social connections or impersonating social connections. An example of impersonating social connections is spear phishing, where an email that appears to be from a legitimate social connection or authority figure requests credentials. The goal of social engineering is to obtain information that will allow the hacker to gain unauthorized access, via human-mediated or computer-mediated methods, to a system in order to compromise the system's integrity, potentially leading to other types of attacks. Human-mediated methods may include impersonation, impersonating a help desk, third-party authorization, phishing through impersonating a trusted authority figure, and snail mail, to name a few (Quader and Janeja 2021).

The question addressed here is how do we detect common social engineering attacks in the network using computational models? A computational data model is discussed next to detect the anomaly in the network data as a result of password theft.

5.2.1 Computational Data Model for Social Engineering

Computational data models are derived on intuitions of how these attacks affect the patterns in the data collected on the network. To build a computational data model for social engineering attacks, specifically password theft, log data from intrusion detection systems, such as Snort log data, can be analyzed. The objective is to derive a data model by which we can detect an anomaly in the network that emulates the behavior of a password theft. This model can be applied to Snort IDS log data or firewall or server log data to identify a potential password theft attack.

Intuition: Let us consider what happens when a password is stolen with malicious intent. It is highly likely that if a password is stolen, the intent could be to generate more attacks inside the network through this compromised system. Alternatively, if the intent is data theft, then several datasets might be moved from this compromised system. Thus, in either case, the traffic would substantially increase after the password was stolen. To distinguish such a change in data pattern of the user, we can also differentiate it from other traditional attacks by eliminating any probes conducted on this system, since traditional hacks into a system are done after a probe and scan in the network. Therefore, the intuition is that if there is no probe or scan in the network and the system under study and the network pattern has substantially changed over time, this then leads to an observation that a password theft may potentially have occurred. While this is a broadly defined intuition, this is not a predictive labeling but an exploratory analysis, as a network administrator would have to evaluate further whether the identified system indeed had a password theft or there is another event signifying change in the traffic patterns. These types of intuitions allow the administrator to focus on a narrower swath of data rather than the entire network traffic at large.

Using this intuition, let us consider how it can be translated into a computational data model. The conditions of the model (Quader and Janeja 2014), depicted in Figure 5.3, are about observing the activities on a user's system and identifying if there is any probe on that machine to gain access. A probe is an attempt to gain access to a computer and its files through a known or probable vulnerability in the computer system. Password theft in this study of social engineering attack is a nonprobing scenario where the intruder may gain access to the password via nonprobing means such as getting hold of a password through human-mediated methods such as impersonation as IT security personnel.

If the log files are evaluated for frequency of IP addresses, then the count of the destination IP would be a small number in a situation when there is no probe. Another condition that can be added is that a single source IP may access several IP addresses in the network after the password theft.

In Figure 5.3, given a set of IP addresses $N = \{n_1, \ldots, n_n\}$, IP n_1 is the source accessing n_2 as the destination, with the number of accesses less than a certain threshold ρ. Threshold computation is elaborated further.

The second condition, as depicted in Figure 5.3, is about significant activity increase on the same machine (IP) as a result of the intruder having access to that machine. Once the target machine becomes a victim, the same machine is used as a source (IP) to potentially attack other machines or send out data. Hence, the activities on the source IP significantly increase over time as a result of password theft.

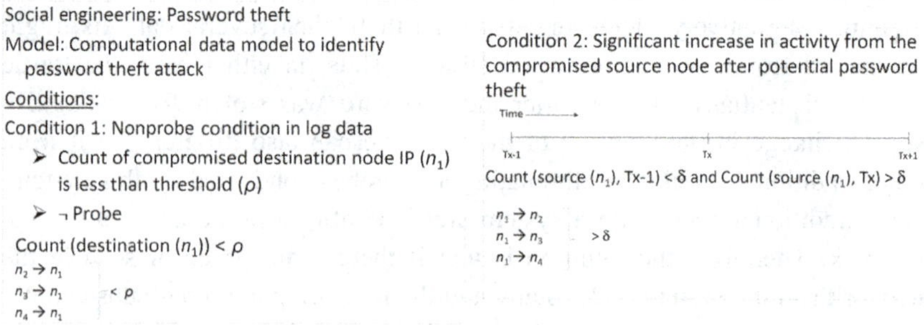

Social engineering: Password theft
Model: Computational data model to identify
    password theft attack
Conditions:

Condition 1: Nonprobe condition in log data
  ➤ Count of compromised destination node IP (n_1)
    is less than threshold (ρ)
  ➤ ¬ Probe

Count (destination (n_1)) < ρ
$n_2 \rightarrow n_1$
$n_3 \rightarrow n_1$ < ρ
$n_4 \rightarrow n_1$

Condition 2: Significant increase in activity from the compromised source node after potential password theft

Time ————▸

|————————|————————————————|
Tx-1   Tx   Tx+1
Count (source (n_1), Tx-1) < δ and Count (source (n_1), Tx) > δ

$n_1 \rightarrow n_2$
$n_1 \rightarrow n_3$ > δ
$n_1 \rightarrow n_4$

Figure 5.3 Computational data model conditions.

In this model, the behavior of the destination IP at time T_{x-1} when this IP has normal behavior is compared to the behavior of the same IP as a source at time T_x when the IP becomes a victim of password compromise. ρ is the threshold, below which a particular destination is identified as having a nonprobing scenario. δ is the threshold, below which the source IP depicts normal activities while the value above the threshold would identify the source to be sending out a large amount of communication to other destinations (for example, data or attacks).

Thus, given a set of IP addresses $N = \{n_1, \ldots, n_n\}$, a compromised IP n_1 is the source and accessing destination n_i more than a certain threshold δ.

Computing Thresholds: The data from log files can be divided into several bins based on the time stamp and for each bin the count for each destination IP can be computed and sorted in ascending order. The mean and standard deviation of the counts can be computed. This mean can be considered as the threshold value for ρ and δ; alternatively, mean + standard deviation can also be used as a slightly restrictive threshold. For example, Figure 5.4 shows example data for both time bins. Thresholds of $\mu + \sigma1$ and $\mu + \sigma2$ are computed to indicate an anomalous communication at time T_x for IP n_5. In general, if subsequent bins show low values as compared to the threshold followed by high values of the counts as compared to thresholds, then this may indicate a period worth investigating. While this is not a predictive method, it may provide an administrator with a way to zoom into unusual communications.

Notice the total count for source IP $n1$ before the password theft on T_{x-1} is 2, which is less than our threshold of 2.28 ($\mu + 2\sigma$). The total count of the source $n1$ goes up significantly after the password is potentially compromised on T_x, which is 5. This count is greater than the threshold of 4.9 ($\mu + 2\sigma$).

It is important to be able to identify the time periods as well where such investigations can be initiated. As a preprocessing task, thresholds can be identified from historic datasets. Overall interesting conditions are when

Condition1	Source	Destination		Destination	Count
Time T-1	n4	n2		n1	2
	n1	n6		n2	2
	n2	n1		n3	1
	n3	n1		n4	1
	n4	n2		n5	1
	n5	n3		n6	1
	n6	n4			
	n2	n5		μ	1.33
				σ	0.47140$
			ρ	1σ	1.80
			ρ	2σ	2.28

Condition2	Source	Destination		Source	Count
Time T	n1	n2		n1	5
	n1	n3		n2	1
	n1	n4		n3	2
	n1	n5		n4	0
	n2	n6		n5	0
	n3	n2		n6	0
	n1	n6			
	n3	n4		μ	1.33
	n2			σ	1.795055
			δ	1σ	3.13
			δ	2σ	4.92

Figure 5.4 Setting the value for ρ and δ.

Count (destination (n_1), T_{x-1}) $< \rho$ and Count (source (n_1), T_x) $> \delta$. Thus, before the password theft occurs, the count (activity) for that IP (as a destination) is going to be lot less at time T_{x-1} and the count (activity) for that same IP (as source) after the password theft is going to be a significantly high at T_x time.

Discovering Frequent Rules: Association rule mining (discussed in Chapter 3) can be used to validate the rules where the activities of the compromised IP increase significantly with a high LIFT value. Association rule mining provides the rules where the compromised source IP targets many destination IPs once the intruder gains access to the source machine via password theft. This source IP from ARM may also show a correspondence with results from the computational data model and show this IP reaching out to many targets (n_2, n_3, n_4), and as a result it should show up in the association rules. The lift value gives us the performance measure and the confidence for the ARM rules gathered from the algorithm.

5.3 Example: Advanced Persistent Threat

One of the fundamental goals of an advanced persistent threat (APT) is to remain undetected on the network for a long period of time in order to carry out the threat's mission. The desire to remain hidden, and the sophisticated measures taken to avoid detection, makes it extremely difficult to identify, analyze, and categorize APTs. APTs are difficult to detect, prevent intrusion from, and remove, as explained next.

Difficult to detect: Use of custom tools that do not have a signature for detection are very challenging to discover. Zero-day exploits avoid detection by signature-based systems. Legitimate third-party applications leveraged for command and control hide in plain sight. Evidence that data have been transferred from the system is deleted or overwritten.

Difficult to prevent intrusion: Attackers target the users of the systems, via socially engineered spear-phishing emails. Up-to-date systems are still vulnerable to zero-day exploits. Attackers have been known to target additional, outside organizations in order to access their true intended victim (Trend Micro 2012).

Difficult to remove: Attackers install backdoors throughout victim networks to maintain footholds, and hence they are very difficult to remove.

Here a review of the APTs such as Mandiant (Binde et al. 2011), McAfee (McAfee 2010, Websense 2011), Symantec (O'Gorman and McDonald 2012), and Trend Micro (SecDev Group 2009, Leyden 2012) and from security

Figure 5.5 Characteristics of advanced persistent threats.

researchers is discussed. Several properties displayed by different APT groups are discussed (as outlined in Quader et al. 2015). Also included in these properties is the pervasiveness of the attacks, victims, the robustness of the infrastructure, as well as other select attributes. By reviewing these attributes, APTs are categorized into groups by their technical sophistication, longevity, persistence, and overall threat.

APTs have specific characteristics, as shown in Figure 5.5, such as attack vectors through which they are initiated, exploits through which they are carried out, tools used to establish the threat, targets that make a target inviting for an APT attack, command and control, and persistence of the attack, which is longer lasting than other traditional attacks.

There are several reported APTs; however, only a very small set of APTs are well known, fully understood, and reported to the general public. Of the known threats, very few holistic pictures are available that detail the tactics, techniques, and procedures. Here the more prominent APTs discovered over the last several years are discussed and broken into individual parts of the APT to study the attack vectors, exploits, tools, targets, command and control, and persistence of each APT. Each attribute is described in the following subsections (Quader et al. 2015, Stauffer and Janeja 2017) and shown in Figure 5.5.

5.3.1 Attributes of APTs

5.3.1.1 Attack Vector

APTs typically follow three primary attack vectors for gaining access to a target's system. No vector is necessarily more sophisticated than any other; however, the level of sophistication is inherent in the quality and thoroughness of the social engineering and spear-phishing techniques.

Several APTs have broadened their potential victim base and use an attack vector known as a *watering hole*. Attackers first identify a vulnerable website and insert malicious code into the site that will redirect visitors to another malicious site hosting the APT's malware (O'Gorman and McDonald 2012). *SQL injection/other* is probably the least utilized vector by APTs. Attackers may use SQL injection to exploit a company's web servers and then proceed with the attack.

5.3.1.2 Exploits

Before an attacker can surreptitiously install their chosen backdoor on a victim machine, vulnerability needs to be available to exploit. Vulnerabilities can be found in many software applications.

Zero day: A zero-day vulnerability is not known by the software developer or security community; it is typically only known by the attacker or a small group of individuals. A zero day is valuable because any victim machine running that software will be vulnerable to the exploit. Thus, Zero-day vulnerabilities are difficult to discover (O'Gorman and McDonald 2012).

Known, but unpatched vulnerabilities: A small window of time exists between the discovery of vulnerability and the time it takes to develop and release a patch. An attacker may take advantage of this time to develop an exploit and use it maliciously.

Known, patched vulnerabilities: Since software developers have to release updates to patch any vulnerability, an opportunity exists for attackers to take advantage of users who do not regularly update their software.

5.3.1.3 Tools

Many attackers use similar, publicly available tools to navigate a victim network once they have established backdoors on victim systems. The difference between APTs lies in the tools they use to maintain access to victims.

Custom tools: Some APTs use custom tools that are not publicly available. Since a considerable amount of time, expertise, and money is needed to develop a family of malware, custom tools will highlight the potential expertise and backing of a group.

Publicly available tools: Many APTs use tools that are publicly available and easily downloadable from many websites dedicated to hacking.

5.3.1.4 Targets

APT targets can be government/military, nongovernmental organizations, commercial enterprises, or the defense industrial base.

5.3.1.5 Command and Control

This highlights the ways in which an attacker communicates with implanted machines:

Trojan-initiated callbacks: This type of communication is marked by the malicious program initiating the connection to an external server. Most attackers use this technique in order to defeat firewalls, which typically allow outbound connections from computers within the network (Mandiant 2013).

Encryption: Encryption is used to hide C2 communications and make such communications more difficult to detect.

Third-party applications: Third-party applications, such as MSN Messenger, are leveraged to communicate with victims. Using trusted applications makes it more difficult for network defenders to identify C2 communications (Mandiant 2013).

Standard/default malware connections: Many publicly available backdoors come with default settings. For example, Poison Ivy uses port 3460 by default. Communications over default settings are more easily detected because they are known by network defenders (Mandiant 2013).

5.3.1.6 Persistence

Persistence is characterized by the length of time a particular APT has been conducting operations, such as more than five years, between two and five years, or less than two years

Figure 5.6 presents an overview of the characteristics of some well-known APTs (SecDev Group 2009, Alperovitch 2011, McAfee Labs 2010, 2011, Chien and O'Gorman 2011, Thakur 2011, Villeneuve and Sancho 2011, Blasco 2013, Mandiant 2013). Taking into account the tools, exploits, and

Name	Attack vector	Exploit	Tools	Targets	Command and control	Persistence
APT1	Spear phishing		Custom	Commercial enterprises, defense industrial base	Trojan-initiated callbacks, third party applications	More than five years
Shady Rat	Spear phishing	Known patched vulnerabilities		Government/military, non governmental organization, commercial enterprises, defense industrial base		Less than two years
Aurora/ Elderwood	Spear phishing Watering hole	Zero day	Custom	Nongovernmental organization, commercial enterprises, defense industrial base	Trojan-initiated callbacks, encryption	Between two and five years
RSA Hack	Spear phishing	Zero day	Publicly available	Commercial enterprises	Trojan-initiated callbacks, standard/default malware connections	Less than two years
Lurid	Spear phishing	Known but unpatched vulnerabilities	Publicly available	Government/military, commercial enterprises, defense industrial base	Trojan -initiated callbacks	
Night Dragon	Spear phishing SQL injection/other	Known patched vulnerabilities	Publicly available	Commercial enterprises	Trojan-initiated callbacks	Between two and five years
Ghost Net	Spear phishing	Known patched vulnerabilities	Publicly available	Government/military, non-governmental organization		Less than two years
Sykipot	Spear phishing Watering hole	Known, but unpatched vulnerabilities	Custom	Government/military, defense industrial base	Trojan-initiated callbacks, encryption	More than five years
Nitro	Spear phishing Watering hole		Publicly available	Non-governmental organization, commercial enterprises	Trojan-initiated callbacks, encryption	Less than two years

Figure 5.6 APT characteristics.

command and control communications, it appears that Elderwood, APT1, and Sykipot present the most substantial threats among the currently reported APTs in terms of the characteristics discussed.

5.3.2 Data Analytics Methods for Persistent Threats

Let us consider how we can use data analytics to discover persistent threat patterns such as those exhibited in an APT, particularly using the network traffic data.

For this, it is useful to evaluate the intrusion detection log data along with other raw log data files and study them over time using data discretization. Once the temporal bins are created to divide the data into chunks of time to study persistent behavior in these time chunks, frequent patterns using the association rule mining can be identified, and the overlapping and nonoverlapping rules across these bins can be determined. The high-priority unusual persistent threats can be isolated, i.e., the rules that occur frequently in the temporal bins but are nonoverlapping across time periods. This will help identify rules that do occur multiple times in a timer period but do not occur across other time periods.

Intuition: An advanced persistent threat is generally unusual and uses stealth mechanisms to not be discoverable. APTs also exhibit signs of system access at unusual times, a high level of backdoor access, and unusual information exchange. These events can be unusual yet frequent – but not necessarily across multiple times. This unusualness comes from the times when these events happen or in some cases the specific systems being targeted. Association rules that are repeatedly occurring across the multiple time periods represent the daily chatter in the log files. However, rules that are frequent but are nonoverlapping across time periods can be deemed unusual and considered as potential persistent threats. Similar to the social engineering example, here the idea is to narrow down the data and time window, which can be further investigated by an administrator. For example, frequent logins at unusual times might be useful for an administrator to follow up on rather than looking at the entire massive dataset. Keeping this intuition in mind, let us consider the mining strategy.

Data discretization: This segregates data into time segments or bins representing the multiple time periods, which makes it easier to evaluate the persistence of the threats across time periods represented by bins. *Given a set of temporally ordered alerts $A = \{a_1, \ldots, a_n\}$ (from the IDS log files such as from Snort logs) where each a_i has a set of features $fi = \{f_{i1}, f_{i2}, \ldots, f_{im}\}$, Bin is a set of temporally ordered segments from A such that $B = \{b_1 = (a_1, \ldots, a_x),$*

$b_2 = (a_{x+1}, \ldots, a_y), \ldots, b_r = (a_{i+1}, \ldots, a_n)\}$, where $|b_1| = |b_2| = \ldots = |b_z| = z$, and where z is the size of the bin. Let us consider equal-sized bins, in this case where z is fixed frequency.

Suspicious network traffic is captured through IDS in an alert log capturing the source and destination IP, with time stamps and the priority. Here priority indicates the severity of an alert (high, medium, or low-level alert). The high-priority threats can be obvious suspicious activities, and the low-priority threats can be potential alerts that may or may not be real. Such high-priority alerts when looked at in combination over a long period of time may turn out to be persistent. In general, an IDS does not capture threats over a period of time, but views each individual alert and assigns priority. Therefore, it is important to evaluate the alert priorities to see, when combined over time, what the overall threat is.

Identify frequent patterns: Analyzing threats individually may not provide the overall persistence of a threat. It is important to study the data from the overall perspective and identify frequent patterns on a given time frame to discover persistent threats. Thus, the data can be mined using association rule mining techniques and isolate the persistent high-priority threats (PHPT) from the individual high-priority threats (Quader et al. 2015). The PHPT are consistent and may indicate APT behaviors. Now given a set of discrete bins B in the log data, frequent pattern set $P = \{p_1, \ldots, p_s\}$ is a set of association rules where each $p_i = \{f_{ij} \rightarrow f_{ik}, f_{il} \rightarrow f_{im}, \ldots, f_{ip} \rightarrow f_{iq}\}$ such that each rule set p_i corresponds to each bin b_i and where $f_i = \{f_{i1}, f_{i2}, \ldots, f_{im}\}$ are features of alert a_i in b_i

Persistent threats: Persistent threats (PT) are unusual threats that stay consistent over a long period of time. The binned datasets and their corresponding frequent patterns can be intersected with each other to isolate the nonintersecting high-priority threats to detect the potential persistent threats. Persistent threat patterns have the following key characteristics: consistent over time (occurs repeatedly); single source (same key players); individually each is a threat, unusual (the pattern may be repeated at an unusual time of the day or a single source accessing different sources repeatedly at the same time of the day); and nonobvious (nonoverlapping).

In Figure 5.7, the PT patterns are located in the nonoverlapping area. Each circle in the figure represents the association rules for a specific bin. Now if the association rules overlap, they are consistent across bins and may be more like probing, which is not consistent with the characteristics of an APT. However, if the association rules do not overlap across bins and are unique to certain time periods, then they can be considered as potential persistent patterns of interest. Note that these are still frequent but not the same across each time period.

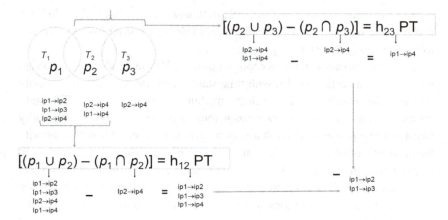

Figure 5.7 Example overlapping and nonoverlapping rules from ARM for Bin1, 2, and 3.

Association rule mining technique with classification-based association can be used to obtain the implied priority on the right-hand side of the rule. This helps identify the potential persistent threats with priority alert labels along with the repetitive nature of the threats. The binning also allows plotting the priorities on a timeline to associate the PT with time periods when these events occur.

In Figure 5.7, we see three time periods T_1, T_2, and T_3 with their corresponding rule sets p_1, p_2, and p_3. For example, p_1 has associations in the form of IP1 $\rightarrow$ IP2. This could imply a source destination relationship where IP1 is sending data to IP2. A union of two consecutive sets is taken and the intersection is subtracted from this set. As a result, the nonoverlapping or nonintersecting part of the two sets is discovered. Finally, after subsequent operations, the most unusual frequent set is identified that is nonintersecting across multiple bins.

In both these examples, the end result is not predictive but exploratory to help narrow down the data and time periods that should be further investigated. Each of this analysis is also based on the intuition of the attack pattern. Even in supervised methods, the intuition is used in formulating the training set with a given distribution. This is true to any data analytics task for identifying a cyberattack. There is no true model that can predict or identify an attack with a 100% certainty. Each detected pattern helps an administrator investigate the potential occurrence of the attack or zeroing into the needle in the haystack of data.

6

Anomaly Detection for Cybersecurity

In this chapter, we focus on what anomalies are, their types, and challenges in detecting anomalies. In Chapter 7, we focus on specific methods for detecting anomalies.

6.1 What Are Anomalies?

An anomaly in a dataset is an observation or a set of observations that are different and inconsistent with respect to the normal observations. An anomaly is also referred to as outlier, peculiarity, exception, and discord, among other terms. "Anomaly" and "outlier" are mostly used interchangeably. An anomaly is always identified with respect to a frame of reference. The frame of reference is the normal or baseline set of observations in the data. An anomaly stands apart from this frame of reference. Therefore, anomaly detection heavily relies on discovering the normal, the frame of reference, or the baseline against which an observation is compared to be termed as an anomaly. The further away the anomaly is from the frame of reference, the more severe is the anomaly.

Anomaly detection is a well-studied area of research, with several surveys describing the state of the art (Patcha and Park 2007, Chandola et al. 2009), and more specifically anomaly detection in areas of cybersecurity (Estevez-Tapiador et al. 2004, Feily 2009, Ten et al. 2011, Hong et al. 2014, Ahmed et al. 2016).

In the area of data analytics, anomaly detection has utilized techniques from supervised, semisupervised, and unsupervised learning to identify anomalies. Anomalies have been characterized as single point, group of points, and contextual anomalies (Chandola et al. 2009), as shown in Figure 6.1. However, these different types of anomalies can be interrelated.

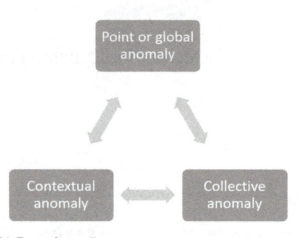

Figure 6.1 Types of anomalies.

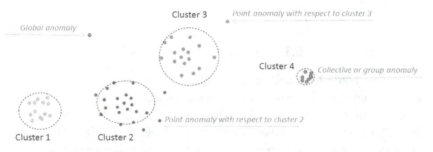

Figure 6.2 Illustrating the types of anomalies in clusters of network traffic data.

To explain the types of anomalies, let us consider Figure 6.2. The figure shows clusters of network traffic data that comprise features such as time to live, datagram length, and total size. Once clustering is performed, we see that certain points do not fall into any of the clusters. We can evaluate this clustering as containing potential anomalies.

Figure 6.2 depicts different types of anomalies. A *point anomaly* is a single data point that is anomalous with respect to a group of neighboring points. There can be different points of references such that an anomaly can be identified with respect to all clusters or with respect to points in a cluster or in some cases the entire dataset. For example, in the figure we can see that there is a single point that is a global anomaly, which is an anomalous with respect to all the three clusters 1, 2, and 3. There some local point anomalies, which are anomalous with respect to specific clusters such as cluster 2 and 3.

In some cases, a small group of points can also be an anomaly, called as a *collective anomaly*, such as cluster 4 in Figure 6.2. This cluster is an anomaly with respect to all the clusters due to the relative size of the cluster and its distance from other clusters. Individual points inside the cluster may not be anomalous on their own; however, when considered together as a group they are anomalous. In the example in Figure 6.2, the point of reference is the other clusters, such that the size of the clusters 1, 2, and 3 is much bigger and the distance of the small cluster 4 to the other clusters is much bigger than the distance between the clusters 1, 2, and 3. Thus, it is clear that a frame of reference is extremely important in discovering anomalies such that points or groups of points are not frivolously identified as anomalous.

Another type of anomaly is a *contextual anomaly*, where the anomaly is identified with the perspective of a certain context. For example, if the network traffic in an e-commerce site at a certain time appears to be very high as compared to the other network traffic points for this site, they may appear to be anomalous or the time period may appear anomalous. However, if there is a specific event that is leading to the high network traffic, such as high sales during holiday time, then this high traffic would not be anomalous. The context here is that the high amount of traffic is generated due to a marketing event or a special sale and not because of a flooding attack or a denial of service attack. In the figure, we provide additional information that the cluster 4 is in fact a group of points where a large file was being uploaded by a specific network admin, which resulted in the massive size of the transfer on the network generating the data point that is different from that of the rest of the traffic. Given the context of the origin of the data, these data should not have been included in the analysis. Thus defining a context can be very important to create a frame of reference. This can be done before the anomaly detection, which is much more robust, to clean up the data of possible frivolous outliers or as a postprocessing step where the outliers are filtered through any context.

6.2 Context

Context can be in the form of attributes within the data that can be used to create demarcations in the data so that data are separated into groups for further analysis. Context can help define homogeneous groups for anomaly detection. Context discovery is a preprocessing step where the groups are identified using contextual attributes (such as shown in Figure 6.3), and then anomaly detection is performed in the contextually relevant groups of data points using the behavioral attributes that measure the phenomena (such as network traffic

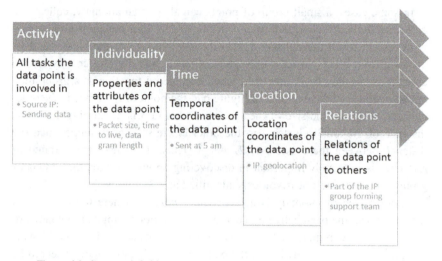

Figure 6.3 Context definition.

density). Context-aware processing allows for accommodating context definition into the algorithmic process.

Context can be defined in the terms of activity, individuality, spatial or
location context, temporal context, and relations context (Zimmermann et al.
2007). Context definition for an example network data point is shown in
Figure 6.3. For example, *a data point, part of the network traffic data, is a
source IP, is sending the data packet at 5 a.m., and is part of the IP address
allocated to the support team.* Thus, if all the support team IPs are sending
similarly sized data and at similar time frame, then this point will be considered
normal. However, if this particular data point is sending data at an unusual
time and is originating from a geolocation outside of the expected locations,
then this could be a potential anomaly. Here the frame of reference is defined
in terms of time, IP location, and the team. Thus, data points with a similar
context should be grouped together, and anomaly detection can be applied to
each of the groups for a well-defined anomaly detection. The point, group, and
contextual anomalies are related to each other since a context can apply to both
a point and groups of outliers. Moreover, in some cases individual point
anomalies can collectively be part of a group anomaly. However, this may
not always be the case since data points that are part of the group may or may
not be individually anomalous.

Anomaly detection has several associated challenges, and these will be
clarified next with the help of a motivating example.

6.3 Motivating Example: BGP Hijacking

Network packets follow certain specific traffic routes on the internet using the announced and available routes maintained in the routing tables. Border Gateway Protocol (BGP) is primarily responsible for exchange of information between autonomous systems (AS) for successful transmission over the published routes. Several types of attacks lead to hijacking of hosts or servers and redirecting traffic to anomalous sites or dumping traffic at random sites. BGP hijacking is one such type of attack. Examples include redirection of Google and YouTube requests in Turkey (Paganini 2014) and erroneous rerouting of YouTube traffic (Sandoval 2008), among others.

BGP anomalies (Al-Musawi et al. 2016) prevent successful exchanges between the AS, leading to loss of data or unauthorized rerouting of the data. Such anomalies may include route flapping, path announcements that delay in-routed packets, malicious redirecting of traffic for unauthorized surveillance purposes, and dropping of packets to unknown destinations. BGP anomalies where path announcements are made may lead to thousands of anomalous updates. BGP first initiates a complete routing table exchange and then subsequently exchanges updates. Thus, if there is an anomaly, then there will be a lot more updates than normal. This can potentially indicate the presence of an anomaly. However, a more specific discovery is needed to identify where (at what location or specific AS) the anomaly originated, as this can provide pertinent information for interpretation of the anomaly, whether it was a simple misconfiguration or a more malicious intent to disrupt or redirect the traffic.

BGP anomalies can also be classified similar to the general anomalies a point or collective anomaly. A single update can be considered as a point anomaly if it has an invalid AS number, invalid IP prefix, or a prefix announced by an illegitimate AS (Wübbeling et al. 2014). A set of updates can be anomalous (collectively) if there are several BGP updates in a short amount of time containing longest and shortest paths or substantial changes in the BGP traffic (Al-Musawi et al. 2015). Such anomaly detection can use data from BGP update messages or routes that packets use. Several repositories are available for such datasets to be analyzed and for discovering anomalies, as shown in Table 6.1. Each of these datasets shows the complexity and massive nature of the data.

Studies have shown that a large number of attributes can be mined to discover BGP anomalies (Li et al. 2005, Al-Rousan et al. 2012). Using these as an example the following section identifies the challenges in understanding and discovering anomalies.

6.4 Challenges in Understanding Anomalies

As data size increases both in terms of the number of data points and the features describing them, the patterns in the data get further embedded deeper into the data space. This is primarily because data are sparse in high dimensions. This means that the patterns may exist in some subspaces in the data and not in others. This is referred to as the curse of dimensionality (Bellman 1961). The curse of dimensionality affects all the data analytics techniques and is even more relevant for anomaly detection, as anomalies are already rare.

Several studies have explored the datasets listed in Table 6.1. Li et al. (2005) used 35 features every one minute to generate decision trees based on past BGP events. Such data are high dimensional and nearly real-time data. Let us consider the dimensionality issue in such data. High-dimensional data can be analyzed in various ways to identify anomalous routes. The full dataset can be considered for the analysis or alternatively a smaller relevant (contextual) subset of the data can be considered. It is possible that a route or a single update can be an outlier in one subset of attributes but not an outlier in another subset. For example, a route is not an outlier in the *updates* attribute but is an outlier in the *location* attribute.

Thus, it is essential to carefully determine whether all the dimensions are to be considered or a selected critical attribute set is considered. This selection of the critical attribute set is also a data mining task in itself, such as through feature selection.

In the example shown in Figure 6.4, the data are comprised of four attributes: *number of BGP announcements, number of BGP updates, number of*

Table 6.1 *BGP data repositories*

Data description	Link
RouteViews	www.routeviews.org/
Réseaux IP Européens	www.ripe.net/manage-ips-and-asns/db
BGPMon	https://bgpmon.net/
Internet route registries	http://irr.net/index.html
CIDR report (bogon prefix lists)	www.cidr-report.org/as2.0/
MaxMind, GeoIP location data	www.maxmind.com/en/open-source-data-and-api-for-ip-geolocation
IP2location	www.ip2location.com/
CAIDA traceroute platform	www.caida.org/proiects/ark/

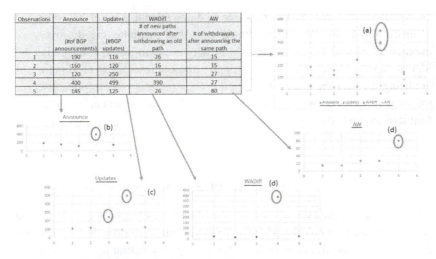

Observations	Announce	Updates	WADiff	AW
	(#of BGP announcements)	(#BGP updates)	# of new paths announced after withdrawing an old path	# of withdrawals after announcing the same path
1	190	116	26	15
2	160	120	16	15
3	120	250	18	27
4	400	499	390	27
5	145	125	26	80

Figure 6.4 Example curse of dimensionality.

new paths announced, and number of withdrawals after announcing the same path. The two-dimensional plot of the data considering all the attributes together (Figure 6.4a) depicts clear anomalies that stand out from the other data points. This anomaly corresponds to observation 4, which shows high values for all attributes with respect to all the other observations. Figure 6.4b–e shows the plot for each attribute. It is clear that observation 4 dominates plots shown in Figure 6.4b–d. However, in Figure 6.4c we see that observation 3, which has a high number of BGP updates, is also deviant with respect to the rest of the data points. Finally, in Figure 6.4d, which plots the attribute AW, which is the number of withdrawals after announcing the paths, it is evident that observation 5 is highly deviant compared to the rest of the data points. This anomaly did not show up in Figure 6.4a and was masked by the other highly deviant values. This clearly shows the challenge of high dimensionality when the patterns are hidden in the subspaces.

Thus, anomaly detection is not only focused on the mechanism of labeling an outlier or anomaly but also carefully identifying the frame of reference in terms of the objects to compare against and also the subset of attributes or subspaces to consider.

Once the frame of reference or context in terms of the data and set of dimensions to be used is determined, then the data mining and analysis could be used to identify the deviation of the route from the normal.

This type of analysis based on a clearly defined context could be useful in selecting the suspicious routes for further investigation. Such analysis can help answer the following: What routes or updates should a point be compared against? What are the critical dimensions that facilitate the discovery of anomalous routes? How can we inform why a certain route is an outlier by identifying the dimensions contributing to the outlierness? If all dimensions are being used for the discovery, then it is also important to explore subsets of the attributes to account for contribution from dimensions and also identify the (outlierness) contributing dimensions.

6.5 Interpretation

Anomalies are in the eyes of the beholder. Anomalies can be a nuisance for an operator or a user who does not want too many alerts to slow them down. For example, in some domains such as the emergency operating centers where complex and multiple systems are used, too many alerts can lead to alert fatigue, desensitizing the end users to the numerous pings from their systems. Indeed, in healthcare environments, this type of alert fatigue has been studied,[1] and it could lead to potential threats such as ransomware, etc. This can affect the overall performance of a system, but more importantly this can desensitize users to click when they should not be clicking. Alternately, for a security officer each anomaly may be a critical alert to portend the arrival of a major attack or a major misconfiguration leaving a gaping hole in a system.

Anomaly interpretation may also change from one domain to another. What appears as a blip in an instrument reading in one domain (such as sensors monitoring water monitoring quality in a stream) may appear to be a major alert in another domain (such as sensors monitoring water in the nuclear power plant). Another example is password attempts. How many failed password attempts are allowed into a system will depend on the function of the system being accessed. A bank may only allow three failed attempts before it locks out the user, whereas an emailing system may allow more attempts. In each of these systems, predicting whether there is a guess password attack will be based on different criteria based on the domain context. Figure 6.5 depicts some of the priorities and discussions at various levels that can impact the discovery and interpretation of an anomaly. The organization's priorities may be connected to the business bottom line, such as reputation, when an attack happens that can translate to millions of dollars lost (Drinkwater 2016). Similarly, an end user is highly driven by the day-to-day functions and how

---

[1] https://psnet.ahrq.gov/primers/primer/28/alert-fatigue Last accessed June 2017.

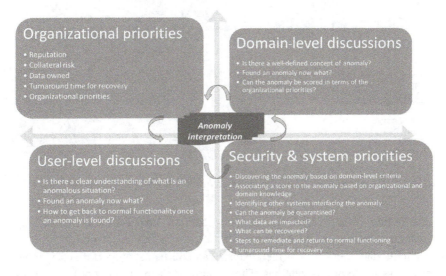

Figure 6.5 Factors governing the interpretation and discovery of anomalies.

fast the functionality can return to normal. The system and security priorities are more directly related to the anomaly detection and scoring. However, these must work in conjunction to the other players' priorities.

Thus, interpretation of anomalies will vary from one type of user to another, one type of system to another, and one domain to another based on the context defined and agreed upon by each.

Many times, two users in the same organization may also not agree on the definition of an anomaly. It is critical to have a well-crafted definition of an anomaly to (a) facilitate the discovery of an anomaly, (b) reduce the false positives, and (c) associate importance to the level of the anomaly for faster recovery and remediation.

6.6 Treating Anomalies

Traditional statistical outlier detection (Barnett and Lewis 1994) has addressed how outliers can be treated once they are discovered, whether they should be accommodated into the analysis or rejected before the analysis.

Accommodation tends to detect the outlier and accommodate the value in the dataset so that the whole set of observations is still intact. It tends to manipulate the observation so that even if an anomaly is in the dataset, the data do not become skewed because of this rogue observation. The idea is that outliers are part of the data: although their removal fits the data into some

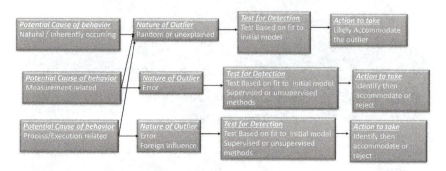

Figure 6.6 Treatment of outliers (adapted from Barnett and Lewis 1994).

distribution or normalizes the data, the outliers' presence could be equally important for the analysis. Hence, the idea is to not reject outliers, but to accommodate them so that the analysis can still be safely performed without any loss of data or observations. Thus, it aims at the robustness of the analysis in the presence of outliers.

Rejection is basically testing an outlier purely from the point of view of rejecting it from the dataset or of identifying it as a feature of special interest and removing it before further analysis is done.

Figure 6.6, adapted from Barnett and Lewis 1994, summarizes the treatment of outliers based on the source of variation and the nature of outliers. If the anomaly is caused due to a measurement error, it is either rejected or corrected, or the detection is repeated. However, if the variation is inherent or due to some real measurement of an event, then the anomaly detection is used, but again in this case the outlier is incorporated in the revised model, identified for a separate study of origin and form. Also, if the anomaly is due to some random reason, then it could be accommodated to see the overall analysis rather than eliminating the observation altogether.

In terms of cybersecurity, in the majority of the cases, the anomaly must be eliminated. For instance, if there is a Trojan discovered in a computer system that disrupts the regular functionality, it has to be eliminated. Similarly, if the BGP updates appear to be anomalous, they need to be corrected for proper communication and movement of the traffic. However, in some cases the anomaly needs to be studied, in which case the anomaly may be detected and traced. This was a concept carried out in a setting called "Jail," where an attacker was traced through the system access and observations collected to learn about the role and activities of the attacker (Cheswick 1992). Similarly, honeypots are set up to collect data and activities of attackers (Spitzner 2003).

We next discuss methods for anomaly detection in Chapter 7.

7

Anomaly Detection Methods

As discussed in Chapter 6, anomalies or outliers are objects or groups of objects that are deviant with respect to other normal objects. This anomalous behavior can be caused by extreme values in some dimensions, which could be an inherent rare property of the anomalous objects. In high-dimensional data, this rarity increases with the increase in the number of dimensions. This is mainly because data become sparse in higher dimensions; this will further aggravate the discovery of outliers. Other situations may be caused due to measurement errors or phenomena that are causing the deviations. This chapter focuses on techniques for anomaly detection addressing these issues and their applicability to cybersecurity problems.

Figure 7.1 shows a broad categorization of anomaly detection techniques to give an idea of the development in this field. Several recent surveys provide a lot more categories and discuss the works in detail (Patcha and Park 2007, Chandola et al. 2009, Garcia-Teodoro et al. 2009, Bhuyan et al. 2014).

Outlier detection techniques have been adopted from the statistical literature and treat the outliers as parametric outlier detection, in which the data are assumed to fit a certain distribution. The tail region of the distribution, such as in a normal distribution, would constitute the outliers. However, in real-world datasets, the data do not fit into a standard statistical distribution. Certain other techniques detect outliers using metrics such as distance, distance from nearest neighbors, density, deviation, and other such measures. Other methods are a byproduct of clustering methods. The data are first clustered using some clustering technique, and the data points, which lie outside of a cluster, are considered to be outliers. There could also be a scenario that part or all of a cluster of data points could be outliers based on the problem being studied. Classification-based techniques identify and predict anomalies based on historic anomaly signatures.

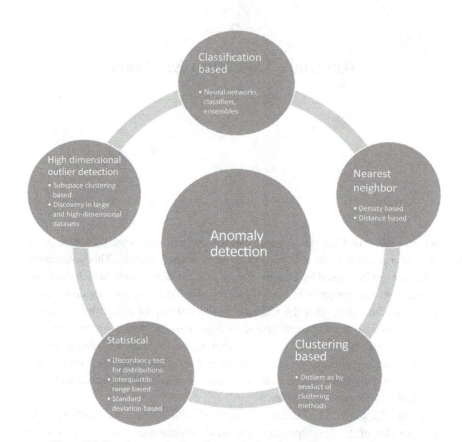

Figure 7.1 Broad categorization of anomaly detection methods.

The discussion in this chapter is limited to key anomaly detection techniques since they are the foundational approaches that are adopted as variations of these methods, such as in the distance-based techniques and discovery of anomalies in large, multidimensional datasets.

7.1 Statistical Outlier Detection Tests

The distribution-based parametric methods are discussed in the statistical outlier detection literature, which assumes that data fit into a prespecified distribution, such as normal distribution, and then identifies the outliers with respect to the model using *discordancy tests* (Barnett and Lewis 1994). The discordancy tests are developed based on the properties of the distribution. Similarly, the Inter Quartile Range based outlier detection method is developed using statistical dispersion.

7.1.1 Discordancy Tests

Discordancy tests evaluate the fit of the data to an assumed distribution. It has two main hypotheses: a working hypothesis and an alternative hypothesis. It assumes a standard distribution of the dataset, and if the discordancy test finds the outliers, then it tries to fit the data to the alternative distribution; however, the underlying assumption is that the data fit a distribution, which might not be the case always, especially for multidimensional real-world data.

As an example, if there is a normal distribution where x_1 and x_n are the extremes, a discordancy test will check if x_n, apart from being an extreme, is also statistically unreasonable; if it is, then it is called a discordant upper outlier. The next step would be to show that the outlier comes from the alternative distribution and not the working distribution. However, this is a difficult task in itself. The key thing to note here is that the discordancy tests are statistical measures used to see if the data element being tested fits a distribution. A key metric is to see the fit of the data point using measures such as deviation/spread statistics such that $d = \frac{\mu - x_1}{s}$, where μ is a measure of central tendency; in this case, the mean and s can be a known measure of spread, such as range. For example, if $d \leq 1$, then x_1 is not an outlier; on the other hand, if $d > 1$, it is an outlier.

There are two major procedures for outlier detection in statistical studies, as shown in Figure 7.2: block procedures and consecutive (or sequential) procedures.

In *consecutive (or sequential) procedures*, sample size is not fixed, but determined in each cycle in relation to the values of earlier observations.

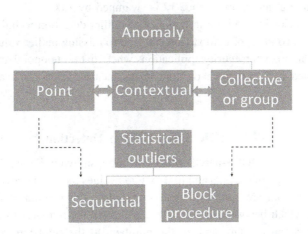

Figure 7.2 Types of anomalies and statistical methods of detection.

Each observation is screened for discordancy in relation to the already screened set of observations. This procedure can be done in two ways: outside inward, which means that the extreme outlier is tested first, then second most extreme, and so on, but more widely preferred way of doing it is the other way around (starting with the least likely element to be an outlier). In *block procedures*, two or more observations are tested together for outlierness.

These procedures have similarity to the point anomaly detection and collective anomaly detection discussed in the data mining literature (Chandola et al. 2009).

Consecutive procedures can suffer from challenges such as masking and swamping (Barnett and Lewis 1994). *Masking* is an erroneous judgment arising out of a single outlier test. Suppose if through a discordancy test observation x_n is declared an outlier with respect to all the $n - 1$ values, then x_{n-1} is further tested. But if x_n is not declared an outlier with respect to all $n - 1$ values then x_{n-1} is not tested. This could be a problem in a scenario where x_n is not an outlier with respect to the adjacent value of x_{n-1}, but both x_n and x_{n-1} are outliers when tested together with respect to all $n - 2$ values. Let us consider a small sample values: 8, 10, 11, 13, 1,000, and 1,005. Now, for example, if tested individually 1,009 will not be declared as an outlier since it is close to 1,000, but if 1,000 and 1,005 are tested together against other values, then they are outliers with respect to all other $n - 2$ values.

Swamping, on the other hand, results from using a block or consecutive procedure to test for discordancy, i.e., testing two values together, as in a sample such as 5, 8, 10, 12, 1,000.

If two values are tested together, then they are considered outliers, but value 12 is not an outlier, so in essence 12 is swamped by 1,000.

This behavior is also seen in majority of outlier detection techniques when the incorrect context for comparison can lead to missing outlier values. This is very relevant to cybersecurity applications where data is temporal and needs to be evaluated as a sequence of time series measurements such as network traffic data.

7.1.2 IQR-Based Outlier Detection

Interquartile range (IQR)–based outlier detection, shown in Figure 7.3, aims to identify the range of the data and find extreme values that are far away from the range. First, data are sorted in increasing order. The median of the data is identified, which becomes the second quartile. All the numbers to the left are smaller than the median, and all the numbers to the right are greater. The median of these left- and right-hand sides are identified as first quartile and

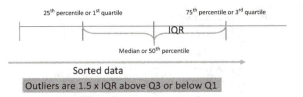

Figure 7.3 IQR-based outlier detection approach.

third quartile respectively. The data are now divided into four chunks of data ordered by the quartiles. The difference between the third quartile and the first quartile is the IQR. IQR-based outlier detection assumes that the IQR should have the majority of the data distribution measuring the spread of the data. Now if this IQR range is further stretched beyond the first and third quartile such that the lower threshold is the first quartile minus IQR times 1.5, and the upper threshold is the third quartile plus the IQR times 1.5. This stretches the range or spread of the data. Points that fall beyond these thresholds at the lower extreme or the upper extreme are the outliers.

IQR is primarily a univariate outlier detection method. An example of IQR-based outlier detection is shown in Figure 7.4, in the network traffic data sample for the attribute "packet size."

In general, statistical outlier detection is a highly developed field and has been well established for a long time. However, for outlier detection using statistical methods, the distribution of the dataset needs to be known in advance and the knowledge of the distribution is the underlying assumption. The properties of the distribution need to be known in advance such as the mean, standard deviation, etc. Outlier detection also has to take into consideration the masking and swamping effects for sequential and block procedures. In general, the modeling process is more complicated, especially in case of multidimensional datasets. The statistical outlier detection mainly works well for univariate variables. Moreover, these techniques do not work well with incomplete or inconclusive data, and computation of the results is expensive.

7.2 Density-Based Outlier Detection: OPTICS-OF Identifying Local Outliers

OPTICS-OF (Breunig et al. 1999) is an extension of the OPTICS density-based clustering algorithm as discussed in Chapter 3. It discovers outliers relative to their neighborhood. Distance-based outliers are good in a global sense, but when different densities of objects exist within the data, distance-based discovery is not adequate. Hence, each outlier is assigned with a degree

Observations	Packet size		
1	7.012472	Outlier	
2	8.771873		
3	9.360618		
4	9.428184		
5	9.456278	9.476627769	Q1
6	9.496977		
7	9.608662		
8	9.881874		
9	9.922703		
10	10.11899		
11	10.47658	Median	Q2
12	10.51159		
13	10.63797		
14	10.91105		
15	10.98602		
16	11.06	11.08674809	Q3
17	11.1135		
18	11.48358		
19	11.69379		
20	11.95874		
21	25	Outlier	
IQR	1.61012		
IQR*1.5	2.41518		
Thresholds	7.061447	Lower threshold	
	13.50193	Upper threshold	

Figure 7.4 Example of IQR-based univariate outlier detection.

by which the object is an outlier. Outliers, relative to their local surrounding space, motivate a formal definition of local outliers. An object is mostly defined as an outlier or not an outlier; however, there could be a degree of outlierness attached to each object based on the local density where position of each object affects the other. The basic concepts of ε-neighborhood and K-distance are adapted from the algorithm DBSCAN, and the concepts of core distance and reachability distance are from the algorithm OPTICS.

OPTICS-OF defines a concept called local reachability, which is measured in terms of the local reachability density of point p given as *Lrd(p) = 1/average reachability distance of minpts nearest neighbors of P.*

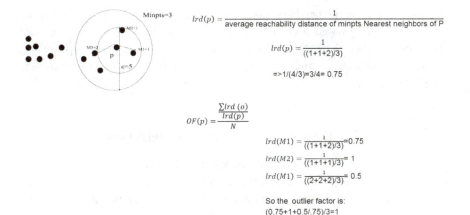

Figure 7.5 Example of OPTICS-OF parameter computation.

Let us consider the example shown in Figure 7.5. Here the *minpts* are set to 3, although there are more than 3 points in the neighborhood. Only reachability distance to the 3 points needs to be measured. Thus, $Lrd(p) = 1/((1 + 1 + 2)/3)$, which is 0.75.

The outlier factor of p is measured in terms of the uniformity in the density of *p's neighborhood*. Thus, it takes into consideration the local reachability density of all the *minpnts'* nearest neighbors of p. In the preceding example, these are $M1$, $M2$, and $M3$. The outlier factor of p is as follows:

$$OF(p) = \frac{\frac{\sum lrd(o)}{lrd(p)}}{N}$$

So in the example from Figure 7.5, the outlier factor is as follows: $(0.75 + 1 + 0.5/0.75)/3 = 1$.

The OF = 1 represents a cluster of uniform density. The lower p's *Lrd* is, and the higher the *Lrd* of p's *minpts'* nearest neighbors is, the higher will be p's outlier factor.

This approach is one of the first and few approaches that quantifies the outlierness of an object. In the case of multidimensional datasets, however, the degree of the outlierness also depends on dimensions that are contributing to the outlierness and possibly the cause of the outlierness. This approach is able to identify the local or global outliers with respect to a set of points. For some applications, both global and local outliers must be pointed out. Moreover, if only distance from the neighbors or *minpts* in the neighborhood are considered, then we overlook the situation when several points are collectively an anomaly compared to others. If several points deviate from the standard, simply relying on the neighborhood or distance measure is not effective. For this, a clustering-based approach is needed where unusual clusters can be identified as anomalous. In graphs and spatial data, other types of approaches look at the collective structure of the anomalous subset with respect to the other data points.

7.3 Distance-Based Outlier Detection

In data mining, distribution of attributes is mostly unknown. Distance-based outlier detection algorithms initially proposed by Knorr et al. (2000) continue the idea of a unified notion of mining outliers, which extends statistical-based outlier detection.

Such an approach generalizes the notion of outliers provided by many of the discordancy tests for known distributions, such as Normal, Poisson, Binomial, etc. Although it proposes a partitioning-based technique for distance-based outlier detection, it also elaborates on how this approach can unify the various discordancy tests available in the statistical/distribution-based outlier detection techniques. The time complexity is linear with respect to number of objects, and the algorithms are efficient for low-dimensional datasets. The key idea that outliers are far away from their neighbors in terms of a distance threshold was proposed and has been adopted by many recent works (for example, Zhang et al. 2009, Sugiyama and Borgwardt 2013, Cao et al. 2014). Ramaswamy et al. (2000) treats the distance-based outlier detection as one relative to K-nearest neighbors.

The distance-based outliers are identified with two parameters, p and D, namely $DB (p, D)$. An object O in a dataset T is a $DB (p, D)$ outlier if at least a fraction p of the objects in T are at a greater distance D from O. For example, in Figure 7.6, the fraction of points p is 3 and distance threshold is 2. Thus, the point O is at least greater than distance 2 from at least 3 points and can be labeled an outlier.

Essentially, these outliers are objects that do not have enough neighbors within a certain distance. This eliminates the computation for fitting the

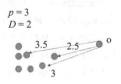

Figure 7.6 Example of a distance-based outlier.

observed distribution into a standard distribution and in selecting the discordancy tests. For many discordancy tests for standard distributions, if an object is shown to be an outlier, then it is also a distance-based outlier.

Parameters p, D are set by a user in case of nonstandard distributions; this is a trial-and-error approach, where the user interactively changes the p, D variables to evaluate the outcome.

This approach identifies outliers based on the distance of a candidate outlier from a set of neighboring points; it is not dependent on the clustering structure of the dataset. The outliers detected, however, are dependent on user input. Different algorithms are proposed that are suitable for different types of datasets. But these algorithms are sensitive to user input such as the distance threshold, or the value of p to identify the number of points for comparison to the candidate point. This approach is not suitable for high-dimensional data since distance measures (such as the Euclidean distance) do not scale well over high dimensions and average out the behavior of the dimensions. The distance metric is a point metric; therefore, it detects outliers that are at a distance greater than a parameter, and it does not take into consideration outliers that could be as a result of a very small distance measure in a subset of the dimensions. This technique is also mainly geared toward detecting global outliers.

Ramaswamy et al. (2000) eliminates the dependency in terms of the user input required for distance threshold. It also proposes outlier detection for large datasets using a pruning technique. This issue is addressed using a structure such as R Tree and CF Tree. This is a modified way of detecting outliers based on a distance threshold; it uses K-NN query and detects global outliers. This technique provides a pruning technique to deal with large datasets. However, it does not handle multidimensional datasets and is unable to account for attributes contributing to outlierness.

In general, distance-based outlier detection methods suffer from the curse of dimensionality (as discussed in Chapter 6). In higher dimensions, data become sparse, and points tend to become equidistant. This adversely affects the methods based on spatial density, unless data follow certain simple distributions. For outlier detection, a subset of the entire attribute set should be enough to detect or indicate the outliers. Aggarwal and Yu (2001) proposed the idea to examine specific projections of high-dimensional data instead of examining all the dimensions. If we consider cross sections of the data in various dimensions, we can find outliers better than in other cross sections. Aggarwal and Yu (2001) define the abnormal lower-dimension projections. There can be many abnormal projections, and this work facilitates the discovery of the best abnormal projections.

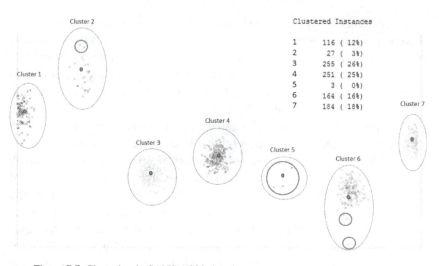

Figure 7.7 Clustering in SANS 1,000-day data.

7.4 Outlier Detection through Clustering

Some clustering algorithms, discussed in Chapter 3, such as DBSCAN, identify outliers as a byproduct of clustering. However, majority of clustering
algorithms have to be postprocessed to discover outliers. Thus, outliers can
be seen as a byproduct of the clustering process.

In traditional clustering, such as K-Means, by the end of the cluster analysis,
we assign each data point to one of the clusters, so basically there are no
unassigned data points. An example of clustering the SANS data,[1] from IDS
sensors around the world for 1,000 days, including attributes of records,
targets, and sources of attacks (from 2017) is shown in Figure 7.7. This
clustering was generated using Weka[2] Simple Kmeans clustering. Since all
the data are assigned to clusters, does that mean that there are no outliers in the
data? If there are still outliers, how do we filter out the outliers? There are a few
possibilities in a clustering output: (a) A point may be placed in a cluster by
itself. (b) A data point may be part of a cluster but far from the centroid. (c)
A small cluster with a lot fewer points than other clusters can be far from the
other clusters. (d) In DBScan-type clustering, points will not be connected or
in a cluster but a distinct outlier.

If a point is placed in its own cluster or is identified by the algorithm as an
outlier, such as in cases (a) and (d), then clearly a point anomaly has been

---

[1] http://isc.sans.edu/submissions_ascii.html, 2017.   [2] www.cs.waikato.ac.nz/ml/weka/.

detected. In the other two cases, postprocessing of the analysis will need to be performed to identify anomalies:

In the case of *small clusters*, if the data are clustered into groups of different density and if there is a cluster with fewer points than the other clusters, this cluster can be a candidate for a collective anomaly. In this case, the density of the candidate cluster is highly deviant than the other clusters. There can be other measures, such as the distance between the candidate cluster and noncandidate cluster, and if the candidate cluster is far from all other noncandidate points, they are potential outliers. In Figure 7.7, we can see a density distribution for each cluster, and cluster 5 appears to have very low density compared to the other clusters. When we consider the three points in this cluster, they represent a very high number of targets, sources, and records, indicating a high level of attack activity. Each of the observations has a time stamp, i.e., the date. If we further investigate the date by a simple Google search for the time period and keyword cyberattack, we see reports of relevant attacks occurring around that time period indicating the unusual activity during the time period. This type of evaluation helps with exploratory analysis of the dataset.

In the case of *larger clusters with scattered points*, there may be bigger clusters where the points in the cluster are not tightly bound around the centroid. In this case, the distance of every point can be measured to the centroid, and the points farthest from the centroid can be identified. This is similar to a distance-based or a K-nearest neighbors–based outlier detection inside such clusters. These clusters can be identified by looking at the sum of squared error (SSE) of the clusters, and the clusters with a high SSE can be candidates for postprocessing for identifying distance-based outliers. For example, in Figure 7.7, clusters 5 and 6 are potential clusters for postprocessing where the circled points could be evaluated as potential outliers.

8

Cybersecurity through Time Series and Spatial Data

As discussed in Chapter 4, the nature of data and data complexity must be addressed carefully in any data analytics methods. This chapter presents a spatial and temporal view of cybersecurity issues. Spatial data generally refer to geospatial data in the context of cybersecurity. The spatial context comes from the origination of the attacks or sources of attacks. In addition, attributes related to the geospatial location may be important to consider, such as socio-economic and geopolitical factors at play in the region. The network layout can also have a spatial context. One example of spatial context in cybersecurity is the geo-origination of anomalies such as massive spam originating from certain spam hubs around the globe. Identifying geolocations for the origins of attacks can provide insightful knowledge to address the defense mechanisms (Hu et al. 2015). Temporal context refers to the time reference of an attack or network traffic in general over a period of time. This could refer to how network traffic evolves over time or how certain trends over time could indicate threats.

This chapter revisits the spatial and temporal nature of the data and the challenges emanating from the data. Spatial and temporal approaches relevant to anomaly detection in cybersecurity are discussed. Finally, examples of spatiotemporal discovery in cybersecurity are discussed.

8.1 Spatial and Temporal Data

8.1.1 Spatial Data

As discussed in Chapter 4, understanding the nature of data is critical for spatial data mining because of the inherent complexities of the spatial data, which consist of data pertaining to space, multidimensional points, lines, rectangles, polygons, cubes, and other geometric objects. Spatial data have large volumes, so much so that they may require an infinitely large database to capture the real world precisely. Spatial data not only pose challenges due to the type of data and volume but also due to the correlation between the objects and their spatial neighbors with a neighborhood. There can be relationships between spatial objects such as topological relationships (e.g., disjoint, meet, overlap, etc.), direction relationships (e.g., north, south, above, below, etc.), metric relationships (e.g., distance greater than), or complex relationships (e.g., overlap with a certain distance threshold in the north), which are based on these basic relationships. Moreover, the data can depict temporal changes, which are inherent in the data.

For the purposes of cybersecurity, we focus on georeferenced data, which include spatial location in terms of latitude, longitude, and other information about spatial and nonspatial attributes. This essentially means that there is some preprocessing on the raw data to extract the georeferenced attributes and some other nonspatial attributes such as geopolitical attributes, other regional attributes affecting the network trends such as network bandwidths, etc. Chapter 11 discusses one such specific geospatial example. Figure 8.1 shows a list of various cyberattack maps that capture this information in a georeferenced manner.

8.1.2 Spatial Autocorrelation

Autocorrelation (Griffith 1987, Haining 2003) refers to the correlation of a variable to itself. Spatial autocorrelation refers to the correlation of the variable with itself in space. It can either be positive (spatial clusters for high–high or low–low values) or negative (high–low or low–high values). Everything is related to everything else but nearby objects are more related than distant objects (Tobler 1970). This is considered to be the core of spatial autocorrelation statistics. Any statistical measure (such as Moran's I, Geary's ratio, or Joint Count; Griffith 1987, Haining 2003) of spatial autocorrelation relies upon this (Tobler's) first law of geography.

8.1.3 Spatial Heterogeneity

Spatial heterogeneity is the spatially varying autocorrelation where autocorrelation can be positive or negative. It refers to the variation in the region that may generate characteristic spatial patterns, which could be due to the underlying geographical processes and geographical features in the region. This behavior can be understood in different scales of spatial variation (Haining 2003), including large (macrovariation as autocorrelation) and medium/small

Cyberattack map	Link	Cyberattack information
Norse	http://map.norsecorp.com/#/	Attack type, attack origin and target country, live attack map
Checkpoint-threatmap	https://threatmap.checkpoint.com/Threat Portal/livemap.html	Attacker, targets, top countries attacked and top attackers
Fireeye	www.fireeye.com/cyber-map/threat-map.html	Source, destination, top industries targeted
Kaspersky	https://cybermap.kaspersky.com/	Interactive based on data sources, threat types
Digital attack map	www.digitalattackmap.com/#anim= 1&color=0&country=ALL&list=0&time=173 88&view=map	Source destination, duration, size
Akamai	www.akamai.com/us/en/solutions /intelligent-platform/visualizing-akamai/real-time-web-monitor.jsp	Network attacks by region
Wordfence	www.wordfence.com/	Wordpress plugin, blocking attacks

Figure 8.1 Cyberattack maps, based on geolocations of attack origins and destinations.

(mesovariation as heterogeneity), as well as error (independent noise or anomalies).

Based on the concept of spatial autocorrelation and heterogeneity, it may be possible that the geospatial trends within United States may be similar due to spatial autocorrelation; however, there may also be inherent variability due to heterogeneity. Let us consider the number of attacks coming into the United States as shown in the various maps in Figure 8.1. However, every location in the United States will not be targeted with the same frequency. While the number of incoming attacks are generally high for the United States, depicting spatial autocorrelation, there is also a spatial heterogeneity due to the relative variation of the attacks to different locations inside the United States. Figure 8.2 shows that United States is the top targeted country; however, the

Figure 8.2 Illustration of spatial autocorrelation and heterogeneity.

number of attacks on the East Coast are much larger than the Midwest due to the richness of targets in the East Coast. Thus, even though there is a bigger class of locations, for a more accurate analysis the locations will need to be subdivided to better evaluate and better allocate resources.

8.1.4 Temporal Data

Let us consider a location or an entity identified by an IP address. This location or entity may have measurements for a variable separated by a regular interval of time. For example, the traffic information originating from the IP address is generated continuously over time (separated by seconds or milliseconds). These traffic data are linked to the geolocation generating the traffic. These data by nature are temporal, as they are time ordered and each measurement is separated by a time tick (seconds, milliseconds, or nanoseconds). The attribute or variable being measured may be the datagram length (dgmLen) or size of the packet. There is also a possibility that the object or entity is the network itself and the variable being measured over time is the number of incoming or outgoing connections to see the health of the network in terms of the network traffic. Similar to spatial data, temporal data also have issues of autocorrelation and heterogeneity.

8.1.5 Temporal Autocorrelation

Two instances of an object in time occurring one after the other (reflected as two attribute values for this object) have a temporal relationship of adjacency.

Since these instances occurred one after the other, they are possibly similar or are related in terms of their values (quantified as temporal autocorrelation). The time difference between the values of the attribute is referred to as lag. For example, for the variable "packet size" for an IP address, the lag is 1 millisecond. An autocorrelation coefficient measures the correlations (such as using Pearson's correlation) between temporal values a certain temporal distance apart. Here autocorrelation measures the correlation (positive or negative) of the data variable to itself with a certain time lag. A few approaches (Zhang et al. 2003) have accounted for this aspect in temporal data mining.

8.1.6 Temporal Heterogeneity

The overall autocorrelation of a temporal data sequence may be positive and high. However, there may be underlying processes that may bring about some patterns, which are averaged out over larger time periods. Although temporal mining accounts for issues such as seasonality, it does not account for the bigger challenge of heterogeneity. Heterogeneity essentially is the property of the temporal data due to which it behaves differently even in close time proximity (Raveh and Tapiero 1980). So a temporal sequence that depicts an ascending trend may give a high value for autocorrelation when considered for a larger time window, and on close observation we may find pockets of variations in these data due to their inherent variability. If autocorrelation exists in temporal data, it can be assumed that data are coming from the same underlying process for the points in a time window. However, heterogeneity indicates that even though the data may be autocorrelated, it may be originating from multiple processes (Basawa et al. 1984) depicting microscale variations.

8.2 Some Key Methods for Anomaly Detection in Spatial and Temporal Data

As discussed in Chapters 6 and 7, anomaly detection deals with discovering nontrivial and intriguing knowledge, in the form of unusual patterns, objects, and relationships. Such a discovery works on the principle of identifying anomalies with respect to similarly behaving partitions in the data. Accounting for heterogeneity within the data in creating these partitions is critical to accurately identify anomalies. To understand the need for such refined anomaly detection, the current approaches to anomaly detection in spatial and temporal data are discussed with an emphasis on identifying the correct partitioning, referred to as neighborhood discovery, in spatial and temporal data. The neighborhoods can also be used as a characterization such that objects that deviate substantially from this characterization can be identified as suspicious. This process is similar to anomaly detection using clustering as discussed in Chapter 7; the key difference is that the preprocessing to form the similar objects into a neighborhood is different for spatial and temporal data due to the properties of the data outlined previously. So essentially the anomaly detection process is similar for all data types, and the key difference is the preprocessing based on different types of data. The next sections discuss this process of preprocessing to form the neighborhoods.

8.2.1 Spatial Anomaly Detection

We discuss the spatial anomaly detection in two parts: (1) spatial outlier detection and (2) anomalous window detection. These two aspects of anomaly detection are representative and important since in one case an individual object or a set of objects can be outliers with respect to neighboring objects, whereas in the other a set of contiguous spatial objects are outliers with respect to the entire data. This follows the types of anomalies discussed in Chapter 6, namely point and collective anomalies. In addition, here the context of location plays a key role in preprocessing the data before the anomaly detection can take place.

8.2.2 Spatial Outlier Detection

A spatial outlier is an object that is deviant in its behavior from its neighboring objects. This behavior is quantified in terms of significant difference in attribute values of the object with similarly behaving objects in a certain proximity (neighbors based on spatial relationships). Thus, the neighborhood definition (Ester et al. 1997, 1998) is a critical aspect for any spatial data mining task. In general, a graph-based neighborhood definition facilitates the accounting of autocorrelation (Shekhar et al. 2001). However, traditional approaches ignore heterogeneity, i.e., when nearby spatial objects may behave differently. Other approaches address both autocorrelation and heterogeneity (Janeja et al. 2010). The issue of outlier detection has been addressed in several approaches and has been extensively studied (Aggarwal 2017). Several techniques consider neighborhoods that are based primarily on spatial relationships, thus they only account for autocorrelation but ignore spatial heterogeneity. Second, the neighborhood formation is not order invariant. Thus, a neighborhood based on cardinality (number of objects in the neighborhood) will lead to different neighborhood formation and outlier detection outcomes with different starting points. Third, the outlier detection considers the deviation in terms of a single attribute only or Euclidean distance between multiple attributes and not inter-relationships between attributes. Some approaches specifically discuss these issues and consider the treatment of both autocorrelation and heterogeneity (Janeja et al. 2009, 2010).

Anomalous window detection deals with the discovery of contiguous set of objects forming an unusual window. In most clustering techniques (such as DBSCAN (Sander et al. 1998), OPTICS (Ankerst et al. 1999), the focus is on the identification of the major groupings in the data, as opposed to unusually ordered groupings. Similar to clustering, outlier detection identifies individual outliers and does not quantify the degree of unusualness of an outlier.

Scan statistic approaches (Naus 1965, Glaz et al. 2001) detect a group of objects behaving anomalously with respect to all the objects in the dataset and detect quantifiable anomalous behavior in multiple attributes in relation to one another. A variation of the simple scan statistic is the spatial and spatiotemporal scan statistic (Kulldorff 1997, Kulldorff et al. 1998), which detects unusual space or space-time windows using circular or cylindrical windows respectively. However, this approach does not account for the combination of both autocorrelation and heterogeneity. Most of these approaches use circle (Openshaw 1987, Besag and Newell 1991, Kulldorff 1997), square, rectangular windows (Neill et al. 2005) and several complex shapes (pyramid with square cross sections) (Iyengar 2004). FlexScan (Tango and Takahashi 2005) identifies flexible shaped scan windows and only considers adjacency as the factor for moving to the next spatial node in the $K-1$ nearest neighbors, and therefore overlooks heterogeneity. Duczmal and Renato (2003) use simulated annealing to identify arbitrarily shaped spatial clusters, by absorbing not only the surrounding regions with nonelevated risks but also faraway regions with nonelevated risk, extended with a compactness measure to penalize very large-sized windows. The linear semantic–based scan statistic (LS^3) (Janeja and Atluri 2005) extends the basic scan statistic approach. Additionally, Janeja and Atluri (2005, 2008), Shi and Janeja (2009) and Tang et al. (2017) propose approaches accounting for heterogeneity with improved results as compared to several other approaches.

Thus, most of the scan statistic–based approaches suffer from two major issues. First, the window shape is not free-form. Second, the anomaly detection is primarily based on autocorrelation only and does not take into account heterogeneity. It is interesting to note that recently spatial heterogeneity has been identified as a major issue in various spatial applications, but its quantifi-cation has suffered from the absence of a clearly outlined definition.

The traditional anomaly detection methods, for example anomalous window detection (window shapes such as a circular window), assume autocorrelation by virtue of the proximity of the spatial objects. Subsequently, the deviation of these objects is compared to the rest of the data. However, spatial analysts have recognized that every location has an intrinsic degree of uniqueness (Miller 2004).

8.2.3 Spatial Neighborhood

The goal of this step is to identify spatial neighborhoods accommodating both spatial autocorrelation and heterogeneity in the region. The neighborhood should not be identified simply by the change in geospatial features or solely on the basis of spatial proximity determined using spatial relationships such as adjacency of objects. Spatial neighborhoods can be considered a characterization of the region (as shown in Janeja et al. 2010). This approach consists of the following distinct steps:

(1) Generate the immediate neighborhood of an object, called a *microneighborhood*, as shown in Figure 8.3a, using Voronoi tessellations. This captures the knowledge about the immediate neighborhood of this object such as the presence or absence of spatial features (e.g., proximity to geopolitical events or prior known cyberattacks from this location) in its proximity and attributes of the object. This will allow us to associate features and attributes to these objects, which can be used to determine similarity or dissimilarity across spatial objects.

(2) Identify *spatial relationships* (such as adjacency) using the spatial attributes of the microneighborhoods to accommodate autocorrelation.

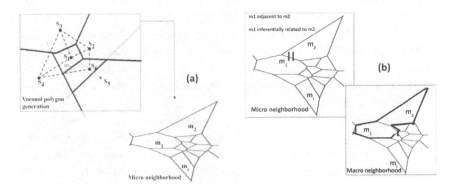

Figure 8.3 (a) Micro neighborhood; (b) macro neighborhood.

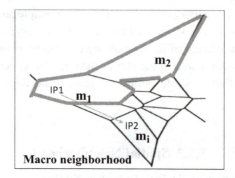

Figure 8.4 Neighborhood as an underlying characterization.

(3) Capture spatial heterogeneity by identifying *semantic relationships* between the nonspatial attributes and features in the microneighborhoods. A semantic relationship is defined using similarity coefficients such as Jaccard and Silhouette coefficients. If there is a spatial and semantic relationship between spatial objects, the microneighborhoods are merged to form *macroneighborhoods* as shown in Figure 8.3b. This facilitates the determination of the local heterogeneous patterns across neighborhood in terms of the attributes associated with each spatial object. Thus, the macroneighborhood captures both autocorrelation and heterogeneity in the neighborhood definitions by not only considering proximity but also the change in the localized features and attributes in the region.

This neighborhood definition can be used as a precursor to the anomaly detection in reference to this neighborhood. Similarly, if an anomaly or an attack event is discovered in one part of this neighborhood, then chances are that the attack can propagate to other parts of the neighborhood given the similarity and homogeneousness in this neighborhood.

Neighborhoods can be seen as an underlying characterization as well. For example, if two IP addresses are communicating with each other (e.g., IP1 sending a packet to IP2), then using geolocation (through databases such as Maxmind[1]), these IP addresses can be located and overlaid on top of the neighborhood definitions, as shown in Figure 8.4. For example, if macroneighborhood m1 has a series of features indicating that it has known prior attacks originating and is a source of geopolitical unrest, then this IP1 gets a certain reputation score and should be monitored carefully. This will help network administrators go beyond the white and black listing of IP

[1] www.maxmind.com/en/home.

addresses and use geolocated information sources as well. One potential challenge to using geolocation information of IP addresses is the vulnerability of an IP address to be spoofed such that an attacker can illicitly impersonate another host by using a forged IP address. We envision geospatially enhanced models to work as a supplementary model that bolsters a network analyst's existing knowledge. Geospatial models may not effectively work for network traffic with high probability of being spoofed, for example in UDP traffic. However, using geospatially enhanced data helps provide geocontextual information as well, potentially enhancing detection accuracy.

8.2.4 Temporal Anomaly Detection

There is a rich literature in temporal data mining and statistical time series analysis. The aspects closest to anomaly detection in temporal data are reviewed here. Specifically, this section looks at approaches that facilitate the discovery of relevant segments in temporal data (equivalent to the neighborhood definition in spatial literature) and discovery of anomalies such as outliers and discords in such datasets are discussed.

Change point detection addresses the discovery of time points at which the behavior of time series data change. Several techniques (Aminikhanghahi and Cook 1994) have been proposed to detect change points in time series data. However, most of these approaches assume that a phenomenon can be approximated by a known model whereas in reality several dynamic models may be in play. Yamanishi and Takeuchi (2002) proposes an approach for outlier and change point detection in nonstationary time series data. Guralnik and Srivastava (1999) outline an approach for event detection from time series data by detecting the change of model or parameters of the model that describe the underlying data.

Discretization has been extensively studied, and many efficient solutions exist for simple discretization techniques, including equal width or equiprobable discretization and piecewise aggregate approximation (PAA) (Lin et al. 2003, Duchene et al. 2004) Although some approaches (Tim et al. 1999, Duchene et al. 2004) have looked at the problem of variable width discretization, they do not address variable number of widths across multiple time series generated in a spatial proximity.

Time series *discords* are subsequences of a longer time series that are maximally different to all the rest of the temporal subsequences. Discord discovery was introduced by Keogh et al. (2005). Ameen and Basha (2006) propose improvements on the discord discovery algorithms. Wei et al. (2006) describe an approach for finding discords in shapes by converting shapes into time series data. Yankov et al. (2007) discover unusual time series or discords with a disk-aware algorithm.

First, most of these approaches consider autocorrelated segments as true segments for pattern discovery. This may ignore heterogeneity in the discovery process, possibly in the form of unequal width segments. Second, most of these approaches do not quantify the unusualness of a patterns discovered in terms of how distinct the pattern is from the data. Similar to spatial behavior, temporal autocorrelation, and heterogeneity are a challenge.

Finally, in the area of spatiotemporal mining, several approaches have explored the spatiotemporal nature of the data (such as Abraham and Roddick 1999, Roddick and Spiliopoulou 1999, and Roddick et al. 2001). As such, there does not exist a generalizable framework that facilitates the accommodation of the properties of space and time in an effective and efficient manner. Additionally, there is no consensus on spatial-dominant or temporal-dominant analysis of spatiotemporal data. Thus, there is a need for a shift that facilitates the analysis based on the properties of space and time (spatial, temporal autocorrelation, and heterogeneity) in a unified framework.

8.2.5 Temporal Neighborhoods

Let us consider a computer network and its connectivity as a time series dataset where we have time stamps associated with a set of attributes such as number of nodes, number of edges, and total traffic. Similar to spatial neighborhood discovery, temporal neighborhoods can be seen as a precursor to anomaly detection. Let us now consider these network properties over time to demarcate temporal neighborhoods.

8.2.5.1 Stationary Distribution-Based Merging

If we consider a time series, with many small time intervals, the end goal is to generate merged intervals (or neighborhoods). The idea here is to generate similarly behaving time segments so that these neighborhoods can be used for anomaly detection within these time segments. One approach models the time series data as a Markov model (Dey et al. 2009, 2014). This approach starts with many small equal frequency bins in the data as the states of a Markov model (Figure 8.5a). The similarity between the bins is computed using a distance measure. A transition matrix based on these similarities is generated for this Markov model and subsequently normalized to obtain a row-stochastic matrix. In order to form the larger time segments or similar temporal neighborhoods, an intuition is used that the adjacent bins in the transition matrix

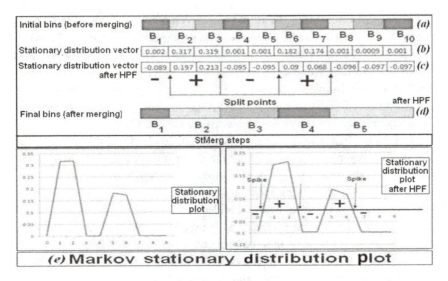

Figure 8.5 Markov stationary distribution-based discretization.

having a high degree of probability of transition should be merged in order to obtain the unequal depth bins.

Thus, a Markov stationary distribution-based merging is used to form the stationary distribution vector (Figure 8.5b, e). The split points in this vector are identified by finding spikes in the stationary distribution vector plot (Figure 8.5e) (Brigham 2002).

This temporal neighborhood indicated by the split time series in Figure 8.5d can be used as a precursor to anomaly detection to identify anomalies in the temporal neighborhoods, which are more homogeneous for an accurate identification of unusual events. Moreover, the spikes in the distribution also may correspond to events of interest. Thus, if we apply this method to the network traffic data or even data about the network connectivity, we can identify the more homogeneous neighborhoods as the regular traffic patterns and the smaller spikes as unusual activity in the network. This approach is fairly robust to small-scale noise or data-to-day fluctuation in the data.

8.3 Cybersecurity through Spatiotemporal Analysis

8.3.1 Spatial Anomalies in Cybersecurity

While cyber threats that target networks are directed toward specific nodes during specific time periods, these nodes are not randomly selected but may be located in specific geographical regions. According to Davies (2012),

Kaspersky reported that Iran is the most common place where the Flame malware was discovered. Cases were also reported in Israel, Palestine, Sudan, Syria, Lebanon, Saudi Arabia, and Egypt. Out of all computer systems that were affected worldwide by Stuxnet, 60% of them belonged to Iran (Halliday 2010, Burns 2012). Also, a recent analysis indicates that most online schemes occur in Eastern Europe, East Asia, and Africa. These schemes and phishing attacks are shifting to other countries like Canada, United States, France, Israel, Iran, and Afghanistan (Bronskill 2012). Thus, the spatial element plays a key role in strengthening the cyber infrastructure, not only computer networks but also in power grids and industrial control systems. Therefore, while identifying locations of cyberattack victims is important in a power grid or computer network, it is also crucial to determine the location of those responsible for these attacks, as it may have serious national security implications. Cyberattacks may be targeted toward specific countries due to sociopolitical factors. It is therefore important to identify the association between a cyberattack, its target, and the origin location.

A spatial aspect to cyber data analysis can be brought through (a) identification of spatial neighborhoods in the network structure to discover the impact of an event in space, (b) studying influence of events in neighborhoods, and (c) studying correlation and associations of events over time.

8.3.2 Neighborhood-Based Anomalies

Several works have studied spatial neighborhood definition in sensor networks (Janeja and Alturi 2008, McGuire et al. 2008, 2012, Janeja et al. 2010, Sun et al. 2012). The neighborhood discovery can be used to describe influence flow among spatial objects. In the network, vertices represent spatial objects, and edges represent the possible influence flow. The weight on each edge indicates the hardship the influence faces to reach from one spatial object to another. Such a weight takes into account the spatial distance and other factors such as barriers, which can be network properties such as number of hops as the distance measure, geopolitical factors such as IP domain, country, etc. So, for instance, Mexico and United States, even though they are in proximity, will have different rates of spread of an event due to differences in the cyber infrastructure. Thus, even though they are in proximity, their links' weight will be less if we are studying event propagation. This was made evident even within the United States when a major breach of social security numbers (Kosner 2012) occurred in South Carolina that did not affect the nearby or any other states. It is obvious that there are other organizational contexts at play that create geospatially heterogeneous behaviors.

Let us consider a network of nodes in a spatial neighborhood, where the spatial nodes are connected by edges, based on spatial relationships, with weights computed from the distance between the spatial and nonspatial attributes through the previously discussed similarity coefficients. So given an event being studied, such as a specific attack if we want to study the propagation of the attack, influence distance can be used to quantify it. The influence distance from one spatial object IP_p to object IP_q is the sum of the weights of the constituent edges of the shortest paths from IP_p to IP_q. If IP_p and IP_q are unconnected, then the influence distance is ∞, such as in the example of South Carolina. If IP_p to IP_q are the same, then the distance is 0.

The difference of the influence distance between events can also be compared. For example, an event such as a local breach only has an influence on spatial objects located on a direct connection, whereas a global event can impact a much larger part of the network.

For example, a phenomenon such as a distributed denial of service (DDoS) attack will have a much larger influence than a single computer infected by a virus. One can argue that even a single infected computer can also lead to a larger impact; however, if we model the network appropriately, then that should be captured in the weights between the edges and subsequently on the influence distance of this infected system.

These concepts can also be used to model attacks in nuclear power plants or highly networked organizations. Similarly, multiple organizations using the same software with a vulnerability can also be modeled using the influence distance.

8.3.3 Spatio temporally Clustered Anomalies

A network can also be seen as in a spatial layout to discover various types of clustered network anomalies. This can be done based on spatial window-based techniques discussed earlier (Kulldorf 1997). Figure 8.6 outlines an example using a scan statistic–based approach. A network can be laid out on a spatial grid based on relationships of network bandwidth usage and usage of the network, as shown in Figure 8.6. Subsequently, using any tcpdmp software the packet data can be extracted into population and case files, where the population file has the overall network usage information extracted from historic data and the case file has the current usage information. Here network usage can be measured in terms of a variable of interest, such as number of packets every minute or average packet size or total packet size. Once the files are created from the raw data, spatial and temporal anomalies can be identified. These anomalies are in the form of (a) nodes on the network that behave anomalously with respect to other nodes (or geospatial points) on the network,

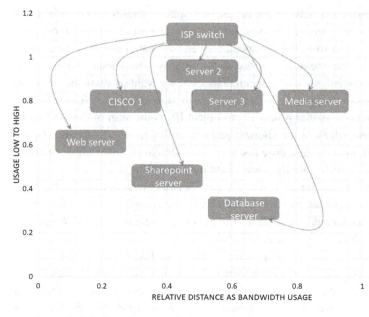

Figure 8.6 Spatio temporally clustered anomalies.

and (b) cluster of network traffic points that are anomalous as a temporal cluster with respect to other neighboring servers.

8.3.4 Insights through Geo-Origination of IP Addresses

The geolocation of IP addresses sending emails can provide insights into origination of spam or phishing activities. Certain parts of the world are more known to be related to spam or phishing activities (for example, top 10 countries[2] that are the worst spam enablers or top phishiest countries[3]). Geolocation[4] of the (nonspoofed) IP address identifies the physical location down to latitude and longitude. Such information can be utilized in tools providing actionable information of user emails. Keim et al. (2005) describe a visualization tool to mine and analyze spatiotemporal aspects of emails. A histomap provides a visualization of spam origination from across the world and within the United States. Email routes can be visualized to discover

---

[2] www.spamhaus.org/statistics/countries/. The world's worst spam enabling countries, last accessed March 2021.
[3] https://news.netcraft.com/archives/2012/12/13/world-map-of-phishing-attacks.html. Phishiest countries, last accessed March 2021.
[4] http://geoiplookup.net/, last accessed August 2017.

unusual locations and routes. This can help users identify potential threat locations, particularly when users are in a sensitive job or secure location.

8.4 Temporal Behaviors in Evolving Networks

Computer network traffic over a period of time can be studied by utilizing the temporal neighborhoods and help draw out several forms of communication patterns, as discussed in Chapter 4. For example, one can identify if some nodes are popular on the network, either as a common source point to all other nodes or consistently a common destination point from all other nodes on the network. One can also determine if the popularity of a node either increases or decreases over time. Studies have discussed various properties in networks. These properties include but are not limited to the centrality of nodes in a network, the densification of a network, and the diameter of a network (Leskovec et al. 2005, Leskovec and Faloutsos 2007, Leskovec 2008, Kang et al. 2009).

Studies have portrayed that networks tend to follow the properties of densification and shrinking diameter of a network (Lescovec et al. 2005), they have been applied to study of communication networks, specifically network traffic flows (Namayanja and Janeja 2015, 2019). More so, these studies have accounted for the importance of nodes on the network and how this may affect the densification of the network and the shrinking diameter over time. These approaches determine how change in the behavior of a central node on the network may impact the overall behavior of the network over time.

Therefore, the mining of large networks can be performed with the aim of understanding the following: Does the structure of the network change over time? Can we define what changes occur as the network evolves? And most importantly, can we identify when these changes in the network take place? By detecting changes in a temporally evolving network, one can drill down and identify the underlying cause of this change in the network, which could have come forth as a result of a threat to the network. For example, the unexpected unavailability of a server system from the network could be due to an unknown denial of service attack. Using a temporal approach can discover inconsistencies in the network and identify times when these inconsistencies occur. This is in turn useful in the efficient allocation of resources for monitoring network activity. Chapter 9 discusses graph-based techniques and using temporal evolution of the network as a way to measure the threat propagation over time.

9

Cybersecurity through Network and Graph Data

Graphs (as discussed in Chapter 4) depict the relationships between various entities. A graph is comprised of nodes and links (or vertices and edges). The node or vertex represents an entity such as an IP address, and the edge or link represents the relationship between the two entities, such as a message sent from one IP address to another. Thus, network traffic data lend themselves to graph representation, which opens up a vast array of graph-based analytics that can be applied to studying cybersecurity issues.

Figure 9.1 depicts the cybersecurity applications that can utilize graphs. These are only some of the major examples from research and application themes:

- **Communication graphs:** Network traffic has been extensively studied as a graphs; here source and destination IP addresses are vertices, and the communication between them is the edge. Various properties such as centrality, density, and diameter have been used to evaluate the state of the graph and study communication patterns over time (Lescovec et al. 2005, Kang et al. 2010, Tartakovsky et al. 2013, Namayanja and Janeja 2014).
- **Attack graphs**: These graphs (Wang et al. 2007a, b) are used to evaluate exploits and their pre- and postconditions. Here the vertex can be an exploit, and the edges connect to the conditions that occur before or after the exploit. Attack graphs can also be used to evaluate conditions in a network model that violate security policies (Jha et al. 2002). Thus, such graphs help in studying various paths that can be taken in a graph that propagate an exploit. Attack graphs should ideally be exhaustive and yet succinct to provide a comprehensive view of the network health in terms of the security policy. Violations discovered can help make a network more robust through enforcement of more stringent security policies.

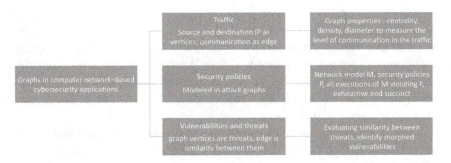

Figure 9.1 Graph-based studies for cybersecurity applications.

- **Threat similarity–based graphs**: Graphs have been used to find relation-ships between known vulnerabilities. In such graphs, known vulnerabilities are the nodes, and the similarity between two vulnerabilities is the edge. The weight on the edge depicts the level of similarity. These types of graphs can be augmented with semantic and contextual information (AlEroud and Karabatis 2013). These graphs can be queried when a new unknown threat is potentially observed, such as a zero-day attack. By computing the simi-larities between the zero-day attack and the known attacks, a score can be provided to indicate the level of threat from this zero day (AlEroud and Karabatis 2014).

- **Threat propagation:** A cyber threat not only impacts an individual entity (one single computer or IP address) but can easily propagate to other connected entities (Ingols et al. 2006, Trinius et al. 2009, Ohm et al. 2020). Studies have been conducted to identify the spread and prevention of threats such as in high-risk groups of IP addresses. Some of these studies and approaches are restricted to individual IP behavior, such as black and white listing IP addresses, which limit the understanding of the dynamics involved in the spread of the threat. Apart from individual behavior, high-risk behavior can also be captured at two other levels: the microsocial level (e.g., personal network), and macro level (through analysis of the network structural factors influencing the transmission mechanism). Computer net-works and communication across the networks provide a framework to study the spread and prevention of high-risk behavior for widespread cyberattacks.

Several relevant graph-based anomaly detection applications are also dis-cussed in Akoglu et al. (2015). In the following sections, this chapter evaluates basic graph properties that can be utilized and discusses some specific types of methods within these themes.

9.1 Graph Properties

Certain graph properties are central to the graph mining used in cybersecurity applications. For a general introduction to graph theory and those properties relevant to anomaly detection, several texts are available, such as Rivest and Vuillemin (1976), Wilson (1986), and Akoglu et al. (2015). Some key properties are described in this section.

Adjacency matrix: A graph can be represented as an adjacency matrix. Let us consider a graph G with E edges and V vertices. The adjacency matrix of G is a V × V matrix where each cell in the matrix has a 0 for no edge between the pair of vertices or 1 for an edge between the pair of vertices. If there are multiple edges between two vertices, then the value of the matrix cell is the number of edges. A vertex degree is the number of edges incident on a node or vertex. In an undirected graph, the matrix is asymmetric, as shown in Figure 9.2a. The sum of the row or column in the asymmetric matrix is the out degree (edges going outward from a node, such as outbound network communication from an IP address) and in degree (edges going inward to a node, such as inbound network communication to an IP address) respectively. In an undirected graph, the matrix is symmetric, as shown in Figure 9.2b. The sum of the row or column is the same, which is the degree of a vertex (such as the total of the inbound and outbound communication for an IP address).

Walk: In a graph, the sequence of edges leading from one vertex to another is called a walk. A walk where no vertex appears more than once is a path. The

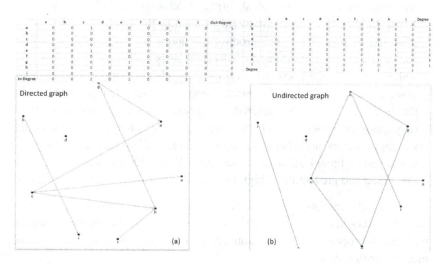

Figure 9.2 (a) Directed and (b) undirected graphs.

distance between two vertices is the shortest path between the two vertices, also referred to as geodesic path. A graph can be disconnected when some parts of the graph are not connected by a path, or if a single node is disconnected it means that there is no edge connecting it to the graph. For example, in the graph in Figure 9.2b, there are three separate (disconnected) components.

Centrality: Centrality in a graph structure indicates prominence of a node in a graph. A node with high centrality will potentially be more influential. A simple type of centrality is the degree centrality (Freeman 1978), which indicates the total number of edges incident on a node in an undirected graph. This can be divided into in-degree and out-degree for directed graphs. Betweenness centrality (Freeman 1978) of a vertex v measures the number of geodesic paths connecting vertices ij that are passing through v, divided by the total number of shortest paths connecting ij. This is summed across all ij to get the overall betweenness centrality of v. Akoglu et al. (2015) provides a detailed survey of several different types of centrality, such as betweenness, closeness, and eigenvector centrality, among others.

Cliques: Traditionally, a clique is defined as any complete subgraph such that each pair of the vertices in the subgraph are connected by an edge, for example nodes **b**, **n**, and **g** in Figure 9.3. Cliques may be mapped to coteries (such as high-risk groups in the context of spreading a virus or DoS attack).

More importantly, the nodes among different cliques may overlap, which indicates a higher relevance of those nodes in high-risk groups.

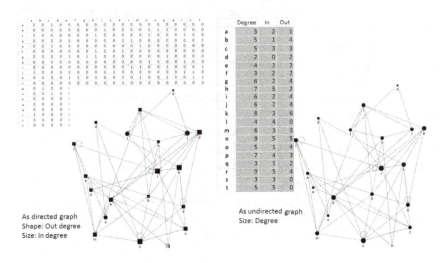

	Degree	In	Out
a	3	2	1
b	5	1	4
c	5	3	3
d	2	0	2
e	4	2	2
f	3	2	2
g	6	2	4
h	7	5	2
i	6	2	4
j	6	2	4
k	8	3	6
l	4	4	0
m	6	3	3
n	9	5	5
o	5	1	4
p	7	4	3
q	3	1	2
r	9	5	4
s	3	3	0
t	5	5	0

As directed graph
Shape: Out degree
Size: In degree

As undirected graph
Size: Degree

Figure 9.3 Graph example.

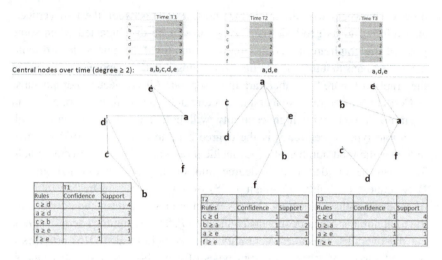

Figure 9.4 Using graph properties to evaluate consistency of nodes across time.

Given the adjacency matrix for the graphs in Figure 9.3, the visualization is generated using NodeXL.[1] Figure 9.3a presents a directed graph view, and Figure 9.3b shows an undirected view of the graph. In Figure 9.3a, it is evident that node **k** has a high out-degree, and nodes **h**, **n**, **r**, and **t** have a high in-degree. Overall, vertex **n** has the highest degree. In terms of centrality in an undirected graph vertex, **n** will be considered the most central node.

Another example of using graph properties is to evaluate consistency of nodes over time. For example, Figure 9.4 depicts three time periods, $T1$, $T2$, and $T3$, with their corresponding graphs. Each time period has a set of nodes **a–f** that communicate with each other as depicted by the edges. The corresponding graphs and degrees are shown in the figure. A degree threshold can be used such that anything less than or equal to the threshold is not central. For example, in this dataset, the threshold is two, then the central nodes are shown that are equal or greater than this threshold. Node **c**, which is central in time period $T1$, does not show up in the other time periods. As discussed in Chapter 3, association rules and their related metrics of confidence and support, showing the likelihood and strength of associations or frequent co-occurrences, can be utilized here. Association rules for each time period are shown that provide a complementary view of the communication in this example. For example, **f**, which is not a central node, is also not frequent, as support is low. However, in all time periods, the rule $f \geq e$ is always present.

---

[1] https://nodexl.com/.

Similarly, the nodes **a** and **d** are consistently central, and the rule $a \geq d$ is consistently a strong rule in terms of support and confidence. On the other hand, $a \geq e$ has high confidence, and both nodes are central; however, the support is low compared to other rules with central nodes. Thus, multiple types of analysis can be used to analyze the network traffic data to provide complementary knowledge.

9.2 Graphs for Cybersecurity: Understanding Evolving Network Communication

Utilizing the temporal neighborhoods, as discussed in Chapter 8, communication networks over a period of time can be evaluated as shown in the example in Figure 9.4. Several forms of communication patterns can be discovered. Examining certain key graph properties can help us understand the overall behavior of a network, as discussed next.

Centrality over time: The level of connectivity to or from a given node can be used to measure the centrality of the node. This level of centrality can be used to determine the importance of a node and how critical this node is on the network, by virtue of its high degree of connectivity in the graph. For example, as discussed earlier, the degree centrality is the number of edges incident to a given node. Page rank provides the number of highly central nodes that are adjacent to a given node. The number of nodes that are connected to a given node and the quality of the nodes that connect to it can both be identified. Intuitively, one can expect to find certain nodes to be consistently central over time periods. Alternatively, a node that is central only at one or few time periods is interesting to study as it may be a source or destination of an attack, or alternatively, due to the period in time, may have taken an important role in the network. The idea here is to not predict an anomalous central node but to narrow down nodes of interest, especially in massive network traffic data, which may lead to a very complex graph.

Densification over time: Studies have indicated that an increase in the number of nodes on the network over a period of time also leads to an increase in the number of edges. This process is referred to as densification of a network (Lescovec et al. 2005). However, these studies have looked at densification of all nodes and edges on the network without looking at evolving densification (Faloutsos et al. 1999, Phillips 1999, Fabrikant et al. 2002, Kang et al. 2010). Densification can also be evaluated in terms of the highly central nodes. Determining the change in the behavior of a central critical node – for example, its unexpected absence from the network – can identify whether this affects the densification of the network. If densification is tracked over a period of time, it is possible to identify time points where the densification is anomalous compared to the overall trend in the network. Such time periods may indicate unusual changes in the network. Now if such changes are consistent over multiple, large time periods (depicting periodicity, for example every year in December), then this can be related to a trend; however, if this happens in only one sample year, then it may indicate an anomalous time period.

Diameter over time: Densification draws nodes closer to each other such that the distance between those nodes that are far apart becomes smaller. As a result, the diameter of the network reduces, a concept commonly described as the shrinking diameter (Lescovec et al. 2005). Similar to densification, changing the diameter of the network over time can provide insights about the health of the network traffic. This analysis can be performed for the central nodes, which is particularly helpful for massive datasets. The change in the behavior of a critical node, for example its unexpected absence from the network, can impact the diameter of the network. Thus, drastic changes in the diameter, such as expanding diameter, can indicate malicious effects on the central nodes.

9.3 Graphs for Cybersecurity: Similarity-Based Redundancy in Router Connectivity

Router configuration can be a difficult and complex task, especially on larger networks, which can typically have hundreds of routers (Caldwell et al. 2004). There is a clear need for automatic router configurations; however, many organizations continue to rely on manual configurations and reconfigurations, leading to several network outages. After several reconfigurations, it is possible that the network topology may be considerably different from the originally planned topology. As a result, problems such as bottlenecks or redundancy may crop up.

A bottleneck router can be a router that is dissimilar to other routers on the network in terms of its connectivity, such that it has a unique function to perform through its unique set of connections. Other parts of the network will rely on it to connect to keep certain parts of the network connected, and if this router is impacted in any way to perform its functionality, then the overall network connectivity may suffer.

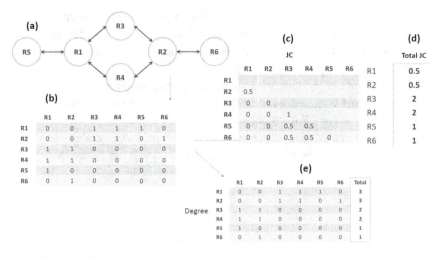

Figure 9.5 Network redundancy.

A redundant router, on the other hand, can be highly similar to other routers in terms of its connectivity. Taking a redundant router offline would probably have little effect on the network connectivity. Such a redundant router can act as a fail-safe if it is similar to some critical network routers. On the other hand, this redundant router can be used for load balancing or reallocating it to other useful roles.

Router connectivity can be considered as a graph, and similarity coefficients can provide an intuitive method of determining whether a router is similar or unique in relation to the other routers connected on the graph representing the network. As discussed in Chapter 3, several similarity coefficients have been studied (Lewis and Janeja 2011). An example use is shown in Figure 9.5 using the Jaccard coefficient (JC). An example graph with various routers connected is shown in Figure 9.5a. The corresponding adjacency matrix is also depicted in Figure 9.5b. Pairwise similarity between each pair of the routers is computed using JC, which is given as positive matches (1–1 match) divided by the sum of positive matches and positive mismatches (0–1 or 1–0 mismatch) as shown in Figure 9.5c. Thus, looking at the two rows of connectivity in the adjacency matrix for routers R4 and R3, we can see that they have perfect set of matches (1–1) and no mismatches (0–1 or 1–0). Thus, JC for similarity between R3 and R4 is 1, and they can be seen as redundant routers that are perfectly similar to replace each other's role in terms of their connectivity. On the other hand, when we look at the total similarity of each node and its degree in Figure 9.5d, e respectively, we can see that nodes R5 and R6 have lowest degree and lowest similarity, thus they are the most vulnerable nodes in terms of connectivity. Similarly, nodes R1 and R2 are highly central but have only some similarity. Thus, they are possible bottleneck nodes due to their unique connectivity and highly central nature.

Such preemptive exploratory analysis using basic graph properties can help facilitate the network management for better response to threats and recovery from network impact. For instance, in the preceding example, if there is better planning in terms of identifying bottlenecks and redundant nodes, the remediation and recovery from a network-based cyberattack can be facilitated.

10

Human-Centered Data Analytics
for Cybersecurity

Humans are a key part of the security infrastructure (Wybourne et al. 2009). Several studies have looked at the human aspect of cyber threats from the user or attacker perspective. Given that more and more users use home computers, systems are becoming vulnerable and susceptible to more cyberattacks, Anderson et al. (2010) hypothesized that psychological ownership of one's computer is positively related to behavioral intentions to protect one's own computer. More and more research has suggested that social, political, economic, and cultural (SPEC) conflicts are a leading cause for cyberattacks (Gandhi et al. 2011). This chapter looks at the different key players' viewpoints in the cyberattack and how they can be strengthened to prevent and mitigate the risks of the attack.

In general, there are two key parties at play in a cyberattack: a user who is a victim and the attacker. In a cyberattack against a business, there are three key parties in play: the *business*, a *user or employee*, and *an attacker*. In addition, there may also be other types of employees involved, such as network administrators or system administrators who are configuring the systems, and programmers who are programming functionalities.

While this is a compartmentalized view of the real-world fluid scenarios, it helps us understand the dynamics of an attack and study ways to prevent it. Each of these parties have a set of constraints and factors that help facilitate or restrict the perpetration of the attack.

A *user or employee* in a business comes with a certain educational background, experiences, and any lessons learned in the past. In addition, a user also has certain psychological traits that impact how they respond to certain types of requests, from clicking of links, downloading content, or providing their credentials.

Businesses have to follow their business model, which could be highly secure or more open. They have a mission and a set of principles they abide by.

137

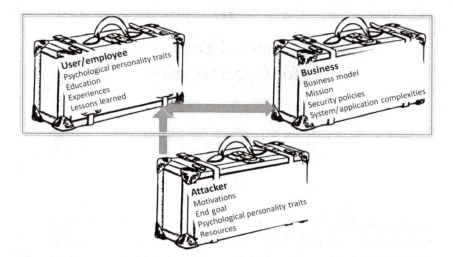

Figure 10.1 Key players in a cyberattack.

Moreover, a business may or may not have a well-defined set of security policies. Lastly, the types of business applications being run in a business may have their own set of complexities and challenges.

In addition to having technological know-how, an *attacker* has certain motivations and an end goal to achieve through perpetrating the attack. An attacker may have certain psychological traits that lead them to instigate these attacks not unlike other types of crimes. Greitzer et al. (2011) has implemented a psychological reasoning for human behavior in cyberattacks and categorized the attackers with disgruntlement, difficulty accepting feedback, anger management issues, disengagement, and disregard for authority.

Additionally, depending on the amount of resources an attacker may have, the extent of the attack may vary from a single computer to a network or entire business being targeted. An attacker targets a user of the business systems, be it a technology worker or an end user, utilizing the business systems. Some of these aspects of the key players in a cyberattack are depicted in Figure 10.1.

This chapter addresses certain types of cyberattacks that have a major influence of the human perspective, such as phishing and insider threats. It outlines data analytics methods to study human behaviors through models extracted from data.

10.1 Human Perspective to Cybersecurity: Phishing

A cyber threat can come in several forms, such as phishing, viruses, and vulnerabilities, to name a few. Let us consider the case of spear phishing, where an individual receives an email claiming to be from an organization known to the individual and is asking for the individual's username and password or interacting with the user through a malicious link in the email. While users with knowledge of security threats may be inclined to check the sender's email address and the validity of the link for authenticity, others may interact with the message, compromising security.

In general, cybersecurity can be aimed toward hardening our systems or taking offensive approaches. However, in this case, cybersecurity cannot simply be seen as an organization-centric issue but an individual user-level issue. In social engineering–type attacks, such as phishing, indeed it is an individual user who may lead to opening up an organization to bigger risks (for example, by clicking on an unsafe link or providing the users credentials). Recent cases of cybersecurity breaches in the commercial (Rashid 2013) and government sectors (Hoffman 2011, Zetter 2011) indicate that in the majority of cases, a user's choice can be attributed as the root cause of the cyberattack. A recent study by Trend Micro found that 91% of all targeted attacks are initiated with a spear-phishing email, potentially leading to advanced persistent threats (APT) (Trend Micro 2012). Therefore, the human perspective is critical to evaluate and address questions such as: what makes a user click on a potentially malicious link? Why would a user open a malicious website or provide their credentials? How do users determine whether an email appears to be fraudulent?

There is also an organizational perspective in a user's behavior. It's important to consider if an organization has checks in place to prevent phishing emails reaching from email inboxes. Are there ways that the organization labels emails? For example, many organizations include messages or tags indicating that the email is external so that it is not incorrectly seen as originating from a supervisor or a colleague in the organization – which is generally the mask in spear phishing emails. This is a simple way to tag emails but may be quite effective.

An evaluation of this perspective can lead to insights into preventing future cyberattacks. Built on prior psychological and behavioral research on phishing (Grazioli 2004, Davinson and Sillence 2010, 2014, Wright and Marett 2010), it can be hypothesized that end users' experience and perception play critical roles in the behavioral process of phishing detection. However, the perceptions of the user can be changed. Specifically, a user's perception of security can be changed based on targeted education and awareness of ways to address cybersecurity threats. Studies to evaluate user perception can include the following:

(a) Evaluating behavioral factors affecting end users' ability to detect phishing, such as through survey-based methods to study users' psychological factors related to phishing detection (Jakobsson 2007, Wright and Merett 2010, Fischer et al. 2013, Pfeiffer et al. 2013).

(b) Evaluating the effectiveness of a simply designed educational intervention and awareness program. The intervention can involve presentation of vignettes, carefully designed to support a diverse user group (those with or without technical background). Zimmermann and Renaud (2021) evaluate the impact of user nudges on decision making, particularly when making choices of picking a secure Wi-Fi channel.

(c) Eye-tracking to determine areas of an interface where attention is focused when performing tasks where threats may be evident (e.g., when interacting online, the user may focus on the security icon on the toolbar). There has been some research in evaluating toolbars in preventing phishing (Wu et al. 2006) and using eye-tracking data to evaluate browser security indicators (Darwish 2012).

(d) Data mining to evaluate patterns observed in the user's eye gaze data and how those patterns affect phishing detection or interaction with threat-prone areas on the user interface. This can include evaluating the focus of the user and associate different foci for different types of users (based on psychological profiles, background, and demographics).

10.2 Human Perspective to Cybersecurity: Insider Threat

Insider threats consist of an authorized user of a system who perpetrates an attack compromising the system's confidentiality, integrity, and availability, which may include illegal copying of data, sending data to unauthorized users, or providing access to unauthorized users. In such scenarios, there is a need for a deeper understanding of cybersecurity from multiple perspectives. Insider threat detection and masquerade detection (Salem et al. 2008, Salem and Stolfo 2011, Garg et al. 2013) can be categorized based on the approaches used namely: system call analysis, graph-based analysis, network mapping/topology analysis, structural anomaly detection, and rule-based analysis.

Brdiczka et al. (2012) propose a hybrid system that combines structural anomaly detection from social and information networks (graph analysis, dynamic tracking, and machine learning) with psychological profiling (dynamic psychological profiling from behavioral patterns). Eberle et al. (2010) describe a graph-based anomaly detection approach for insider threat detection. The approach is quite robust with few false positives, but falls short on dynamic graphs and while handling numeric values in structural analysis. Across the multiple areas of study discussed here, there is no work that brings together multiple facets from data and behavioral perspectives for discovering insider threats. Insider threats remain one of the hardest types of threats to detect.

Studying how network traffic changes over time, which locations are the sources, where is it headed, how are people generating this traffic, and how people respond physiologically (such as through stress indicators) when involved in these events – all these aspects become critical in distinguishing the normal from the abnormal in the domain of cybersecurity. This requires shifting gears to view cybersecurity as a people problem rather than a purely technological problem.

As discussed in Chapter 2, several features can be utilized from disparate domains, as shown in Figure 10.2, such as computer usage including CPU, memory, and kernel modules, network traffic features including source, destination IP, port, protocol, derived geolocation, and other location-related features, such as geopolitical event information and physiological sensors providing knowledge of affective behaviors, including features such as emotion and stress variations. Each of these domains provides insights into the workings of a networked information system over a period of time. Each domain individually is not sufficient to indicate an insider threat. When combined, these disparate data streams can facilitate detection of potentially anomalous user traffic for deeper inspection. These features can be evaluated individually and in conjunction to provide knowledge of potential insider threats.

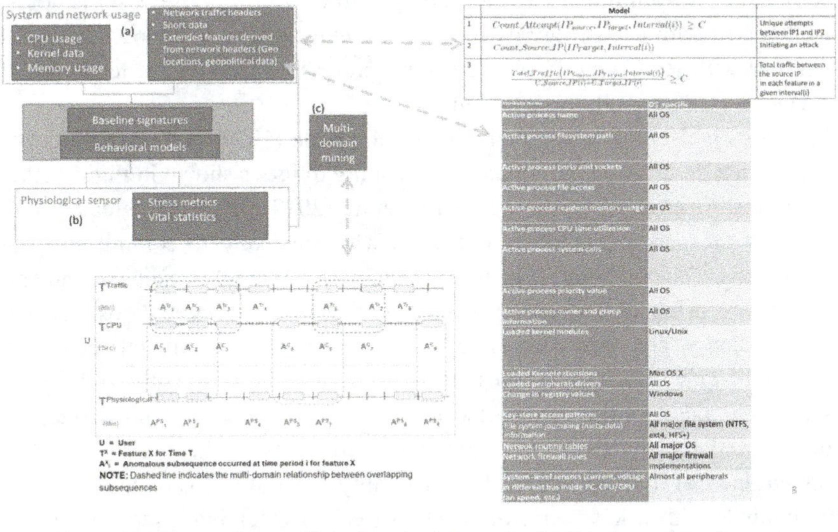

Figure 10.2 Integrating multiple domain datasets for insider threat detection.

Figure 10.2 indicates relating multiple factors for insider threat evaluation:

- A user's systems usage changes over time; similarly, network traffic evolves over time, and communication patterns change over time. These key changes, which are deviant from the normal changes, can be associated with anomalies in the network traffic and system usage.
- Any type of attack has common underpinnings of how it is carried out; this has not changed from physical security breaches to computer security breaches. Thus, data representing the user's behavior from both the usage of the systems and affective behaviors (such as stress indicators) provide important knowledge. This knowledge can be leveraged to identify behavioral models of anomalies where patterns of misuse can be identified.
- Studying multiple types of datasets and monitoring users through the application of affective computing techniques (Picard 2003) can have ethical and privacy implications. Effective adversarial monitoring techniques need to be developed such that they are ethical and respect user privacy.

Utilizing data-based and human behavioral aspects of learning, new knowledge from the vast array of processes can lead to new insights of understanding the challenges faced in this important domain of cybersecurity.

10.3 User/Employee Viewpoint

A cyberattack victim may be a technology-savvy user or a user who is not as well versed with technology use. While one may assume that those users less familiar with technology would be more prone to cyberattacks, technology-savvy users are equally prone to attacks.

Goldberg (1990) and Roddick and Spiliopoulou (1999) outline the big five factors that describe an individual's personality traits, as shown in Figure 10.3.

Shropshire et al. (2006) and McBride et al. (2012) propose to create a link between the personality traits and users who are likely to commit security infractions. These could be unknowingly or through malicious intent. Shropshire et al. (2006) propose the hypothesis that conscientiousness and agreeableness are positively related to IT security compliant behavior. McBride et al. (2012) establishes that individuals react differently to different scenarios, and therefore the cybersecurity training approach should be adopted to differentiate between personality types. McBride et al. (2012) also provide a fine-grained evaluation within the personality types. For example, agreeable individuals with a low sense of sanction (fear of receiving a reprimand) are more likely to violate security policies.

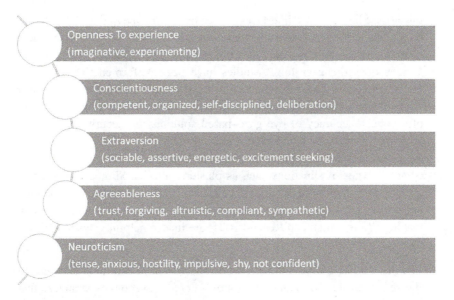

Figure 10.3 Big five personality factors.

As such, there is a very limited number of studies that establish the relationships between personality traits and IT security incidents where an insider or an unknowing user was responsible for the perpetration of the attack.

Certain key aspects of human behavior and personality traits can manifest in technological viewpoints, as follows:

- **User interaction**: How a user interacts with a system is telling of their personalities and their preferences. One common example is setting passwords and saving passwords, which is considered to be one of the biggest points of risk for systems (Yildirim and Mackie 2019). Setting the same passwords for multiple applications is a big security threat and in some regards a single point of failure. Saving passwords on the system, or on a piece of paper, while convenient, may be a security threat, especially if the device is located in a somewhat nonsecure location. Similarly, use of mechanisms such as two-factor authentication have to be carefully evaluated for the types of proposed users of the systems (Das et al. 2020).
- **Interface design**: A very busy interface can leave average nontechnical users confused. This is true for new users who may be starting to use an interface in a new job or for experienced users after a change from the systems they are used to. In some cases, it is also possible that highly technical systems with several parameters may leave users vulnerable to

mistakes. Simple-to-use interfaces can be helpful in alleviating this. Studies (Abdellahi et al. 2020) have also presented user interface security assessment models that can help evaluate user interactions from a security perspective.

- **Where does the user look**: Studies have been performed (Katsini et al. 2020) where user views are tracked to identify the level of interest of a user while interacting with an interface such as a browser. There is indeed a trade-off between accuracy of eye gaze–based solutions for security. Moreover, there may be privacy concerns to use such methods.
- **Education**: A basic cyber education can be critical in averting the more common types of situations such as phishing attacks. Similarly, educating users to keep their systems up to date is also very important to avert known attacks. Nudging users in the right direction and giving indicators in decision making (Zimmerman and Renaud 2021) are indeed helpful ways to increase user awareness.

While these aspects appear to be straightforward, they need to be enumerated and carefully evaluated in an organization's context to avoid cyberattacks that can be averted with better design principles from a user interaction perspective.

10.4 Attacker Viewpoint: Anomaly Detection Methods

A data-oriented approach can be developed to understand how an attack is carried out or what the behavioral aspect of an attack is. In cyberattacks, the intruder will first choose a target and then initiate attacks. Before the attack succeeds or fails, the intruder will have to try multiple times, and they will continue trying different methods until they are successful or eventually give up. This is the nature of the cyberattacks and almost universal in all attacks. This may vary for attacks by insiders where they may know the system well and do not need to scan the system and try multiple methods.

Another behavioral factor in cyberattacks is that the attackers will target relatively few targets each time, and most times only attack one target at a time. This provides a clue that when the attack happens, usually they will focus on one target in a short period of time. The attackers assumed to be human will usually not spend a prolonged time on one target. After they have tried extensively on one target in a short period of time, they will switch targets. These behavioral factors provide hints in developing behavioral models of anomalies. The intruders will essentially leave a trace of activities in network monitors such as in the intrusion detection system (IDS) logs. IDS logs (for example, snort alert logs) can be utilized to generate behavioral models of anomalies.

	Model	
1	$Count\_Attempt(IP_{source}, IP_{target}, Interval(i)) \geq C$	Unique attempts between IP1 and IP2
2	$Count\_Source\_IP(IP_{target}, Interval(i))$	Initiating an attack
3	$\dfrac{Total\_Traffic(IP_{source}, IP_{target}, Interval(i))}{U\_Source\_IP(i) + U\_Target\_IP(i)} \geq C$	Total traffic between of source IP in each feature in a given interval(i)

Figure 10.4 Models describing attacker behaviors.

Let us consider all the visitors V of a network N, for each visitor of the network, V in N, a source IP address, IP_{source}, and a target IP address, IP_{target}, are displayed in the IDS log. The alert information indicates the actions from the source IP addresses. The IDS logs do not always categorize the attacks as such since they observe it in isolation. The alerts in combination may be potentially related to identify the collective behavior of attackers. Let us consider three user patterns and build them into three models to exhibit attacker behavior (Chen and Janeja 2014), as shown in Figure 10.4.

- **Model 1:** When a cyberattack occurs, the attacker usually will not be successful the first time. The attacker will attempt different methods in order to gain access to the target. As discussed in Liu et al. (2008), when an attack happens, it takes multiple steps: probe, scan, intrusion, and goal. Let us say each attacker is represented by a unique IP source, and each attempt is differentiated by the alert messages. If the time when the attack will happen is not known, then data can be divided into temporal neighborhoods, as discussed in Chapter 3. This will reduce the number of instances analyzed each time. It also helps to show the attacks in a smaller subset of the data. If the count of number of unique attempts between IP_1 and IP_2 in a given Interval(i) is greater than a threshold, then this action can be considered anomalous and this source IP address is a potential attacker. Here C represents empirical criteria to differentiate attacks and nonattacks. This is based on the context of a network. If it is at a commercial network, C will be larger than in a private network. Heuristically, we can consider C as three times the average attempts of regular users. If an IP_{source} is identified as an attacker IP address, its activities before or after the actions will be considered part of the attack because its other incidents are likely to be in the probe or scanning stage and in preparation for the following attacks.
- **Model 2:** When an attack happens, the target address usually is unique or relatively a few addresses. The attackers will target the unique targets persistently until success or failure. If a target IP address is accessed by a

much higher number of unique IP addresses than usual within a short period of time, this target IP address is potentially being accessed anomalously.

- **Model 3:** A common attack method is when there are a massive number of attempts in a short time in order, for example, to obtain the password information. Hence, if an IP_{target} is experiencing much higher than normal traffic from a single or a few IP_{source}, this IP_{target} is under attack. This represents the percentage of total traffic between two IP addresses in a given interval (i). If this exceeds a threshold C, an alert can be raised. C can be an empirical criteria to differentiate attacks and nonattacks, and this can be based on experimental assessments and evaluating historic traffic patterns.

All these models are based on intuitions on potential attacker behavior, represented by data on a network. Other models can be developed based on psychological behavioral models such as those discussed in Chapter 5 for social engineering threats.

11

Future Directions in Data Analytics
for Cybersecurity

This chapter discusses some key future directions and new and emerging threats in a complex landscape of machine learning and AI models. This chapter outlines cyberphysical systems, with a subcategory of the Internet of Things (IoT), multidomain mining, and how outputs from disparate systems can be fused for an integrative anomaly detection. This chapter also outlines deep learning and generative adversarial networks and discusses emerging challenges in model reuse. These areas are selected due to the emerging threats and technology landscapes. At the end of this chapter, we also present an important topic of ethical thinking in the data analytics process.

11.1 Data Analytics in Cyberphysical Systems

11.1.1 Cyberphysical Systems

Cyberphysical systems are formed as a result of an integration and interaction of the cyber and physical systems. This introduces many interesting issues in managing, monitoring, and analyzing these interactions and interfaces. One major category of CPS is the industrial control systems (ICS).

Traditionally, ICS is comprised of supervisory control and data acquisition (SCADA) systems, distributed control systems (DCS), and programmable logic controllers (PLC) found in the industrial sectors and critical infrastructures. These are used for industries such as electrical, water, oil, gas, and energy.

Traditionally, ICS has been considered a much more physical process-oriented space as compared to traditional information technology systems (see Figure 11.1). As a result, a cyberattack on an ICS will have much bigger impact on the health and safety of people and impact the economy. These

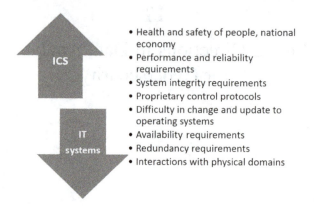

- Health and safety of people, national economy
- Performance and reliability requirements
- System integrity requirements
- Proprietary control protocols
- Difficulty in change and update to operating systems
- Availability requirements
- Redundancy requirements
- Interactions with physical domains

Figure 11.1 ICS vs. IT systems.

systems will also have a higher emphasis on reliability and accurate perform-ance. System integrity and availability have much more emphasis, as these systems cannot be offline for long periods. In addition, there are redundancy requirements in events of failure. All these are also brought into focus with the interactions with the physical domains (Stouffer et al. 2009).

One of the key vulnerability identified in the *Guide to Industrial Control Systems (ICS) Security (*Stouffer et al. 2009) is a lack of redundancy in critical components that could lead to a single point of failure. The signals sent between the various sensors and the control units can be mapped similar to a network communication flow between IP addresses. Let's consider the scen-ario in Figure 11.2, where the various signals or signal pathways are shown. The ICS systems may be comprised of sensors measuring a signal and actuators or movers acting on the signal. Anomaly detection is an important security application to evaluate risks in ICS, such as water monitoring sensor networks (Lin et al. 2018).

Sensor networking (such as in spatial data, discussed in Chapter 8) and its applications can be adapted to industrial control systems (ICS) and computer networks for supporting cybersecurity. Let us consider a part of the sensor network where the nodes A, B, C, and D (comprising of sensors and actuators, with the lines indicating the potential connections and communication between them) are shown in Figure 11.2a, b. We evaluate the nodes based on connec-tions or number of links in Figure 11.2a. Using concepts of graph-based metrics, as discussed in Chapter 9, we can evaluate these communication patterns. Here nodes A and C can be considered important as they are connecting hubs, where a large number of edges are incident, indicating a high degree of communication. Similarly, node B can be considered important

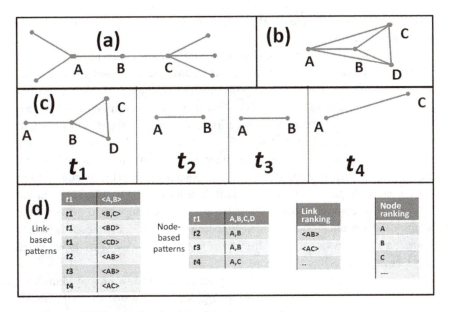

Figure 11.2 Temporal evaluation of a sensor network.

because it is a connector between the two hubs. However, in Figure 11.2b we
see a different scenario, where it is difficult to determine the clear importance
based on links. Thus, simply using metrics such as centrality, focusing on the
number of edges incident on a node, may not be the best approach or even
feasible. Evaluating the critical nodes based on their behavior over time is much
more useful here. This behavior can be captured in terms of relationships based
on edges between nodes, which could represent data transfers between nodes,
such as in a computer network or an ICS network. For example, in Figure 11.2c,
the data transfers at time t_1, t_2, t_3 for the network in Figure 11.2b are shown.
These can now be used for link-based or node-based patterns to produce a
ranking of links and nodes by importance, in terms of how many times they
appear in the temporal windows, as shown in Figure 11.2d. These can be mined
in an association rule–based method. Certain time periods may be more important, and thus may be given more weight, which may be mined using quantitative
association rule–based methods. This brings together concepts of temporal
evolution of a network, as discussed in Chapter 9.

11.1.2 Internet-of-Things (IoT)

IoT is interchangeably used and considered complementary to CPS
(Simmon et al. 2015, Blasch et al. 2017). Other studies have distinguished

IoT as a class of CPS (Nunes et al. 2015) or seen it as intersecting with CPS (Calvaresi et al. 2017).

IoT has indeed become a big share of the CPS space due to the explosion of the number of devices and advancements of smart devices and sensors. Even though estimates vary, they are projected to grow upto 31 billion devices worldwide by 2025 (Statista 2021). This is a very large number of devices by any estimate and creates more security challenges given the highly unregulated and nonstandard market for IoT devices. One such space where smart devices have created this interesting intersection between cyberphysical and Internet of Things is a smart car. We are making our vehicles smart: fully connected with the internet to view real-time traffic and weather, talk on the phone with Bluetooth, listen to the radio, watch video, as well as get real-time status of automobile's mechanical functions. However, this smart interface comes at a price, which is the vulnerability to threats as well as malfunctions to mechanical parts of the vehicle.

Other areas where IoT has taken a big role is in home security systems with fire alarms, CO monitors, door and garage sensors, alarms, and temperature control sensors. Figure 11.3 depicts the complex landscape of IoT.

Let us consider a smart home with a series of devices measuring various phenomena around them. In such a setting, depicted in Figure 11.3, several smart devices collect the information from a location with different levels of

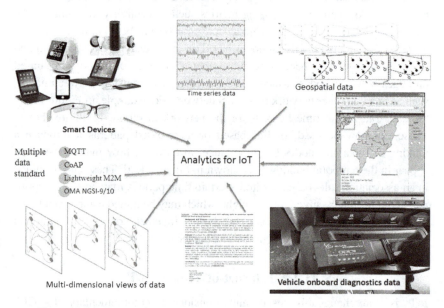

Figure 11.3 IoT examples: car and home sensors.

precision, collecting different data streams, perhaps using different standards. We may want to evaluate behavioral aspects, such as, how are we using our devices? Are there behavioral trends? We may also want to evaluate aspects of something anomalous in this complex space, such as, are there deviations from trends? How do we discover threats and attacks?

The data collected in the IoT space are often of different modalities, including spatial, temporal, image, and text data. The data can also sliced in a multidimensional view over time. The attack space is simply unmanageable. Let us consider an example of a case study evaluating an incident at a university that had close to 5,000 systems making DNS lookups every 15 minutes (Verizon 2017). In our current connected environments, edge devices, vending machines, environmental systems, alarm systems, and every other connected device on a university campus can lead to a massive attack space. This truly becomes a needle in the haystack problem.

Unlike companies and businesses where the responsibility of preventing and mitigating an attack is on the system administrators, where does this responsibility lie in an IoT scenario? It lies both with the device maker and the user. This still creates difficult scenarios where IoT use is occurring in a public or shared space. This landscape is one of the frontiers of cybersecurity and development of novel data analytics solutions for such a space.

11.2 Multidomain Mining

Data in real world are generated by multiple sources and are often heterogeneous in terms of the types of attributes in each dataset. To be preemptive and provide actionable insights, data from multiple sources need to be analyzed to. This type of mining is referred to as multidomain mining, where "domain" refers to distinct sources of data, and these distinct sources may be completely disparately generated. Here a couple of examples are discussed to highlight the challenges and potential solutions to analyzing disparate data sources to provide actionable knowledge for events.

11.2.1 Integrating Multiple Heterogeneous Data

In a computer network, there are various mechanisms to allow for analyzing the network traffic data. However, there may be scenarios where we want to expand the decision criteria, especially when we may not have access to any traffic data, such as payload, but only header information in the network traffic. If we want to detect IP addresses with malicious intent, it becomes harder, as the data would be limited. In such a scenarios, we can augment the header information with other types of data. One such view point is that of geospatial data, which can enhance the knowledge of the IP session or even the IP reputation score itself.

Current reputation systems pursue classification into a white and black list, i.e., binary categorization. Separate lists for URLs and IP addresses are maintained. Some tools that provide rudimentary reputation services include Cisco SenderBase (www.senderbase.org/), VirusTotal IP reputation (www.virustotal.com/), and Spam and Open Relay Blocking System (SORBS) (www.sorbs.net/). Most of these tools and lists are based on smaller feature sets from one source, with no correlation across other data sources. Such a shortcoming degrades a system's effectiveness for detecting sophisticated attacks and terminating malicious activities, such as zero-day attacks.

The set of attributes that the reputation scoring considers can be enriched, providing an expressive scoring system that enables an administrator to understand what is at stake, and increasing robustness by correlating the various pieces of information while factoring in the trustworthiness of their sources. IP reputation scoring model can be enriched using network session features and geocontextual features such that the incoming session IP is labeled based on the most similar IP addresses, both in terms of network features and geocontextual features (Sainani et al. 2020). This can provide better threat assessment by considering not only the network features but also additional context, such as the geospatial context information collected from external sources.

Indeed, in some countries, networks may encounter or even host large quantities of attacks as compared to others. This may be due to shortage of cybersecurity expertise, level of development, the abundance of resources, corruption levels, or the computing culture in these countries (Mezzour 2015). Identifying these factors and quantifying them can provide insights into security policies and have a positive impact on the attack incidents. These scenarios not only impact the countries facing such cybersecurity crises but also impact other countries and end users due to the level of connectivity in today's day and age. In addition, studies have also identified regions across the world that are prone to hosting certain types of attacks. For example, studies have indicated that Trojans, worms, and viruses are most prevalent in Sub-Saharan Africa (Mezzour 2015), some families of malware preferentially target Europe and US (Caballero et al. 2011). Yet other studies (Wang and Kim 2009) have explained broad categories of worldwide systemic risks and country-specific risks where country-specific risks include aspects of economy, technology, industry, and international cooperation in enforcement of laws and policies.

Figure 11.4 Sources of geospatial data relevant to cybersecurity events with geopolitical aspects.

Thus, geospatial data not only provide additional context but offer a framework to accommodate additional geopolitical information that often plays a big role in hactivism or politically inspired attacks. Figure 11.4 provides a set of rich sources to access geospatial data for countries and in some cases even at a granular level of cities. Some of these sources, such as Ip2location, provide a way to identify a user location based on IP address in a nonintrusive manner. Several other data sources such as World Bank Open Data (https://data .worldbank.org/), PIOR-GRID (http://grid.prio.org/#/), and the Armed Conflict Location and Event Data Project (ACLED) (www.acleddata.com/) data provide sociopolitical and geopolitical conflict data. Such data can be used to create geospatial characterization of regions (for example, using methods proposed by Janeja et al. 2010, as discussed in Chapter 8). When an IP address is encountered, it can be geolocated using the IP location databases such as Ip2location or Maxmind. As shown in Figure 11.5, based on its geolocation the location score from the characterization can be attributed to it. In addition the geospatial attributes for this region can be appended to the network attributes for this IP (Sainani 2018, 2020). Any additional security intelligence can be appended to provide an aggregate reputation score to this IP.

The data heterogeneity in terms of types of attributes, namely categorical versus continuous, can be addressed using methods that are capable of handling mixed attribute datasets (such as Misal et al. 2016).

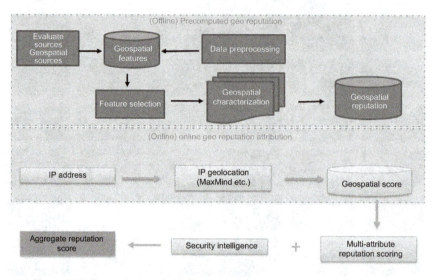

Figure 11.5 Reputation scoring with geospatial context.

11.2.2 Integrated Alerts from Multiple Sources

Computer networks are increasingly facing the threat of unauthorized access. In addition to computer networks, other networks, such as sensor networks and industrial control systems, also face similar threats. Intrusion detection aims at identifying such threats using signatures of unauthorized access or attacks. There are very few systems that address the issue of zero-day attacks, where the attack signature is not known before-hand.

Let us consider a scenario, as outlined in Chapter 1, where the threat is two pronged: first, there is an attack on the organization; and second, there is an attack on a partner that shares key resources. In the first part of the attack, intruders take advantage of vulnerabilities in public-facing web servers. In addition, hackers secretively scout the network from compromised worksta-tions that have already been targeted beforehand as part of a coordinated prolonged attack. The second part of the attack starts with spear-phishing. Instead of casting out thousands of emails randomly, spear phishers target select groups of people with something in common, such as a common employer, a similar banking or financial institution, the same college, etc. The emails are deceptive since they appear to be from organizations from which victims are expecting emails. So potentially a second group of hackers institutes a spear-phishing attack on the organization's major business partners, with which it shares network resources. The hackers are able to obtain a

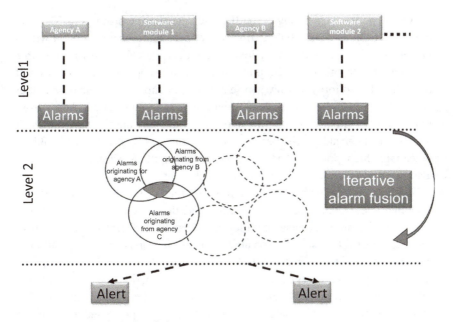

Figure 11.6 Alarm data fusion.

privileged account and compromise a root domain controller that is shared by the organization and its partner. When the intruders try to recreate and assign privileges, they trigger an alarm.

In this scenario where the attack is distributed, it may be difficult to integrate these alarms to identify if this is a single malicious attack or if the attack was spread out over time. This requires the discovery of an integrated alert from alarms generated from disparate sources across a prolonged period of time, as shown in Figure 11.6. Each alarm generated has a set of attributes such as the source and destination of the data, port, length of data packet, etc. Each source generating the alarm is also described through a set of attributes, such as type, port frequently used, etc.

The series of alarms received in such a complex application domain is composed of the raw messages received from multiple sources, and an alert is the processed and aggregated output generated from these alarms. Such an approach for the alarm data fusion would include alarm source characterization and alarm clustering using source characterization and temporal lag determination. The alarms could be generated from a single source as a series of bursts, or from multiple sources such as multiple agencies or multiple software modules, as shown in Figure 11.6. Another scenario (Janeja et al. 2014) is when the alarms are being generated from multiple IDS systems.

We can perform clustering of the IDS log data after preprocessing. The data are in the form of parsed IDS alarms, where each alarm is a data point with a priority level: high, medium, or low. These data are collected from multiple IDS sources. In this case, the premise is that a low-priority alarm may not really be a low-priority alarm when seen in conjunction with some of the other alarms from different IDS systems. Since we are looking at all alarms from multiple IDS systems, we have the opportunity to study the similarity between alarms and then judge whether an alarm is truly a low priority or could be potentially high priority. The end goal is that multiple similar low-priority alarms could potentially indicate cyberattacks.

To distinguish whether these alarms are true alerts, we would need to examine if the sources have similar characteristics. A source characterization based on the features associated with sources can be performed. Here "source" refers to either IDS systems associated with various parts of an organization or even multiple organizations; similarly, "source" could also refer to an application source or even an agency in a multiagency scenario. Sources could also refer to sensors in an ICS example, as discussed earlier in this chapter. This approach is adaptable if the alarm can be sufficiently preprocessed in a uniform manner across different types of alarm data.

Clusters of alarms based on attributes can be generated. For each cluster, the set of sources associated with each cluster and the alarm cardinality of each cluster, which is the number of alarms in a cluster, are identified:

- If only one source is generating alarms in a cluster, then the source is flagged for investigation. If alarm cardinality of a cluster is greater than a preset threshold and if all of the alarms in the cluster are from one source, then this can lead to raising an alert. Let us consider a sensor generating alarms in an ICS. If a single sensor is generating alarms, then this sensor should be investigated. Moreover, if data from the sensors are clustered and readings from one sensor dominates the cluster, this could further raise the alert.
- Next, for every source in a particular characterization (based on similarly behaving sources) such that this source is not equal to the source in the cluster, if the source s is in not in any other cluster it implies that potentially the other sources in the characterization as well are not generating alarms. This cluster can be flagged as a possible false positive for further investigation. This really means that if a source is part of a cluster but the other sources from this characterization are not in any of the clusters, then this source may be a false positive.

After removing the clusters representing the false positives, among the remaining clusters of alarms, two cases may occur: (a) a cluster comprises a significant number of alarms, but these alarms do not belong to one single source in a characterization; and (b) no single cluster has a significant number of alarms:

- In the case of the first scenario, an aggregated alert can be generated if there is any cluster that has alarms greater than a preset threshold.
- In the case of the second scenario, we can identify the overlap between the clusters, using measures such as silhouette coefficient and entropy, to find *mutually related alarms* to generate an aggregated alert. The greater the overlap, the more strongly related are the alarms.

Once an alert is generated, sources can be associated with it. The set of sources of the alarms is the sources of the alarms in the cluster, or in the other scenario, the sources of the alarms in the overlap. These sources can be aggregated by grouping the feature vectors of all the sources, thus generating a composite feature vector of the source of the alert.

11.3 Advanced Machine Learning Models

11.3.1 Deep Learning

The output of a machine learning algorithm is only as good as the data that are fed to train the model. Machine learning models such as classification learn to predict the outcome of a task based on a set of features that are provided to the training algorithm. Essentially, the model is trained based on the set of features. For example, based on the packet features, can a packet be labeled as anomalous or benign? Here feature selection is a major task. The features provide a representation of the data. If the features or representations of the data are not correctly selected, this can lead to erroneous results.

Deep learning is a type of machine learning that learns the features through multiple layers of abstractions. For example, if the task is learning to recognize a picture of an individual, the deep learning model may start with various levels of abstractions, starting with the most basic pixels in an image, to an abstraction of an outline of the nose to the outline of the facial structure. Deep learning algorithms compute the representations of one layer by tuning the parameters from the previous layers (Le Cun et al. 2015). As the amount of data increases, performance of most machine learning algorithms plateaus. However, performance of deep learning algorithms increases as the amount of input data increases.

An example deep learning model is shown in Figure 11.7, where the input is translated into several features or representations in layer 1. Some of these

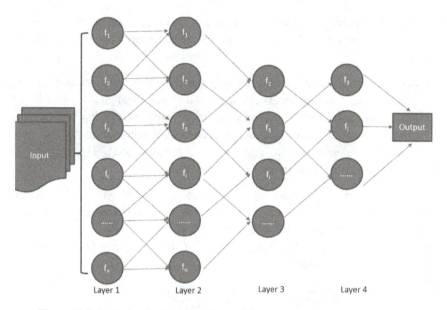

Figure 11.7 Example of a deep learning model.

representations can be dropped in subsequent layers, and throughout the layers the representations are weighted based on the reduction in a loss function until the model converges to the output, which is the prediction task. Deep learning has found a major application in computer vision, where images can be labeled based on their most basic of features and abstracting to the higher-level composition of the images. Deep learning has also found applications in anomaly detection (Naseer et al. 2018).

Deep learning emulates how human brain learns through connections of neurons. The most fundamental level of learning comes from neural networks that were in vogue in the early 1960s and have now had a renewed interest due to deep learning algorithms. The difference is now we have the availability of massive amounts of data and computing capacity, which has resulted in stronger models and learning algorithms. In cybersecurity applications, higher accuracy and lower false positive rates are very important to label truly anomalous events. Deep learning methods such as deep belief networks, recurrent neural networks, and convolutional neural networks have the capacity to learn from unlabeled data and produce better outcomes (Xin et al. 2018).

However, deep learning suffers from several challenges, as summarized in Figure 11.8. Deep learning models have several hyperparameters that need to

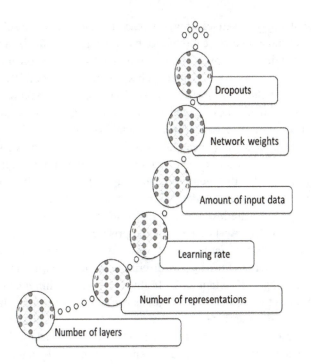

Figure 11.8 Deep learning challenges.

be predetermined and tuned, including number of layers, number of nodes in each layer, network weights, and dropouts in each layer. Some of these factors are also interdependent and can also impact the learning rate of the model. Moreover, if the input data are not large, the model cannot be trained well. Thus, the true strength of deep learning is possible in massive datasets and requires heavy parameter tuning. The challenge also comes in with explainability of how these parameters are impacting the outputs and the interpretation of the final outcomes. However, this area is constantly evolving, and methods such as deep reinforcement learning (Nguyen and Reddi 2019) are finding use in cybersecurity applications to provide adaptive, responsive, and scalable methods of threat detection.

11.3.2 Generative Adversarial Networks

Increasingly, cybersecurity challenges have started emerging with image and data manipulation. As machine learning models are increasingly being used for cybersecurity applications, so are ways to manipulate these systems from an adversarial standpoint. Attacks may increase the chances of misclassification of outcomes from a predictive model; for example, poison attacks may add bad data into the training samples, and evasion attacks may distort input data so that they are not correctly classified (Yinka-Banjo and Ugot 2019). Attacks may also emerge due to model reuse (as discussed in the next section). It is imperative that such types of generative samples are part of the learning strategy for accurate detection of truly anomalous samples.

Generative models have been explored with pioneering work in 1996 (Revow et al. 1996), where an expectation maximization algorithm was used to identify the model that generated an image of a handwritten digit. This approach not only labeled the data but also explained the model generating it.

Recent work (Goodfellow et al. 2014) formalized the idea of a generative adversarial network (GAN) as a model comprising two components: a generative model and a discriminative model. As shown in Figure 11.9, each of these models has a different function. A discriminator takes input and labels the input as belonging to a certain class. In this example, the input can be images and the output is the label for the images as belonging to a certain class. On the other hand, the generator can take the images (or distributions as a starting point) and learn from the distribution to produce new outputs, in this case new images. The new images may not be realistically comparable to the original but emulate the distribution.

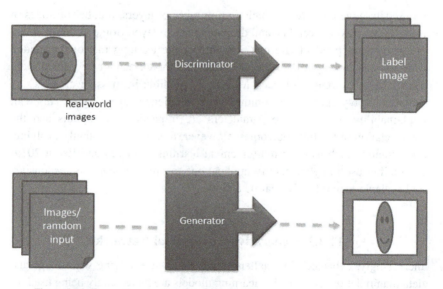

Figure 11.9 Generative vs. discriminative functions.

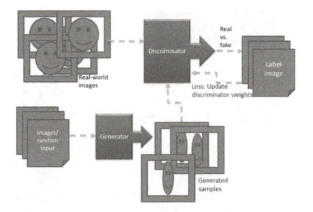

Figure 11.10 Generative adversarial network.

In a GAN, the two components interact in a two-player game where each is trying to win over the other maximizing the similarity to the original distribution. Here the generative model emulates the probability distribution to match the original data, and the discriminative model tries to distinguish whether the generated sample came from the original distribution or from the generative model.

As shown in Figure 11.10, we can see that the two components are pitted against each other. Here an input (a combination of noise and random images) is provided to the generator, which generates samples. On the other hand, the discriminator, which is trained on the real-world images, examines these generated samples. These samples are labeled as real or fake. In addition, the discriminator also learns from the loss of labeling the samples incorrectly and corrects the weights in the discriminator. This process can iteratively improve the learning from a discriminator.

Based on game theoretic concepts, an "adversarial" concept is generally used; however, this could also be a "cooperative" setting where the discriminator can share the information with the generator (Goodfellow 2016). Other types of adversaries, such as adaptive adversaries, have also been discussed in a request-answer game theoretic setting (Ben-David et al. 1994, Gormley et al. 2000). While such adaptations have not been shown in computational deep learning models yet, these types of models can be used to make the machine learning samples more robust against adversarial attacks.

11.3.3 Model Reuse

As machine learning and in general data analytics models become more easily available, they are being pervasively used and reused. Many repositories have

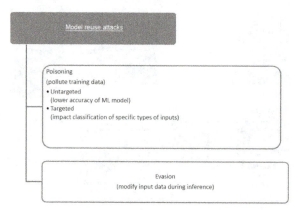

Figure 11.11 Model reuse attacks.

emerged where models are checked in by researchers and others are reusing these. Examples include the Open Neural Network Exchange (ONNX) format[1], Azure AI gallery[2], and Caffe Model Zoo[3]. It is only a matter of time before models are as easily available and searchable as public datasets. However, there is a clear danger in reusing machine learning models without understanding the provenance of the models and the model pipelines. This has been a well-studied problem in software reuse (Paul and Taylor 2002, Kath et al. 2009). Vulnerability databases have been established to study known software defects to prevent propagating them to other users and applications. If reuse of vulnerable software and code in general is not prevented, it can lead to massive disruptions and attacks such as in the case of the heart bleed bug (Carvalho et al. 2014).

This level of understanding has been well established in machine learning models. Recently some studies have shown that manipulating even simple building blocks of a machine learning model can lead to model reuse attacks (Ji et al. 2018) where corrupted models can lead the host systems to behave anomalously when certain types of input triggers are introduced into the system. These threats in model reuse and training data manipulation (Ji et al. 2018) can be summarized as shown in Figure 11.11.

To understand the impacts of such an attack, consider an autonomous vehicle that has to evaluate several images from multiple camera inputs in an ensemble learning system. In such a complex system, if a trigger results in an anomalous decision, this can have far-reaching impacts for the immediate

---

[1] http://onnx.ai/   [2] https://gallery.azure.ai//
[3] http://caffe.berkeleyvision.org/model_zoo.html

vicinity where the vehicle is driving and also in the long term for the company that has developed the autonomous vehicle and the systems processing the images. Indeed, studies have shown how researchers have hacked into driver-less cars (Versprille 2015) and studied potential risks in smart car functional-ities (Weimerskirch and Dominic 2018). Model reuse attacks can bring in a new wave of cyberattacks where complex systems that rely on machine learning behave erratically when certain trigger inputs are introduced.

11.4 Ethical Thinking in the Data Analytics Process

Data analytics, developed using data-driven technologies from artificial intelli-gence, machine learning, and statistics, are extremely beneficial for cyberse-curity if used well. These systems can lead to substantial benefits in terms of the speed, cost, and scalability of decision making compared to human deci-sion making, and they often lead to better and more reliable decisions, espe-cially in cases where system administrators are flooded with data from massive organizational computer networks. If implemented appropriately, these systems also have the potential to be more robust in identifying accurate alerts. Since the same procedure is applied across massive amounts of data, achieving such robustness may simply not be possible for a network administrator. However, because of the far-reaching scalability of the data analysis, data and algorithms being implemented also need to be considered from ethical viewpoints.

Ethics generally works on the principles of do no harm (Janeja 2019). Although research protocols to protect human beings have been in place for a while now, the pervasiveness of multiple types of data and their use make it less clear where the impact on human beings is in the data analytics processes. Thus, harm is not only direct based on exposing identifiable data for individ-uals, but also indirect resulting from the reuse of easily available data and combining multiple datasets, as we have discussed in various examples of data manipulation throughout the book.

In particular for data analytics, there is a need to develop ethical critical thinking while analyzing the data. Throughout the entire life cycle of the data analytics in the knowledge discovery process, there are many opportunities for ethical decision making that need to be evaluated to consider the human and societal impacts.

Here the harms are not only in terms of privacy, for example through identification of personally identifiable information (PII), but also other types of data and algorithms that may not necessarily fall under the direct purview of traditional privacy protections. There may be yet other types of data that may have impacts for the society as a whole. Consider data such as location data collected on a phone, driving data collected through on board diagnostics (OBD), or atmospheric data collected through sensors in a community. Now let us consider the types of patterns one may discover if they have access to such data. For example, the GPS data on the phone may pinpoint the geospatial coordinates of secure locations where an individual is carrying the phone; OBD driving data may provide insights into driving behavior; systems may falsely label anomalous behavior. Data collection is another very important element where ethical considerations (in addition to legal considerations) are important.

As we think through the examples, we can also think of the uses of the data while integrating them with data from other sources. For example, if the data of IP addresses are combined with geographical distribution of demographics, does that identify vulnerable populations, especially if the system being used is not robust to false positives? Can the driver behavior, discovered through OBD or the information on the neighborhoods that the driver passes through, lead to additional security risks? Even in these limited examples we can see beginnings of questions of bias and risk to individuals as more and more systems relying on data analytics are being used. Indeed, such systems are beginning to be used in augmented decision making that can impact lives and livelihoods.

We all have come to accept recommendations made by data-driven analytics algorithms in our day-to-day lives, such as in spam labels for emails and fraud alerts from our credit card companies. Things start getting tricky if these data analytics systems are being used to make decisions that would generally take a lot of thought and deliberation – for example, who should receive bail or not, who could be a criminal or not, or if a facial recognition system should be used or not.

The vast complexity of data, the data's easy availability, and algorithmic tools requires vigilance around access, privacy, provenance, curation, interoperability, issues of fairness, accountability, and transparency. In studying data analytics algorithms and systems such as for the security alert mechanisms discussed in this book, it is clear that there are several checkpoints where a system follows a pathway based on the choices that the creator of that system made or the user of the system made. It is important to know what those choices are and how they can impact lives and livelihoods. It is also important to explain the outcomes from such systems and ensure they are not disproportionately impacting certain groups or individuals. Just like we would carefully hire an employee, supervise them, and give them advice in making critical decisions, we need to have sensible extensions so that we do the same for data analytics algorithms and systems.

References

Abad, C., Taylor, J., Sengul, C., et al. (2003). "Log correlation for intrusion detection: a proof of concept." *19th Annual Computer Security Applications Conference, 2003. Proceedings.*, 2003, pp. 255–264, doi: 10.1109/CSAC.2003.1254330.

Abdellahi, S., Lipford, H. R., Gates, C., and Fellows, J. (2020). "Developing a User Interface Security Assessment method." *USENIX Symposium on Usable Privacy and Security (SOUPS) 2020.* August 9–11, 2020, Boston.

Abedin, M., Nessa, S., Khan, L., Al-Shaer, E., and Awad, M. (2010). "Analysis of firewall policy rules using traffic mining techniques." *International Journal of Internet Protocol Technology*, 5(1–2), 3–22.

Abraham, T. and Roddick, J. F. (1999). "Survey of spatio-temporal databases." *GeoInformatica*, 3(1), 61–99.

Aggarwal, C. C. (2017). "Spatial outlier detection." *Outlier Analysis.* Springer International Publishing, 345–368.

Aggarwal, C. C. and Yu, P. S. (2001, May). "Outlier detection for high dimensional data." *ACM Sigmod Record*, 30(2) 37–46.

Agrawal, R., Gehrke, J., Gunopulos, D., and Raghavan, P. (1998). "Automatic subspace clustering of high dimensional data for data mining applications." *Proceedings of the 1998 ACM SIGMOD International Conference on Management of Data.* ACM Press, 94–105.

Agrawal, R. and Srikant, R. (1994). "Fast algorithms for mining association rules." *Proceedings of the 20th International Conference on Very Large Data Bases, VLDB*, J. B. Bocca, M. Jarke, and C. Zaniolo (Eds.). Morgan Kaufmann, 487–499.

Agarwal, S., Farid, H., Gu, Y., et al. (2019, June). "Protecting world leaders against deep fakes." *Proceedings of the IEEE/CVF Conference on Computer Vision and Pattern Recognition (CVPR) Workshops*, 38–45.

Ahmed, M., Mahmood, A. N., and Hu, J. (2016). "A survey of network anomaly detection techniques." *Journal of Network and Computer Applications*, 60, 19–31.

Akamai. (2016). "Q4 2016 state of the internet/security report." www.akamai.com/newsroom/press-release/akamai-releases-fourth-quarter-2016-state-of-the-internet-connectivity-report. Last accessed November 2021.

Akamai. (2019). "Web attacks and gaming abuse, 2019." www.akamai.com/us/en/multimedia/documents/state-of-the-internet/soti-security-web-attacks-and-gaming-abuse-report-2019.pdf. Last accessed November 2021.

Akoglu, L., Tong, H., and Koutra, D. (2015). "Graph based anomaly detection and description: a survey." *Data Mining and Knowledge Discovery*, 29(3), 626–688.

Al-Musawi, B., Branch, P., and Armitage, G. (2015, December). "Detecting BGP instability using Recurrence Quantification Analysis (RQA)." *Computing and Communications Conference (IPCCC), 2015 IEEE 34th International Performance*. IEEE, 1–8.

Al-Musawi, B., Branch, P., and Armitage, G. (2016). "BGP anomaly detection techniques: a survey." *IEEE Communications Surveys & Tutorials*, 19(1) 377–396.

Al-Rousan, N. M. and Trajković, L. (2012, June). "Machine learning models for classification of BGP anomalies." *2012 IEEE 13th International Conference on High Performance Switching and Routing (HPSR)*. IEEEV, 103–108.

Al Shalabi, L., Shaaban, Z., and Kasasbeh, B. (2006). "Data mining: a preprocessing engine." *Journal of Computer Science*, 2(9), 735–739.

Aleroud, A. and Karabatis, G. (2013). "A system for cyber attack detection using contextual semantics." *7th International Conference on Knowledge Management in Organizations: Service and Cloud Computing*, L. Uden, F. Herrera, J. B. Pérez, and J. M. Corchado Rodríguez (Eds.). Springer, 431–442.

Aleroud, A. and Karabatis, G. (2014, September). "Detecting zero-day attacks using contextual relations." *International Conference on Knowledge Management in Organizations*, L. Uden, D. Fuenzaliza Oshee, I. H. Ting, and D. Liberona (Eds.). Springer, 373–385.

Alperovitch, D. (2011). "Revealed: Operation Shady RAT." www.csri.info/wp-content/uploads/2012/08/wp-operation-shady-rat1.pdf. Last accessed November 2021.

Alseadoon, I., Chan, T., Foo, E., and Gonzales, N. J. (2012). "Who is more susceptible to phishing emails? A Saudi Arabian study." *Proceedings of the 23rd Australasian Conference on Information Systems*. ACIS, 1–11

Ameen, J. and Basha, R. "Mining time series for identifying unusual sub-sequences with applications." *ICICIC'06: Proceedings of the First International Conference on Innovative Computing, Information and Control*. IEEE Computer Society, 574–577.

Aminikhanghahi, S. and Cook, D. J. (2017). A survey of methods for time series change point detection. *Knowledge and Information Systems*, 51(2), 339–367.

Anderson, L. C. and Agarwal, R. (2010, September). "Practicing safe computing: a multimethod empirical examination of home computer user security behavioral intentions." *MIS Quarterly*, 34(3), 613–643.

Ankerst, M., Breunig, M. M., Kriegel, H. P., and Sander, J. (1999, June). "OPTICS: ordering points to identify the clustering structure." *Proceedings of the 1999 ACM SIGMOD International Conference on Management of Data (SIGMOD '99)*. ACM, 49–60. doi: 10.1145/304182.304187.

Azari, A., Janeja, V. P., and Levin, S. (2017). "MILES: multiclass imbalanced learning in ensembles through selective sampling." *ACM Symposium on Applied Computing, Data Mining*. ACM, 811–816. doi: 10.1145/3019612.3019667.

Azari, A., Namayanja, J. M., Kaur, N., Misal, V., and Shukla, S. (2020, May). "Imbalanced learning in massive phishing datasets." *2020 IEEE 6th*

International Conference on Big Data Security on Cloud (BigDataSecurity), IEEE International Conference on High Performance and Smart Computing (HPSC) and IEEE International Conference on Intelligent Data and Security (IDS). IEEE, 127–132.

Banerjee, A., Venkatasubramanian, K. K., Mukherjee, T., and Gupta, S. K. S. (2012). "Ensuring safety, security, and sustainability of mission-critical cyber–physical systems." *Proceedings of the IEEE*, 100(1), 283–299.

Barnes, R. (2013, August 8). "Geocoding router log data." http://resources .infosecinstitute.com/geocoding-router-log-data/#gref. Last accessed November 2021.

Barnett, V. and Lewis, R. (1994). *Outliers in Statistical Data.* John Wiley and Sons.

Basawa, I. V., Billard, L., and Srinivasan, R. (1984). "Large-sample tests of homogeneity for time series models." *Biometrika*, 71(1), 203–206.

Bellman, R. (1961). *Adaptive Control Processes: A Guided Tour.* Princeton University Press.

Ben-David, S., Borodin, A., Karp, R., Tardos, G., and Wigderson, A. (1994). "On the power of randomization in on-line algorithms." *Algorithmica*, 11(1), 2–14.

Ben Salem, M., Hershkop, S., and Stolfo, S. J. (2008). "A survey of insider attack detection research." *Insider Attack and Cyber Security: Advances in Information Security*, vol. 39, S. J. Stolfo, S. M. Bellovin, A. D. Keromytis, S. Hershkop, S. W. Smith, and S. Sinclair (Eds.). Springer, 1–19.

Ben Salem, M. and Stolfo, S. J. (2011). "Modeling user search behavior for masquerade detection." *Insider Attack and Cyber Security: Advances in Information Security*, vol. 39, S. J. Stolfo, S. M. Bellovin, A. D. Keromytis, S. Hershkop, S. W. Smith, and S. Sinclair (Eds.). Springer. doi: 10.1007/978-0-387-77322-3_5.

Besag, J. and Newell, J. (1991). "The detection of clusters in rare diseases." *Journal of the Royal Statistical Society Series A*, 154, 143–155.

Beyer, M. A. and Laney, D. (2012). *The Importance of "Big Data": A Definition.* Gartner.

Bhuyan, M. H., Bhattacharyya, D. K., and Kalita, J. K. (2014). "Network anomaly detection: methods, systems and tools." *IEEE Communications Surveys and Tutorials*, 16(1), 303–336.

Binde, B. E., McRee, R., and O'Connor, T. (2011, May). "Assessing outbound traffic to uncover advanced persistent threat." doi: 10.13140/RG.2.2.16401.07520.

Blasch, E., Kadar, I., Grewe, L. L., et al. (2017, May). "Panel summary of cyber-physical systems (CPS) and internet of things (IoT) opportunities with information fusion." *Signal Processing, Sensor/Information Fusion, and Target Recognition XXVI*, vol. 10200, International Society for Optics and Photonics, 02000O.

Blasco, J. (2013, March 21). "New Sykipot developments." https://cybersecurity.att .com/blogs/labs-research/new-sykipot-developments. Last accessed November 2021.

Brdiczka, O., Liu, J., Price, B., et al. (2012). "Proactive insider threat detection through graph learning and psychological context." *2012 IEEE Symposium on Security and Privacy Workshops (SPW).* IEEE, 142–149.

Breiman, L. (1996). "Bagging predictors." *Machine Learning*, 24(2), 123–140.

Breiman, L. (2001). "Random forests." *Machine Learning*, 45(1), 5–32.

Breunig, M. M., Kriegel, H. P., Ng, R. T., and Sander, J. (1999, September). "Optics-of: identifying local outliers." *Principles of Data Mining and Knowledge Discovery. PKDD 1999*, J. M. Żytkow and J. Rauch (Eds.) Lecture Notes in Computer Science, vol. 1704. Springer. doi: 10.1007/978-3-540-48247-5_28.

Brigham, E. O. (2002). *The Fast Fourier Transform*. Prentice Hall.

Bright, A. (2007). "Estonia accuses Russia of 'cyberattack'." www.csmonitor.com/2007/0517/p99s01-duts.html. Last accessed March 2020.

Bronskill, J. (2012, November 9). "Govt fears Canada becoming host country for cyber-attacker." https://winnipeg.ctvnews.ca/canada-becoming-host-country-for-cyber-attackers-government-fears-.1032064. Last accessed November 2021.

Burns, C. (2012, June 1). "Stuxnet virus origin confirmed: USA and Isreali governments." www.slashgear.com/stuxnet-virus-origin-confirmed-usa-and-isreali-gov ernments-01231244/. Last accessed November 2021.

Caballero, J., Grier, C., Kreibich, C., and Paxson, V. (2011, August). "Measuring pay-per-install: the commoditization of malware distribution." Proceedings of the 20th USENIX Conference on Security (SEC'11), 13.

Cai, L. and Hao, C. (2011). "TouchLogger: inferring keystrokes on touch screen from smartphone motion." *HotSec*, 11(2011), 9–9.

Caldwell, D., Gilbert, A., Gottlieb, J., et al. (2004). "The cutting EDGE of IP router configuration." *ACM SIGCOMM Computer Communication Review*, 34(1), 21–26.

Calvaresi, D., Marinoni, M., Sturm, A., Schumacher, M., and Buttazzo, G. (2017, August). "The challenge of real-time multi-agent systems for enabling IoT and CPS." *Proceedings of the International Conference on Web Intelligence*. ACM, 356–364.

Cao, L., Yang, D., Wang, Q., Yu, Y., Wang, J., and Rundensteiner, E. A. (2014, March). "Scalable distance-based outlier detection over high-volume data streams." *2014 IEEE 30th International Conference on Data Engineering (ICDE)* . IEEE, 76–87.

Carvalho, M., DeMott, J., Ford, R., and Wheeler, D. A. (2014). "Heartbleed 101." *IEEE Security & Privacy*, 12(4), 63–67.

Chandola, V., Banerjee, A., and Kumar, V. (2009). "Anomaly detection: a survey." *ACM Computing Surveys (CSUR)*, 41(3), 15.

Chandrashekar, G. and Sahin, F. (2014). "A survey on feature selection methods." *Computers & Electrical Engineering*, 40(1), 16–28.

Chapman, P., Clinton, J., Kerber, R., et al. (2000). CRISP-DM 1.0, Step-by-Step Data Mining Guide. CRISP-DM Consortium; SPSS: Chicago, IL, USA.

Check Point. (2020). "Threat map." https://threatmap.checkpoint.com/. Last accessed March 2020.

Chen, M., Mao, S., and Liu, Y. (2014). "Big data: a survey." *Mobile Networks and Applications* 19(2), 171–209.

Chen, S. and Janeja, V. P. (2014). "Human perspective to anomaly detection for cybersecurity." *Journal of Intelligent Information Systems*, 42(1), 133–153.

Cheok, R. (2014). "Wire shark: a guide to color my packets detecting network recon-naissance to host exploitation." GIAC Certification Paper. SANS Institute Reading Room.

Cheswick, B. (1992, January). "An evening with Berferd in which a cracker is lured, endured, and studied." *Proceedings of the Winter USENIX Conference, San Francisco*, 20–24.

Chi, M. (2014). "Cyberspace: America's new battleground." www.sans.org/reading-room/whitepapers/warfare/cyberspace-americas-battleground-35612.   Last accessed November 2021.

Chien, E. and O'Gorman, G. (2011). "The nitro attacks, stealing secrets from the chemical industry." *Symantec Security Response* (2011), 1–8.

CIA. (2021). "World Factbook." Last accessed November 2021.

Cleary, J. G. and Trigg, L. E. (1995). "K*: an instance-based learner using an entropic distance measure." *Machine Learning Proceedings 1995*, A. Prieditis and S. Russell (Eds.). Morgan Kaufmann, 108–114.

Cloud Security Alliance. (2014). Big data taxonomy. https://downloads .cloudsecurityalliance.org/initiatives/bdwg/Big_Data_Taxonomy.pdf. Last accessed April 13, 2017.

Cohen, E., Datar, M., Fujiwara, S., et al. (2001). "Finding interesting associations without support pruning." *IEEE Transactions on Knowledge and Data Engineering*, 13(1), 64–78.

Cohen, W. W. (1995, July). "Fast effective rule induction." *Proceedings of the Twelfth International Conference on Machine Learning*. Morgan Kaufmann, 115–123.

Cooper, G. F. and Herskovits, E. (1992). "A Bayesian method for the induction of probabilistic networks from data." *Machine Learning*, 9, 309–347.

Cortes, C. and Vapnik, V. (1995). "Support-vector networks." *Machine Learning*, 20 (3), 273–297.

Cover, T. and Hart, P. (1967). "Nearest neighbor pattern classification." *IEEE Transactions on Information Theory*, 13(1), 21–27.

Dark Reading. (2011). "PNNL attack: 7 lessons: surviving a zero-day attack." www .darkreading.com/attacks-and-breaches/7-lessons-surviving-a-zero-day-attack/d/d-id/1100226. Last accessed March 2020.

Darwish, A. and Bataineh, E. (2012, December 18–20). "Eye tracking analysis of browser security indicators." *2012 International Conference on Computer Systems and Industrial Informatics (ICCSII)*, 1, 6. doi: 10.1109/ ICCSII.2012.6454330. Last accessed November 2021.

Das, A., Ng, W.-K., and Woon, Y.-K. 2001. "Rapid association rule mining." *Proceedings of the Tenth International Conference on Information and Knowledge Management*. ACM Press, 474–481.

Das, S., Kim, A., Jelen, B., Huber, L., and Camp, L. J. (2020). "Non-inclusive online security: older adults' experience with two-factor authentication." *Proceedings of the 54th Hawaii International Conference on System Sciences*, 6472.

Dash, M. and Liu, H. (1997). "Feature selection for classification." *Intelligent Data Analysis*, 1(1–4), 131–156.

Davies, C. "Flame cyber-espionage discovered in vast infection net." (2012, May 28). www.slashgear.com/flame-cyber-espionage-discovered-in-vast-infection-net-28230470/. Last accessed November 2021.

Davinson, N. and Sillence, E. (2010). "It won't happen to me: Promoting secure behaviour among internet users." *Computers in Human Behavior*, 26(6), 1739–1747.

Davinson, N. and Sillence, E. (2014). "Using the health belief model to explore users' perceptions of 'being safe and secure' in the world of technology mediated financial transactions." *International Journal of Human–Computer Studies*, 72 (2), 154–168.

Dempster, A. P., Laird, N. M., and Rubin, D. B. (1977). "Maximum likelihood from incomplete data via the EM algorithm." *Journal of the Royal Statistical Society. Series B (Methodological)*, 39(1), 1–22.

Deokar, B. and Hazarnis, A. (2012). "Intrusion detection system using log files and reinforcement learning." *International Journal of Computer Applications* 45(19), 28–35.

Dey, S., Janeja, V. P., and Gangopadhyay, A. (2009). "Temporal neighborhood discovery through unequal depth binning." *IEEE International Conference on Data Mining (ICDM'09)*, 110–119.

Dey, S., Janeja, V. P., and Gangopadhyay, A. (2014). "Discovery of temporal neighborhoods through discretization methods." *Intelligent Data Analysis*, 18(4), 609–636.

Ding, Y., Yan, E., Frazho, A., and Caverlee, J. (2009, November). "Pagerank for ranking authors in co-citation networks." *Journal of the American Society for Information Science and Technology*, 60(11), 2229–2243.

Domo. (2017). "Data never sleeps." www.domo.com/learn/data-never-sleeps-5?aid= ogsm072517_1&sf100871281=1. Last accessed November 2021.

Drinkwater, D. (2016). "Does a data breach really affect your firm's reputation?" www .csoonline.com/article/3019283/data-breach/does-a-data-breach-really-affect-your-firm-s-reputation.html. Last accessed June 2017.

Duchene, F., Garbayl, C., and Rialle, V. (2004). "Mining heterogeneous multivariate time-series for learning meaningful patterns: application to home health telecare." *arXiv preprint cs/0412003*.

Duczmal, L. and Renato, A. (2004). "A simulated annealing strategy for the detection of arbitrarily shaped spatial clusters." *Computational Statistics and Data Analysis*, 45(2), 269–286.

Eberle, W., Graves, J., and Holder, L. (2010). "Insider threat detection using a graph-based approach." *Journal of Applied Security Research*, 6(1), 32–81.

ENISA (European Union Agency for Network And Information Security). (2016, Jan). "Threat Taxonomy: a tool for structuring threat information." https://library .cyentia.com/report/report_001462.html. Last accessed November 2021.

Ester, M., Frommelt, A., Kriegel, H.-P., and Sander, J. (1998). "Algorithms for characterization and trend detection in spatial databases." *Proceedings of the Fourth International Conference on Knowledge Discovery and Data Mining (KDD'98)*, 44–50.

Ester, M., Kriegel, H., and Sander, J. (1997). "Spatial data mining: a database approach." *The 5th International Symposium on Advances in Spatial Databases*, Springer-Verlag, 47–66.

Ester, M., Kriegel, H. P., Sander, J., and Xu, X. (1996, August). "A density-based algorithm for discovering clusters in large spatial databases with noise." *KDD*, 96 (34), 226–231.

Estevez-Tapiador, J. M., Garcia-Teodoro, P., and Diaz-Verdejo, J. E. (2004). "Anomaly detection methods in wired networks: a survey and taxonomy." *Computer Communications*, 27(16), 1569–1584.

Fabrikant, A., Koutsoupias, E., and Papadimitriou, C. H. (2002). "Heuristically optimized trade-offs: a new paradigm for power laws in the Internet." *International Colloquium on Automata, Languages and Programming.* Springer, 110–122.

Faloutsos, M., Faloutsos, P., and Faloutsos, C. (1999). "On power-law relationships of the internet topology." *The Structure and Dynamics of Networks*, M. Newman, A.-L. Barabási, and D. J. Watts (Eds.). Princeton University Press, 195–206.

Famili, A., Shen, W. M., Weber, R., and Simoudis, E. (1997). "Data preprocessing and intelligent data analysis." *Intelligent Data Analysis*, 1(1–4), 3–23.

Fayyad, U., Piatetsky-Shapiro, G., and Smyth, P. (1996). "From data mining to knowledge discovery in databases." *AI Magazine* 17(3), 37.

Feily, M., Shahrestani, A., and Ramadass, S. (2009, June). "A survey of botnet and botnet detection." *Third International Conference on Emerging Security Information, Systems and Technologies, 2009. SECURWARE'09.* IEEE, 268–273.

Ferebee, D., Dasgupta, D., and Wu, Q. (2012, December). "A cyber-security storm map." *2012 International Conference on Cyber Security (CyberSecurity).* IEEE, 93–102.

FireEye. (2019). "Mandiant Purple Team Assessment data sheet." www.fireeye.com/content/dam/fireeye-www/services/pdfs/pf/ms/ds-purple-team-assessment.pdf. Last accessed November 2021.

Fischer, P., Lea, S. E., and Evans, K. M. (2013). "Why do individuals respond to fraudulent scam communications and lose money? The psychological determinants of scam compliance." *Journal of Applied Social Psychology*, 43(10), 2060–2072.

Fodor, I. K. (2002). "A survey of dimension reduction techniques." *Center for Applied Scientific Computing, Lawrence Livermore National Laboratory* 9, 1–18.

Frank, E., and Witten, H. I. (1998). "Generating accurate rule sets without global optimization." *Proceedings of the 15th International Conference on Machine Learning (ICML'98), Madison, Wisconsin*, E. Frank and I. H. Witten (Eds.). Morgan Kaufmann, 144–151.

Frank, L., Greitzer, R., and Hohimer, E. (2011, Summer). "Modeling human behavior to anticipate insider attacks." *Journal of Strategic Security: Strategic Security in Cyber Age*, 4(2), 25–48.

Freeman, L. C. (1978). "Centrality in social networks conceptual clarification." *Social Networks*, 1(3), 215–239.

Frei, S., May, M., Fiedler, U., and Plattner, B. (2006, September). "Large-scale vulnerability analysis." *Proceedings of the 2006 SIGCOMM Workshop on Large-Scale Attack Defense.* ACM, 131–138.

Freund, Y. and Schapire, R. E. (1996). "Experiments with a new boosting algorithm." *Proceedings of the 13th International Conference on Machine Learning.* Morgan Kaufmann, 148–146.

Gandhi, R., Sharma, A., Mahoney, W., et al. (2011). "Dimensions of cyber-attacks: cultural, social, economic, and political." *IEEE Technology and Society Magazine*, 30(1), 28–38.

Garcia, S., Luengo, J., Sáez, J. A., Lopez, V., and Herrera, F. (2013). "A survey of discretization techniques: taxonomy and empirical analysis in supervised learning." *IEEE Transactions on Knowledge and Data Engineering*, 25(4), 734–750.

Garcia-Teodoro, P., Diaz-Verdejo, J., Maciá-Fernández, G., and Vázquez, E. (2009). "Anomaly-based network intrusion detection: techniques, systems and challenges." *Computers and Security*, 28(1), 18–28.

Garg, A., Upadhyaya, S., and Kwiat, K. (2013). "A user behavior monitoring and profiling scheme for masquerade detection." *Handbook of Statistics: Machine Learning: Theory and Applications*, 31, 353.

Geenens, P. (2020). "FireEye hack turns into a global supply chain attack." https://securityboulevard.com/2020/12/fireeye-hack-turns-into-a-global-supply-chain-attack/. Last accessed November 2021.

Gennari, J. H., Langley, P., and Fisher, D. (1989). "Models of incremental concept formation." *Artificial Intelligence*, 40(1–3), 11–61.

Gesenhues, A. (2014). "Google Dorking: it's all fun & games until the hackers show up." http://searchengineland.com/google-dorking-fun-games-hackers-show-202191. Last accessed November 2021.

Glaz, J., Naus, J., and Wallenstein, S. (2001). *Scan Statistics*. Springer Verlag.

Goldberg, L. R. (1990). "An alternative 'description of personality': the big-five factor structure." *Journal of Personality and Social Psychology*, 59(6), 1216.

Golnabi, K., Min, R. K,. Khan, L., and Al-Shaer, E. (2006). "Analysis of firewall policy rules using data mining techniques." *2006 IEEE/IFIP Network Operations and Management Symposium, NOMS 2006*. IEEE/IFIP, 205–315.

Goodfellow, I. (2016). "NIPS 2016 tutorial: generative adversarial networks." *arXiv:1701.00160*.

Goodfellow, I., Pouget-Abadie, J., Mirza, M., et al. (2014). "Generative adversarial nets." *Proceedings of the 27th International Conference on Neural Information Processing Systems – Volume 2 (NIPS'14)*. MIT Press, 2672–2680.

Gopalani, S. and Arora, R. (2015). "Comparing Apache Spark and Map Reduce with performance analysis using K-means." *International Journal of Computer Applications*, 113(1), 8–11.

Gormley, T., Reingold, N., Torng, E., and Westbrook, J. (2000). "Generating adversaries for request-answer games." *Proceedings of the 11th ACM-SIAM Symposium on Discrete Algorithms*. ACM-SIAM, 564–565.

Grazioli, S. (2004). "Where did they go wrong? An analysis of the failure of knowledgeable internet consumers to detect deception over the internet." *Group Decision and Negotiation*, 13(2), 149–172.

Griffith, D. A. (1987). *Spatial Autocorrelation: A Primer*. Association of American Geographers.

Grover, A., Gholap, J. Janeja, V. P., et al. (2015). "SQL-like big data environments: case study in clinical trial analytics." *Proceedings of 2015 IEEE International Conference on Big Data*, 2680–2689.

Gu, G., Zhang, J., and Lee, W. (2008, February). "BotSniffer: detecting botnet command and control channels in network traffic." *Proceedings of the 15th Annual Network and Distributed System Security Symposium*, vol. 8, 1–18.

Guardian, The. (2016). "Norway, the country where you can see everyone's tax returns." www.theguardian.com/money/blog/2016/apr/11/when-it-comes-to-tax-transparency-norway-leads-the-field. Last accessed November 2021.

Guha, S., Rastogi, R., and Shim, K. (1998, June). "CURE: an efficient clustering algorithm for large databases." *ACM Sigmod Record*, 27(2), 73–84.

Guha, S., Rastogi, R., and Shim, K. (2000). "ROCK: a robust clustering algorithm for categorical attributes." *Information Systems*, 25(5), 345–366.

Gupta, H., Sural, S., Atluri, V., and Vaidya, J. (2016). "Deciphering text from touchscreen key taps." *IFIP Annual Conference on Data and Applications Security and Privacy*. Springer International Publishing, 3–18.

Guralnik, V. and Srivastava, J. (1999). "Event detection from time series data." *KDD'99: Proceedings of the Fifth ACM SIGKDD International Conference on Knowledge Discovery and Data Mining*. ACM, 33–42.

Haining, R. (2003). *Spatial Data Analysis: Theory and Practice.* Cambridge University Press.

Halevi, T., Lewis, J., and Memon, N. (2013, May). "A pilot study of cyber security and privacy related behavior and personality traits." *Proceedings of the 22nd International Conference on World Wide Web Companion*. International World Wide Web Conferences Steering Committee, 737–744.

Halliday, J. (2010, September 24). "Stuxnet worm is the 'work of a national government agency'." www.guardian.co.uk/technology/2010/sep/24/stuxnet-worm-national-agency. Last accessed November 2021.

Han, J., and Fu, Y. (1995, September). "Discovery of multiple-level association rules from large databases." *VLDB'95, Proceedings of 21th International Conference on Very Large Data Bases*, U. Dayal, P. Gray, and S. Nishio (Eds.). Morgan Kaufmann, 420–431.

Han, J., Pei, J., and Yin, Y. (2000, May). "Mining frequent patterns without candidate generation." *ACM Sigmod Record*, 29(2), 1–12.

Hellerstein, J. L., Ma, S., and Perng, C.-S. (2002). "Discovering actionable patterns in event data." *IBM Systems Journal*, 41(3), 475–493.

Heron, S. (2007). "The rise and rise of the keyloggers." *Network Security* 2007(6), 4–6.

Hinneburg, A., and Keim, D. A. (1998, August). "An efficient approach to clustering in large multimedia databases with noise." *KDD*, 98, 58–65.

Hoffman, S. (2011). "Cyber attack forces internet shut down for DOE lab, on July 8." www.crn.com/news/security/231001261/cyber-attack-forces-internet-shut-down-for-doe-lab.htm. Last accessed February 23, 2014.

Hong, J., Liu, C. C., and Govindarasu, M. (2014). "Integrated anomaly detection for cyber security of the substations." *IEEE Transactions on Smart Grid*, 5(4), 1643–1653.

Hu, M. and Liu, B. (2004, August). "Mining and summarizing customer reviews." *Proceedings of the Tenth ACM SIGKDD International Conference on Knowledge Discovery and Data Mining*. ACM, 168–177.

Hu, Z., Baynard, C. W., Hu, H., and Fazio, M. (2015, June). "GIS mapping and spatial analysis of cybersecurity attacks on a Florida university." *2015 23rd International Conference on Geoinformatics*. IEEE, 1–5.

Hu, Z., Wang, H., Zhu, J., et al. (2014). "Discovery of rare sequential topic patterns in document stream." *Proceedings of the 2014 SIAM International Conference on Data Mining*, 533–541.

Huang, Y., Pei, J., and Xiong, H. (2006). "Mining co-location patterns with rare events from spatial data sets." *GeoInformatica*, 10(3), 239–260.

Hussain, M., Al-Haiqi, A., Zaidan, A. A., Zaidan, B. B., Kiah, M. M., Anuar, N. B., and Abdulnabi, M. (2016). "The rise of keyloggers on smartphones: A survey and insight into motion-based tap inference attacks." *Pervasive and Mobile Computing*, 25, 1–25.

Ingols, K., Lippmann, R., & Piwowarski, K. (2006, December). "Practical attack graph generation for network defense." *Computer Security Applications Conference, 2006. ACSAC'06. 22nd Annual.* IEEE, 121–130.

Iyengar, V. S. (2004). "On detecting space-time clusters." *KDD'04: Proceedings of the Tenth ACM SIGKDD International Conference on Knowledge Discovery and Data Mining.* ACM Press, 587–592.

Jain, A. K. (2010). "Data clustering: 50 years beyond K-means." *Pattern Recognition Letters*, 31(8), 651–666.

Jakobsson, M. (2007). "The human factor in phishing." *Privacy & Security of Consumer Information*, 7(1), 1–19.

Janeja, V. P. (2019). *Do No Harm: An Ethical Data Life Cycle, Sci on the Fly.* AAAS.

Janeja, V. P., Adam, N. R., Atluri, V., and Vaidya, J. (2010). "Spatial neighborhood based anomaly detection in sensor datasets." *Data Mining and Knowledge Discovery*, 20(2), 221–258.

Janeja, V. P. and Atluri, V. (2005). "LS3: A linear semantic scan statistic technique for detecting anomalous windows. *Proceedings of the 2005 ACM Symposium on Applied Computing*, 493–497.

Janeja, V. P. and Atluri, V. (2005). "FS3: A random walk based free-form spatial scan statistic for anomalous window detection." *Fifth IEEE International Conference on Data Mining (ICDM'05).* IEEE Computer Society, 661–664.

Janeja, V. P, and Atluri, V. (2008). "Random walks to identify anomalous free-form spatial scan windows." *IEEE Transactions on Knowledge and Data Engineering*, 20(10), 1378–1392.

Janeja, V. P. and Atluri, V. (2009). "Spatial outlier detection in heterogeneous neighborhoods." *Intelligent Data Analysis*, 13(1), 85–107.

Janeja, V. P., Azari, A., Namayanja, J. M., and Heilig, B. (2014, October). "B-dids: Mining anomalies in a Big-distributed Intrusion Detection System." In 2014 *IEEE International Conference on Big Data* (Big Data) (pp. 32–34). IEEE.

Jarvis, R. A. and Patrick, E. A. (1973). "Clustering using a similarity measure based on shared near neighbors." *IEEE Transactions on Computers*, 100(11), 1025–1034.

Jha, S., Sheyner, O., and Wing, J. (2002). "Two formal analyses of attack graphs." *Computer Security Foundations Workshop, 2002. Proceedings. 15th IEEE.* IEEE, 49–63.

Ji, Y., Zhang, X., Ji, S., Luo, X., and Wang, T. (2018, October). "Model-reuse attacks on deep learning systems." *Proceedings of the 2018 ACM SIGSAC Conference on Computer and Communications Security.* ACM, 349–363.

Joachims, T. (2002, July). "Optimizing search engines using clickthrough data." *Proceedings of the Eighth ACM SIGKDD International Conference on Knowledge Discovery and Data Mining.* ACM, 133–142.

John, O. P. and Srivastava, S. (1999). "The big-five trait taxonomy: history, measurement, and theoretical perspectives." *Handbook of Personality: Theory and Research*, vol. 2., L. A. Pervin and O. P. John (Eds.). Guilford Press, 102–138.

Kang, I., Kim, T., and Li, K. (1997). "A spatial data mining method by Delaunay triangulation." *Proceedings of the 5th ACM International Workshop on Advances in Geographic Information Systems.* ACM, 35–39.

Kang, U., Tsourakakis, C., Appel, A., Faloutsos, C., and Leskovec, J. (2010). "Radius plots for mining tera-byte scale graphs: algorithms, patterns, and observations." *Proceedings of the 2010 SIAM International Conference on Data Mining (SDM)*, 548–558.

Kang, U., Tsourakakis, C., and Faloutsos, C. (2009). "Pegasus: a peta-scale graph mining system – implementation and observations." *2009 Ninth IEEE International Conference on Data Mining*, 229–238.

Karypis, G., Han, E. H., and Kumar, V. (1999). "Chameleon: hierarchical clustering using dynamic modeling." *Computer*, 32(8), 68–75.

Kaspersky. (2020). "Cyberthreat real-time map." https://cybermap.kaspersky.com/. Last accessed November 2020.

Kath, O., Schreiner, R., and Favaro, J. (2009, September). "Safety, security, and software reuse: a model-based approach." *Proceedings of the Fourth International Workshop in Software Reuse and Safety*. www.researchgate.net/publication/228709911_Safety_Security_and_Software_Reuse_A_Model-Based_Approach. Last accessed November 2021.

Kato, K. and Klyuev, V. (2017, August). "Development of a network intrusion detection system using Apache Hadoop and Spark." *2017 IEEE Conference on Dependable and Secure Computing*. IEEE, 416–423.

Katsini, C., Abdrabou, Y., Raptis, G. E., Khamis, M., and Alt, F. (2020, April). "The role of eye gaze in security and privacy applications: survey and future HCI research directions." *Proceedings of the 2020 CHI Conference on Human Factors in Computing Systems*, 1–21.

Kaufman, L. and Rousseeuw, P. (1987). *Clustering by Means of Medoids*. North-Holland.

Kaufman, L. and Rousseeuw, P. J. (1990). *Finding Groups in Data: An Introduction to Cluster Analysis*. John Wiley & Sons.

Keim, D. A., Mansmann, F., Panse, C., Schneidewind, J., and Sips, M. (2005). "Mail explorer – spatial and temporal exploration of electronic mail." *Proceedings of the Seventh Joint Eurographics/IEEE VGTC Conference on Visualization*, 247–254.

Keim, D. A., Mansmann, F., and Schreck, T. (2005). "Analyzing electronic mail using temporal, spatial, and content-based visualization techniques." *Informatik 2005–Informatik Live!*, vol. 67, 434–438.

Keogh. E., Lin. J., and Fu. A. (2005). "Hot sax: efficiently finding the most unusual time series subsequence." *Fifth IEEE International Conference on Data Mining (ICDM'05)*, doi: 10.1109/ICDM.2005.79.

Kianmehr, K. and Koochakzadeh, N. (2012). "Learning from socio-economic characteristics of IP geo-locations for cybercrime prediction." *International Journal of Business Intelligence and Data Mining*, 7(1/2), 21–39

Kim, S., Edmonds, W., and Nwanze, N. 2014. "On GPU accelerated tuning for a payload anomaly-based network intrusion detection scheme." *Proceedings of the 9th Annual Cyber and Information Security Research Conference (CISR '14)*. ACM, 1–4. doi: 10.1145/2602087.2602093.

Kim Zetter Security. (2013). "Someone's been siphoning data through a huge security hole in the internet." www.wired.com/2013/12/bgp-hijacking-belarus-iceland/. Last accessed December 2016.

Knorr, E. M., Ng, R. T., and Tucakov, V. (2000). "Distance-based outliers: algorithms and applications." *VLDB Journal – The International Journal on Very Large Data Bases*, 8(3–4), 237–253.

Koh, Y. S. and Ravana, S. D. (2016). "Unsupervised rare pattern mining: a survey." *ACM Transactions on Knowledge Discovery from Data (TKDD)*, 10(4), 45.

Koh, Y. S. and Rountree, N. (2005). "Finding sporadic rules using apriori-inverse." *PAKDD (Lecture Notes in Computer Science)*, vol. 3518. T. B. Ho, D. Cheung, and H. Liu (Eds.). Springer, 97–106.

Koike, H. and Ohno, K. (2004). "SnortView: visualization system of snort logs." *Proceedings of the 2004 ACM Workshop on Visualization and Data Mining for Computer Security (VizSEC/DMSEC '04).* ACM, 143–147. doi: 10.1145/1029208.1029232.

Kosner, A. W. (2012). "Cyber security fails as 3.6 million social security numbers breached in South Carolina." www.forbes.com/sites/anthonykosner/2012/10/27/cyber-security-fails-as-3-6-million-social-security-numbers-breached-in-south-carolina/?sh=5f3637784e9e. Last accessed March 2021.

Kotsiantis, S. and Pintelas, P. (2004). "Recent advances in clustering: a brief survey." *WSEAS Transactions on Information Science and Applications*, 1(1), 73–81.

Kotsiantis, S. B., Zaharakis, I. D., and Pintelas, P. E. (2006). "Machine learning: a review of classification and combining techniques." *Artificial Intelligence Review*, 26(3), 159–190.

Kulldorff, M. (1997). "A spatial scan statistic." *Communications of Statistics – Theory Meth.*, 26(6), 1481–1496.

Kulldorff, M., Athas, W., Feuer, E., Miller, B., and Key, C. (1998). "Evaluating cluster alarms: a space-time scan statistic and brain cancer in Los Alamos." *American Journal of Public Health*, 88(9), 1377–1380.

Kurgan, L. A. and Musilek, P. (2006, March). "A survey of knowledge discovery and data mining process models." *Knowledge Engineering Review*, 21(1) 1–24. doi: 10.1017/S0269888906000737.

L24. (2016). "First national cyber security exercise Cyber Shield." http://l24.lt/en/society/item/150489-first-national-cyber-security-exercise-cyber-shield-2016-will-be-held. Last accessed April 12, 2017.

LeCun, Y., Bengio, Y., and Hinton, G. (2015). "Deep learning." *Nature*, 521(7553), 436.

Lee, G., Yun, U., Ryang, H., and Kim, D. (2015). "Multiple minimum support-based rare graph pattern mining considering symmetry feature-based growth technique and the differing importance of graph elements." *Symmetry*, 7(3), 1151.

Leskovec, J. (2008). "Dynamics of large networks." Dissertation. ProQuest Dissertations Publishing.

Leskovec, J., Chakrabarti, D., Kleinberg, J., and Faloutsos, C. (2005). "Realistic, mathematically tractable graph generation and evolution, using Kronecker multiplication." *European Conference on Principles and Practice of Knowledge Discovery in Databases: PKDD 2005*, A. M. Jorge, L. Torgo, P. Brazdil, R. Camacho, and J. Gama (Eds.). Lecture Notes in Computer Science, vol. 3721. Springer. doi: 10.1007/11564126_17.

Leskovec, J. and Faloutsos, C. (2007). "Scalable modeling of real graphs using kronecker multiplication." *International Conference on Machine Learning (ICML '07)*. ACM, 497–504. doi: 10.1145/1273496.1273559.

Leskovec, J., Kleinberg, J., and Faloutsos, C. (2005, August). "Graphs over time: densification laws, shrinking diameters and possible explanations." *Proceedings of the Eleventh ACM SIGKDD International Conference on Knowledge Discovery in Data Mining*. ACM, 177–187.

Leskovec, J., Kleinberg, J., and Faloutsos, C. (2007). "Graph evolution: densification and shrinking diameters." *ACM Transactions on Knowledge Discovery from Data (TKDD)*, 1, 2-es. doi: 10.1145/1217299.1217301.

Lewis, D. M. and Janeja, V. P. (2011). "An empirical evaluation of similarity coefficients for binary valued data." *International Journal of Data Warehousing and Mining (IJDWM)*, 7(2), 44–66. doi: 10.4018/jdwm.2011040103.

Lewis, J. A. (2005). "Computer espionage, Titan Rain and China." http://csis.org/files/media/csis/pubs/051214_china_titan_rain.pdf. Last accessed March 2020.

Leyden, J. (2012, March 29). "NSA's top spook blames China for RSA hack." www.theregister.co.uk/2012/03/29/nsa_blames_china_rsa_hack/. Last accessed November 2021.

Li, J., Dou, D., Wu, Z., Kim, S., and Agarwal, V. (2005). "An Internet routing forensics framework for discovering rules of abnormal BGP events." *ACM SIGCOMM Computer Communication Review*, 35(5), 55–66.

Li, X., Wang, L., & Sung, E. (2008). AdaBoost with SVM-based component classifiers. *Engineering Applications of Artificial Intelligence, 21*(5), 785–795.

Lin, J., Keogh, E., Lonardi, S., and Chiu, B. (2003). "A symbolic representation of time series, with implications for streaming algorithms." *DMKD '03: Proceedings of the 8th ACM SIGMOD Workshop on Research Issues in Data Mining and Knowledge Discovery*. ACM, 2–11.

Lin, Q., Adepu, S., Verwer, S., and Mathur, A. (2018, May). "TABOR: a graphical model-based approach for anomaly detection in industrial control systems." *Proceedings of the 2018 on Asia Conference on Computer and Communications Security (ASIACCS)*. ACM, 525–536. doi: 10.1145/3196494.3196546.

Liu, B., Hsu, W., and Ma, Y. (1999a). "Mining association rules with multiple minimum supports." *Proceedings of the 5th ACM SIGKDD International Conference on Knowledge Discovery and Data Mining*. ACM, 337–341.

Liu, H., Hussain, F., Tan, C. L., and Dash, M. (2002). "Discretization: an enabling technique." *Data Mining and Knowledge Discovery*, 6(4), 393–423.

Liu, Z., Wang, C., and Chen, S. (2008). "Correlating multi-step attack and constructing attack scenarios based on attack pattern modeling." *International Conference on Information Security and Assurance, 2008. ISA 2008*. IEEE, 214–219.

Limmer, T. and Dressler, F. (2010). "Dialog-based payload aggregation for intrusion detection." *Proceedings of the 17th ACM Conference on Computer and Communications Security (CCS '10)*. ACM, 708–710. doi: 10.1145/1866307.1866405.

Lockheed Martin. (2015). "Gaining the advantage, applying Cyber Kill Chain® methodology to network defense 2015." Technical report. www.lockheedmartin.com/content/dam/lockheed-martin/rms/documents/cyber/Gaining_the_Advantage_Cyber_Kill_Chain.pdf. Last accessed November 2021.

Luengo, J., García, S., and Herrera, F. (2012). "On the choice of the best imputation methods for missing values considering three groups of classification methods." *Knowledge and Information Systems*, 32(1), 77–108.

Ma, S. and Hellerstein, J. L. (2001a). "Mining mutually dependent patterns." *Proceedings of the 2001 International Conference on Data Mining (ICDM'01), San Jose, CA, November 2001*. IEEE, 409–416.

Ma, S. and Hellerstein, J. L. (2001b). "Mining partially periodic event patterns with unknown periods." *Proceedings of the 2001 International Conference on Data Engineering (ICDE'01), Heidelberg, Germany, April 2001*. IEEE, 205–214.

MacQueen, J. (1967, June). "Some methods for classification and analysis of multivariate observations." *Proceedings of the Fifth Berkeley Symposium on Mathematical Statistics and Probability*. University of California Press, vol. 1, no. 14, 281–297.

Mandiant. (2013). "APT1: exposing one of China's cyber espionage units." www .mandiant.com/resources/apt1-exposing-one-of-chinas-cyber-espionage-units. Last accessed November 2021.

Manyika, J., Chui, M., Brown, B., et al. (2011). Big data: The next frontier for innovation, competition, and productivity. McKinsey Global Institute.

Maron, M. and Kuhns, J. (1960). "On relevance, probabilistic indexing, and information retrieval." *Journal of the Association for Computing Machinery* 7, 216–244.

Massicotte, F., Whalen, T., and Bilodeau, C. (2003). "Network mapping tool for real-time security analysis." *RTO IST Symposium on Real Time Intrusion Detection*, 12-1–12-10.

McAfee. (2010). "Protecting your critical assets." www.wired.com/images_blogs/ threatlevel/2010/03/operationaurora_wp_0310_fnl.pdf. Last accessed November 2021.

McAfee. (2011). "Global energy cyberattacks: "Night Dragon." www.heartland.org/ publications-resources/publications/global-energy-cyberattacks-night-dragon. Last accessed November 2021.

McAfee. (2018). "The economic impact of cybercrime – no slowing down." McAfee, Center for Strategic and International Studies (CSIS). www.mcafee.com/enter prise/en-us/solutions/lp/economics-cybercrime.html.

McBride, M., Carter, L., and Warkentin, M. (2012). "Exploring the role of individual employee characteristics and personality on employee compliance with cybersecurity policies." *RTI International Institute for Homeland Security Solutions*, 5(1), 1.

McGuire, M. P., Janeja, V.P., and Gangopadhyay, A. (2008, August). "Spatiotemporal neighborhood discovery for sensor data." *International Workshop on Knowledge Discovery from Sensor Data*. Springer, 203–225.

McGuire, M. P., Janeja, V. P., and Gangopadhyay, A. (2012). "Mining sensor datasets with spatio-temporal neighborhoods." *Journal of Spatial Information Science (JOSIS)*, 2013(6), 1–42.

Meng, X., Bradley, J., Yavuz, B., et al. (2016). "Mllib: machine learning in Apache Spark." *Journal of Machine Learning Research*, 17(1), 1235–1241.

Mezzour, G. (2015). "Assessing the global cyber and biological threat." Thesis, Carnegie Mellon University. doi: 10.1184/R1/6714857.v1.

Miller, H. J. (2004). "Tobler's first law and spatial analysis." *Annals of the Association of American Geographers*, 94(2), 284–289.

Miller, W. B. (2014). "Classifying and cataloging cyber-security incidents within cyber-physical systems." Doctoral dissertation, Brigham Young University.

Misal, V., Janeja, V. P., Pallaprolu, S. C., Yesha, Y., and Chintalapati, R. (2016, December). "Iterative unified clustering in big data." *2016 IEEE International Conference on Big Data (Big Data)*. IEEE, 3412–3421.

Mitra, B., Sural, S., Vaidya, J., and Atluri, V. (2016). "A survey of role mining." *ACM Computing Surveys (CSUR)*, 48(4), 1–37.

MITRE ATT&CK. (2020). ATT&CK Matrix for Enterprise. https://attack.mitre.org/. Last accessed November 2021.

Molina, L. C., Belanche, L., and Nebot, À. (2002). "Feature selection algorithms: a survey and experimental evaluation." *2002 IEEE International Conference on Data Mining, 2002. ICDM 2003. Proceedings.* IEEE, 306–313.

Namayanja, J. M. and Janeja, V. P. (2014, October). "Change detection in temporally evolving computer networks: a big data framework." *2014 IEEE International Conference on Big Data.* IEEE, 54–61.

Namayanja, J. M. and Janeja, V. P. (2015, May). "Change detection in evolving computer networks: changes in densification and diameter over time." *2015 IEEE International Conference on Intelligence and Security Informatics (ISI).* IEEE, 185–187.

Namayanja, J. M. and Janeja, V. P. (2017). "Characterization of evolving networks for cybersecurity." *Information Fusion for Cyber-Security Analytics*, I. Alsmadi, G. Karabatis, and A. Aleroud (Eds.). Studies in Computational Intelligence, vol. 691. Springer International Publishing, 111–127. doi: 10.1007/978-3-319-44257-0_5.

Namayanja, J. M. and Janeja, V. P. (2019). "Change detection in large evolving networks." *International Journal of Data Warehousing and Mining*, 15(2), 62–79.

Naseer, S., Saleem, Y., Khalid, S., et al. (2018). "Enhanced network anomaly detection based on deep neural networks." *IEEE Access*, 6, 48231–48246.

Naus, J. (1965). "The distribution of the size of the maximum cluster of points on the line." *Journal of the American Statistical Association*, 60, 532–538.

Neill, D., Moore, A., Pereira, F., and Mitchell, T. (2005). "Detecting significant multidimensional spatial clusters." *Advances in Neural Information Processing Systems 17*, MIT Press, 969–976.

Netscout. (2020). "A global threat visualization." www.netscout.com/global-threat-intelligence. Last accessed November 2020.

Ng, R. T. and Han, J. (1994, September). "Efficient and effective clustering methods for spatial data mining." *Proceedings of the 20th International Conference on Very Large Data Bases (VLDB '94).* Morgan Kaufmann , 144–155.

Ng, R. T., Lakshmanan, L. V. S., Han, J., and Pang, A. 1998. "Exploratory mining and pruning optimizations of constrained associations rules." *Proceedings of the 1998 ACM SIGMOD International Conference on Management of Data (SIGMOD '98).* ACM,13–24.

Nguyen, T. T. and Janapa Reddi, V. (2019). "Deep reinforcement learning for cyber security." *arXiv:1906.05799.*

Nicosia, V., Tang, J., Mascolo, C., et al. (2013). "Graph metrics for temporal networks." *Temporal Networks: Understanding Complex Systems*, P. Holme and J. Saramäki (Eds.). Springer, 15–40. doi: 10.1007/978-3-642-36461-7_2.

NIST (National Institute of Standards and Technology). (2015). NIST Big Data Interoperability Framework (NBDIF), V1.0. https://bigdatawg.nist.gov/V1_output_docs.php. Last accessed April 12, 2017.

NIST. (2017). National vulnerability database. http://nvd.nist.gov/. Last accessed September 2017.

Nunes, D. S., Zhang, P., and Silva, J. S. (2015). "A survey on human-in-the-loop applications towards an internet of all." *IEEE Communications Surveys and Tutorials*, 17(2), 944–965.

O'Gorman, G. and McDonald, G. (2012). "The Elderwood Project." www.infopoint-security.de/medien/the-elderwood-project.pdf. Last accessed November 2021.

Ohm, M., Sykosch, A., and Meier, M. (2020, August). "Towards detection of software supply chain attacks by forensic artifacts." *Proceedings of the 15th International Conference on Availability, Reliability and Security (ARES '20)*. ACM, 1–6. doi: 10.1145/3407023.3409183.

Openshaw, S. (1987). "A mark 1 geographical analysis machine for the automated analysis of point data sets." *International Journal of GIS*, 1(4), 335–358.

OSQuery. (2016). https://osquery.io/. Last accessed March 2020.

Otoum, S., Kantarci, B., and Mouftah, H. (2019, May). "Empowering reinforcement learning on big sensed data for intrusion detection." *2019–2019 IEEE International Conference on Communications (ICC)*. IEEE, 1–7.

Paganini, P. (2014). "Turkish government is hijacking the IP for popular DNS providers." http://securityaffairs.co/wordpress/23565/intelligence/turkish-government-hijacking-dns.html. Last accessed June 2017.

Parekh, J. J., Wang, K., and Stolfo, S. J. (2006). "Privacy-preserving payload-based correlation for accurate malicious traffic detection." *Proceedings of the 2006 SIGCOMM Workshop on Large-Scale Attack Defense (LSAD '06)*. ACM, 99–106. doi: 10.1145/1162666.1162667.

Patcha, A. and Park, J. M. (2007). "An overview of anomaly detection techniques: existing solutions and latest technological trends." *Computer Networks*, 51(12), 3448–3470.

Paul, R. J. and Taylor, S. J. E. (2002). "Improving the model development process: what use is model reuse: is there a crook at the end of the rainbow?" *Proceedings of the 34th Conference on Winter Simulation: Exploring New Frontiers (WSC '02)*. Winter Simulation Conference, 648–652.

Pei, J. and Han, J. (2000). "Can we push more constraints into frequent pattern mining?" *Proceedings of the Sixth ACM SIGKDD International Conference on Knowledge Discovery and Data Mining*. ACM Press, 350–354.

Peña, J. M., Lozano, J. A., and Larrañaga, P. (2002). "Learning recursive Bayesian multinets for data clustering by means of constructive induction." *Machine Learning*, 47(1), 63–89.

Pfeiffer, T., Theuerling, H., and Kauer, M. (2013). "Click me if you can! How do users decide whether to follow a call to action in an online message?" *Human Aspects of Information Security, Privacy, and Trust. HAS 2013*, L. Marinos and I.

Askoxylakis (Eds.). Lecture Notes in Computer Science, vol. 8030. Springer, 155–166. doi: 10.1007/978-3-642-39345-7_17.

Phillips, G., Shenker, S., and Tangmunarunkit, H. (1999). "Scaling of multicast trees: comments on the Chuang–Sirbu scaling law." *Proceedings of the Conference on Applications, Technologies, Architectures, and Protocols for Computer Communication (SIGCOMM '99)*. ACM, 41–51. doi: 10.1145/316188.316205.

Picard, R. W. (2003). "Affective computing: challenges." *International Journal of Human-Computer Studies*, 59(1), 55–64.

Press, S. J. and Wilson, S. (1978). "Choosing between logistic regression and discriminant analysis." *Journal of the American Statistical Association*, 73(364), 699–705.

Qiu, J., Gao, L., Ranjan, S., and Nucci, A. (2007, September). "Detecting bogus BGP route information: Going beyond prefix hijacking." *In 2007 Third International Conference on Security and Privacy in Communications Networks and the Workshops-SecureComm 2007* (pp. 381–390). IEEE.

Quader, F., and Janeja, V. (2014). *Computational Models to Capture Human Behavior In Cybersecurity Attacks*. Academy of Science and Engineering (ASE).

Quader, F., and Janeja, V. P. (2021). Insights into Organizational Security Readiness: Lessons Learned from Cyber-Attack Case Studies. Journal of Cybersecurity and Privacy, 1(4), 638–659.

Quader, F., Janeja, V., and Stauffer, J. (2015, May). "Persistent threat pattern discovery." *2015 IEEE International Conference on Intelligence and Security Informatics (ISI)*. IEEE, 179–181.

Quinlan, J. R. (1979). *Discovering Rules by Induction from Large Collections of Examples: Expert Systems in the Micro Electronic Age*. Edinburgh University Press.

Quinlan, J. R. (1993). *C4.5: Programs for Machine Learning*. Morgan Kaufmann.

Ramaswamy, S., Rastogi, R., and Shim, K. (2000, May). "Efficient algorithms for mining outliers from large data sets." *ACM Sigmod Record*, 29(2), 427–438).

Rashid, F. Y. (2013, April 4). "DHS: spear phishing campaign targeted 11 energy sector firms." www.securityweek.com/dhs-spear-phishing-campaign-targeted-11-energy-sector-firms. Last accessed February 23, 2014.

Raveh, A. and Tapiero, C. S. (1980). "Periodicity, constancy, heterogeneity and the categories of qualitative time series." *Ecology*, 61(3), 715–719.

Revow, M., Williams, C. K., and Hinton, G. E. (1996). "Using generative models for handwritten digit recognition." *IEEE Transactions on Pattern Analysis and Machine Intelligence*, 18(6), 592–606.

Risk Based Security. (2014). "A breakdown and analysis of the December, 2014 Sony hack." www.riskbasedsecurity.com/2014/12/05/a-breakdown-and-analysis-of-the-december-2014-sony-hack/. Last accessed November 2021.

Rivest, R. L. and Vuillemin, J. (1976). "On recognizing graph properties from adjacency matrices." *Theoretical Computer Science*, 3(3), 371–384.

Roddick, J. F. and Hornsby, K., (Eds.). (2001). *Temporal, Spatial, and Spatio-Temporal Data Mining, First International Workshop TSDM 2000 Lyon, France, September 12, 2000, Revised Papers*. Lecture Notes in Computer Science, vol. 2007. Springer-Verlag.

Roddick, J. F., Hornsby, K., and Spiliopoulou, M. (2001). "An updated bibliography of temporal, spatial, and spatio-temporal data mining research." *Temporal, Spatial, and Spatio-Temporal Data Mining, First International Workshop TSDM 2000 Lyon, France, September 12, 2000, Revised Papers.* Springer-Verlag, 147–164.

Roddick, J. F. and Spiliopoulou, M. (1999). "A bibliography of temporal, spatial and spatio-temporal data mining research." *SIGKDD Explorations Newsletter*, 1(1), 34–38.

Roman, J. The Hadoop Ecosystem Table. https://hadoopecosystemtable.github.io/. Last accessed April 13, 2017.

Rousseeuw, P. J. (1987). "Silhouettes: a graphical aid to the interpretation and validation of cluster analysis." *Computational and Applied Mathematics.* **20**, 53–65.

Sadhwani, H. (2020). "Introduction to threat hunting." https://medium.com/@hirensadh wani2619/introduction-to-threat-hunting-8dff62ba52ca. Last accessed November 2021.

Sainani, H. (2018). "IP reputation scoring – a perspective on clustering with meta-features augmentation." Thesis.

Sainani, H., Namayanja, J. M., Sharma, G., Misal, V., and Janeja, V. P. (2020). "IP reputation scoring with geo-contextual feature augmentation." *ACM Transactions on Management Information Systems (TMIS)*, 11(4), 26:1–26:29.

Samuel, A. W. (2004). "Hactivism and future of political participation." www.alexan-drasamuel.com/dissertation/pdfs/Samuel-Hacktivism-entire.pdf. Last accessed November 2021.

Sander, J., Ester, M., Kriegel, H. P., and Xu, X. (1998). "Density-based clustering in spatial databases: the algorithm GDBSCAN and its applications." *Data Mining and Knowledge Discovery*, 2(2), 169–194.

Sandoval, G. (2008). "YouTube blames Pakistan network for 2-hour outage." www .cnet.com/news/youtube-blames-pakistan-network-for-2-hour-outage/. Last accessed June 2017.

Schlamp, J., Carle, G., and Biersack, E. W. (2013). "A forensic case study on as hijacking: the attacker's perspective." *ACM SIGCOMM Computer Communication Review*, 43(2), 5–12.

Schlosser, A. E., White, T. B., and Lloyd, S. M. (2006). "Converting web site visitors into buyers: how web site investment increases consumer trusting beliefs and online purchase intentions." *Journal of Marketing*, 70(2), 133–148.

SecDev Group. (2009). "Tracking GhostNet: investigating a cyber espionage network." www.nartv.org/mirror/ghostnet.pdf. Last accessed November 2021.

Shashanka, M., Shen, M., and Wang, J. (2016). "User and entity behavior analytics for enterprise security." *2016 IEEE International Conference on Big Data (Big Data)*. IEEEE. 1867–1874. doi: 10.1109/BigData.2016.7840805.

Shearer, C. (2000). "The CRISP-DM model: the new blueprint for data mining." *Journal of Data Warehousing*, 5, 13–22.

Shekhar, S., Lu, C., and Zhang, P. (2001). "Detecting graph-based spatial outliers: algorithms and applications." *Proceedings of the 7th ACM SIGKDD International Conference on Knowledge Discovery and Data Mining*, 371–376.

Sheng, S., Holbrook, M., Kumaraguru, P., Cranor, L. F., and Downs, J. (2010). "Who falls for phish? A demographic analysis of phishing susceptibility and effective-ness of interventions." *Proceedings of the SIGCHI Conference on Human Factors in Computing Systems.* ACM, 373–382.

Shi, L. and Janeja, V. P. (2009, June). "Anomalous window discovery through scan statistics for linear intersecting paths (SSLIP)." *Proceedings of the 15th ACM SIGKDD International Conference on Knowledge Discovery and Data Mining.* ACM, 767–776.

Shropshire, J., Warkentin, M., Johnston, A., and Schmidt, M. (2006). "Personality and IT security: an application of the five-factor model." *AMCIS 2006 Proceedings.* Association for Information Systems AIS Electronic Library (AISeL), 415.

Simmon, E., Sowe, S. K., and Zettsu, K. (2015). "Designing a cyber-physical cloud computing architecture." *IT Professional*, (3), 40–45.

Simmons, C., Ellis, C., Shiva, S., Dasgupta, D., and Wu, Q. (2009). AVOIDIT: A cyber attack taxonomy. *9th Annual Symposium on Information Assurance*, 2–12. https://nsarchive.gwu.edu/sites/default/files/documents/4530310/Chris-Simmons-Charles-Ellis-Sajjan-Shiva.pdf. Last accessed November 2021.

Skariachan, D. and Finkle, J. (2014). "Target shares recover after reassurance on data breach impact." www.reuters.com/article/us-target-results/target-shares-recover-after-reassurance-on-data-breach-impact-idUSBREA1P0WC20140226. Last accessed March 2020.

Sklower, K. (1991, Winter). *A Tree-Based Packet Routing Table for Berkeley UNIX.* USENIX.

SMR Foundation. (2021). NodeXL. www.smrfoundation.org/nodexl/. Last accessed November 2021.

Snare. (2020). Snare. www.snaresolutions.com/central-83/. Last accessed March 2020.

Snort. (2020). Snort Rules Infographic. https://snort-org-site.s3.amazonaws.com/production/document_files/files/000/000/116/original/Snort_rule_infographic.pdf?X-Amz-Algorithm=AWS4-HMAC-SHA256&X-Amz-Credential=AKIAIXACIED2SPMSC7GA%2F20210316%2Fus-east-1%2Fs3%2Faws4_request&X-Amz-Date=20210316T191343Z&X-Amz-Expires=172800&X-Amz-SignedHeaders=host&X-Amz-Signature=bcfc7d75d223ab40badd8bd9e89ded29cc98ed3896f0140f55320ee9bcdf1383. Last accessed March 2020.

Spitzner, L. (2003). *Honeypots: Tracking Hackers*, vol. 1. Addison-Wesley.

Srikant, R. and Agrawal, R. (1996). "Mining quantitative association rules in large relational tables." *Proceedings of the 1996 ACM SIGMOD international Conference on Management of Data.* ACM Press, 1–12.

Statista. (2020). eCommerce report 2020 Statista Digital Market Outlook. www.statista.com/study/42335/ecommerce-report/. Last accessed November 2021.

Statista. (2021, March). Digital population worldwide. www.statista.com/statistics/617136/digital-population-worldwide/. Last accessed November 2021.

Statista. "IoT market – forecasts." www.statista.com/statistics/1101442/iot-number-of-connected-devices-worldwide/. Last accessed November 2021.

Stauffer, J. and Janeja, V. (2017). "A survey of advanced persistent threats and the characteristics. Technical report.

Stephens, G. D. and Maloof, M. A. (2014, April 22) "Insider threat detection." U.S. Patent No. 8,707,431.

Stouffer, K., Falco, J., and Scarfone, K. (2009). "Guide to industrial control systems (ICS) security." Technical report, National Institute of Standards and Technology.

Stubbs, J., Satter, R., and Menn, J. (2020). "U.S. Homeland Security, thousands of businesses scramble after suspected Russian hack." www.reuters.com/article/

global-cyber/global-security-teams-assess-impact-of-suspected-russian-cyber-attack-idUKKBN28O1KN. Last accessed November 2021.

Stutz, J. and Cheeseman, P. (1996). "AutoClass – a Bayesian approach to classification." *Maximum Entropy and Bayesian Methods.* Springer, 117–126.

Sugiura, O. and Ogden, R. T. (1994). "Testing change-points with linear trend." *Communications in Statistics – Simulation and Computation*, 23(2), 287–322. doi: 10.1080/03610919408813172.

Sugiyama, M. and Borgwardt, K. (2013). "Rapid distance-based outlier detection via sampling." *Proceedings of the 26th International Conference on Neural Information Processing Systems – Volume 1 (NIPS'13).* Curran Associates, 467–475.

Tan, Y., Vuran, M. C., and Goddard, S. (2009, June). "Spatio-temporal event model for cyber-physical systems." *29th IEEE International Conference on Distributed Computing Systems Workshops, 2009. ICDCS Workshops' 09.* IEEE, 44–50.

Tang, X., Eftelioglu, E., Oliver, D., and Shekhar, S. (2017). "Significant linear hotspot discovery." *IEEE Transactions on Big Data*, 3(2), 140–153.

Tango, T. and Takahashi, K. (2005). "A flexibly shaped spatial scan statistic for detecting clusters." *International Journal of Health Geographics*, 4(11). doi: 10.1186/1476-072X-4-11.

Tao, F., Murtagh, F., and Farid, M. (2003). "Weighted association rule mining using weighted support and significance framework." *Proceedings of the Ninth ACM SIGKDD International Conference on Knowledge Discovery and Data Mining, KDD'03.* ACM Press, 661–666.

Tartakovsky, A. G., Polunchenko, A. S., and Sokolov, G. (2013). "Efficient computer network anomaly detection by changepoint detection methods." *IEEE Journal of Selected Topics in Signal Processing*, 7(1), 4–11.

Ten, C. W., Hong, J., and Liu, C. C. (2011). "Anomaly detection for cybersecurity of the substations." *IEEE Transactions on Smart Grid*, 2(4), 865–873.

Thakur, V. (2011, December 8). "The Sykipot Attacks." www.symantec.com/connect/blogs/sykipot-attacks. Last accessed November 2021.

Tim, O., Firoiu, L., and Cohen, P. (1999). "Clustering time series with hidden markov models and dynamic time warping." Presented at IJCAI-99 Workshop on Sequence Learning.

Tobler, W. R. (1970). "A computer model simulation of urban growth in the Detroit region." *Economic Geography*, 46(2), 234–240.

Townsend, M., Rupp, L., and Green, J. (2014). "Target CEO ouster shows new board focus on cyber attacks." www.bloomberg.com/news/2014-05-05/target-ceo-ouster-shows-new-board-focus-on-cyber-attacks.html. Last accessed November 2021.

Trend Micro Incorporated. (2012a). "Detecting APT activity with network traffic analysis." www.trendmicro.com/cloud-content/us/pdfs/security-intelligence/white-papers/wp-detecting-apt-activity-with-network-traffic-analysis.pdf. Last accessed November 2021.

Trend Micro Incorporated. (2012b), "Spear-phishing email: most favored APT attack bait."

Trinius, P., Holz, T., Göbel, J., and Freiling, F. C. (2009, October). "Visual analysis of malware behavior using treemaps and thread graphs." *6th International Workshop on Visualization for Cyber Security, 2009. VizSec 2009.* IEEE, 33–38.

Tsuchiya, P. F. (1988). "The landmark hierarchy: a new hierarchy for routing in very large networks." *Symposium Proceedings on Communications Architectures and Protocols (SIGCOMM '88)*. ACM, 35–42.

Vaarandi, R. and Podiņš, K. (2010). "Network IDs alert classification with frequent itemset mining and data clustering." *2010 International Conference on Network and Service Management*. IEEE, 451–456.

Vaidya, J., Atluri, V., and Guo, Qi. (2007). "The role mining problem: finding a minimal descriptive set of roles." *Proceedings of the 12th ACM Symposium on Access Control Models and Technologies*. ACM, 175–184.

Van Mieghem, V. (2016). "Detecting malicious behaviour using system calls." Master's thesis, Delft University.

Venkatasubramanian, K., Nabar, S., Gupta, S. K. S., and Poovendran, R. (2011). "Cyber physical security solutions for pervasive health monitoring systems." *E-Healthcare Systems and Wireless Communications: Current and Future Challenges*, M. Watfa (Ed.). IGI Global, 143–162.

Verizon Wireless. (2017). "Data breach digest." https://enterprise.verizon.com/ resources/articles/2017-data-breach-digest-half-year-anniversary/. Last accessed November 2021.

Verma, J. P. and Patel, A. (2016, March–September). "Comparison of MapReduce and Spark programming frameworks for big data analytics on HDFS." *International Journal of Computer Science and Communication*, 7(2), 80–84.

Versprille, A. (2015). "Researchers hack into driverless car system, take control of vehicle." www.nationaldefensemagazine.org/articles/2015/5/1/2015may-research ers-hack-into-driverless-car-system-take-control-of-vehicle. Last accessed November 20201.

Villeneuve, N. and Sancho, D. (2011). "The 'lurid' downloader." www.trendmicro.com/ cloud-content/us/pdfs/security-intelligence/white-papers/wp_dissecting-lurid-apt.pdf. Last accessed November 2021.

Vishwanath, A., Herath, T., Chen, R., Wang, J., and Rao, H. R. (2011). "Why do people get phished? Testing individual differences in phishing vulnerability within an integrated, information processing model." *Decision Support Systems*, 51(3), 576–586.

Wall, M. E., Rechtsteiner, A., and Rocha, L. M. (2003). "Singular value decomposition and principal component analysis." *A Practical Approach to Microarray Data Analysis*, D. P. Berrar, W. Dubitzky, and M. Granzow (Eds.). Springer, 91–109. doi: 10.1007/0-306-47815-3_5.

Wang, H., Wu, B., Yang, S., Wang, B., and Liu, Y. (2014). "Research of decision tree on YARN using MapReduce and Spark." *World Congress in Computer Science, Computer Engineering, and Applied Computing*. American Council on Science and Education, 21–24.

Wang, K., He, Y., and Han, J. (2003). "Pushing support constraints into association rules mining." *IEEE Transactions Knowledge Data Engineering*, 15(3), 642–658.

Wang, K. and Stolfo, S. J. 2004. "Anomalous payload-based network intrusion detection." *Recent Advances in Intrusion Detection. RAID 2004*, E. Jonsson, A. Valdes, and M. Almgren (Eds.). Lecture Notes in Computer Science, vol. 3224. Springer, 89–96.

Wang, K., Yu, H., and Cheung, D. W. 2001. "Mining confident rules without support requirement." *Proceedings of the Tenth International Conference on Information and Knowledge Management*. ACM Press, 89–96.

Wang, L., Singhal, A., and Jajodia, S. (2007a, July). "Measuring the overall security of network configurations using attack graphs." *IFIP Annual Conference on Data and Applications Security and Privacy*. Springer, 98–112.

Wang, L., Singhal, A., and Jajodia, S. (2007b, October). "Toward measuring network security using attack graphs." *Proceedings of the 2007 ACM Workshop on Quality of Protection*. ACM, 49–54.

Wang, P. A. (2011). "Online phishing in the eyes of online shoppers." *IAENG International Journal of Computer Science*, 38(4), 378–383.

Wang, Q. H. and Kim, S. H. (2009). *Cyber Attacks: Cross-Country Interdependence and Enforcement*. WEIS.

Wang, W., Yang, J., and Muntz, R. (1997, August). "STING: A statistical information grid approach to spatial data mining." *VLDB*, 97, 186–195.

Ward, J. S. and Barker, A. (2013). "Undefined by data: a survey of big data definitions." *arXiv:1309.5821*.

Washington Post. (2013). "Target data flood stolen-card market." www.washingtonpost .com/business/economy/target-cyberattack-by-overseas-hackers-may-have-comprom ised-up-to-40-million-cards/2013/12/20/2c2943cc-69b5-11e3-a0b9-249bbb34602c_ story.html?utm_term=.42a8cd8b6c0e. Last accessed November 2016.

Websense. (2011). "Advanced persistent threat and advanced attacks: threat analysis and defense strategies for SMB, mid-size, and enterprise organizations Rev 2." Technical report.

Wei, L., Keogh, E., and Xi, X. (2006). "SAXually explicit images: finding unusual shapes." *ICDM'06: Proceedings of the Sixth International Conference on Data Mining*. IEEE Computer Society, 711–720.

Weimerskirch, A. (2018). *Derrick Dominic Assessing Risk: Identifying and Analyzing Cybersecurity Threats to Automated Vehicles*. University of Michigan,

Wilson, R. J. (1986). *Introduction to Graph Theory*. John Wiley & Sons.

Wireshark. (2021). www.wireshark.org. Last accessed November 2021.

Wright, R., Chakraborty, S., Basoglu, A., and Marett, K. (2010). "Where did they go right? Understanding the deception in phishing communications." *Group Decision and Negotiation*, 19(4), 391–416.

Wright, R. T. and Marett, K. (2010). The influence of experiential and dispositional factors in phishing: an empirical investigation of the deceived. *Journal of Management Information Systems*, 27(1), 27.

Wu, M., Miller, R. C., and Garfinkel, S. L. (2006). "Do security toolbars actually prevent phishing attacks?" *Proceedings of the SIGCHI Conference on Human Factors in Computing Systems (CHI '06)*. ACM, 601–610.

Wu, X., Kumar, V., Quinlan, J. R., et al. (2008). "Top 10 algorithms in data mining." *Knowledge and Information Systems*, 14(1), 1–37.

Wübbeling, M., Elsner, T., and Meier, M. (2014, June). "Inter-AS routing anomalies: improved detection and classification." *6th International Conference on Cyber Conflict (CyCon 2014), 2014*. IEEE, 223–238.

Wybourne, M. N., Austin, M. F., and Palmer, C. C. (2009). *National Cyber Security. Research and Development Challenges. Related to Economics, Physical*

Infrastructure and Human Behavior. I3P: Institute for Information Infrastructure Protection.

Xu, X., Ester, M., Kriegel, H. P., and Sander, J. (1998, February). "A distribution-based clustering algorithm for mining in large spatial databases." *Proceedings, 14th International Conference on Data Engineering, 1998.* IEEE, 324–331.

Xu, X., Jäger, J., and Kriegel, H. P. (1999). "A fast parallel clustering algorithm for large spatial databases." *High Performance Data Mining.*, Y. Guo and R. Grossman (Eds.). Springer US, 263–290.

Yamanishi, K. and Takeuchi, J. (2002). "A unifying framework for detecting outliers and change points from non-stationary time series data." *KDD'02: Proceedings of the Eighth ACM SIGKDD International Conference on Knowledge Discovery and Data Mining.* ACM, 676–681.

Yang, S.-C., and Wang, Y.-L. (2011, May). "System dynamics based insider threat modeling." *International Journal of Network Security and Its Applications* 3(3), doi: 10.1109/ICDM.2007.61.

Yang, X., Kong, L., Liu, Z., et al. (2018). "Machine learning and deep learning methods for cybersecurity." *IEEE Access*, 6, 35365–35381.

Yankov, D., Keogh, E., and Rebbapragada, U. (2007). "Disk aware discord discovery: finding unusual time series in terabyte sized datasets." *Seventh IEEE International Conference on Data Mining (ICDM 2007)*, 381–390. doi: 10.1109/ICDM.2007.61.

Yıldırım, M. and Mackie, I. (2019). "Encouraging users to improve password security and memorability." *International Journal of Information Security*, 18(6), 741–759.

Yinka-Banjo, C. and Ugot, O.-A. (2019). "A review of generative adversarial networks and its application in cybersecurity." *Artificial Intelligence Review*, 53, 1721–1736. doi: 10.1007/s10462-019-09717-4.

Yun, H., Ha, D., Hwang, B., and Ryu, K. H. (2003, September 15). "Mining association rules on significant rare data using relative support." *Journal of Systems and Software*, 67(3) 181–191.

Yanan, S., Janeja, V. P., McGuire, M. P, .and Gangopadhyay, A. (2012). "Tnet: tensor-based neighborhood discovery in traffic networks." *2012 IEEE 28th International Conference on Data Engineering Workshops*, 331–336. doi: 10.1109/ICDEW.2012.72.

Zetter, K. (2011, April 20). "Top federal lab hacked in spear-phishing attack." www .wired.com/threatlevel/2011/04/oak-ridge-lab-hack/. Last accessed February 23, 2014.

Zhang, K., Hutter, M., and Jin, H. (2009). "A new local distance-based outlier detection approach for scattered real-world data." *Advances in Knowledge Discovery and Data Mining. PAKDD 2009*, T. Theeramunkong, B. Kijsirikul, N. Cercone, and T. B. Ho (Eds.). Lecture Notes in Computer Science, vol. 5476. Springer, 813–822. doi: 10.1007/978-3-642-01307-2_84.

Zhang, P., Huang,, Y., Shekhar, S., and Kumar, V. (2003). "Correlation analysis of spatial time series datasets: a filter-and-refine approach." *Advances in Knowledge Discovery and Data Mining. PAKDD 2003*, K. Y. Whang., J. Jeon, K. Shim, and J. Srivastava (Eds.). Lecture Notes in Computer Science, Vol. 2637 Springer. doi: 10.1007/3-540-36175-8_53.

Zhang, T., Ramakrishnan, R., and Livny, M. (1996, June). "BIRCH: an efficient data clustering method for very large databases." *ACM Sigmod Record*, 25(2), 103–114.

Zhao, Q., and Bhowmick, S. S. (2003). "Sequential pattern mining: a survey." Technical report, CAIS Nayang Technological University Singapore, 1–26.

Zhou, B., Cheung, D. W., and Kao, B. (1999, April). "A fast algorithm for density-based clustering in large database." *Methodologies for Knowledge Discovery and Data Mining. PAKDD 1999*, N. Zhong and L. Zhou (Eds.). Lecture Notes in Computer Science, Vol. 1574. Springer Berlin Heidelberg. doi: 10.1007/3-540-48912-6_45.

Zimmermann, A., Lorenz, A., and Oppermann, R. (2007, August). "An operational definition of context." *Modeling and Using Context. CONTEXT 2007*, B. Kokinov, D. C. Richardson, T. R. Roth-Berghofer, and L. Vieu (Eds.). Lecture Notes in Computer Science, Vol. 4635. Springer Berlin Heidelberg. doi: 10.1007/978-3-540-74255-5_42.

Zimmermann, V. and Renaud, K. (2021). "The nudge puzzle: matching nudge interventions to cybersecurity decisions." *ACM Transactions on Computer–Human Interaction* (TOCHI), 28(1), 1–45.

Index